PUBLISHED *by* PARABLES
Earthly Stories with a Heavenly Meaning

CARROLL WALKER

A PATRIOT'S DEVOTIONAL

BY
CARROLL WALKER

PUBLISHED by PARABLES
Earthly Stories with a Heavenly Meaning

Carroll Walker

A Patriot's Devotional
Carroll Walker

Published By Parables
September, 2019

ISBN 978-1-951497-03-3
Printed in the United States of America

Readers should be aware that Internet Web sites offered as citations and/or sources for further information may have been changed or disappeared between the time this was written and the time it is read.

A Patriot's Devotional

By
Carroll Walker

PUBLISHED by PARABLES
Earthly Stories with a Heavenly Meaning

CARROLL WALKER

Dedication

A Patriot's Devotional is dedicated to all veterans of every branch
of service in the United States of America.
All gave some. Some gave all.

Acknowledgements

A few years ago, Wiley Landon Graham, a fellow veteran, asked that I write a book based on the devotions I give at the monthly meetings of the Jeff Davis County Veterans Association, Inc., where I serve as chaplain. Thank you, Landon, for your wonderful words of encouragement, as *A Patriot's Devotional* is the direct result of your suggestion.

There are others whom I would like to thank, most of all my wife, Susan, for not running me off during the long process of penning and publishing a book. She and Victoria Williams helped type the manuscript, for which I'll always be grateful. To my friends, Scott Worth and Wadis Davis of Jeff Davis Monument Company, I appreciate both of you for having a fax machine and knowing how to use it. I also thank my brother-in-law Greg for his knowledge of computers, as technology left me behind years ago. Much gratitude goes to my sister Judy for helping me with the English and grammar portions of the book, and also to Mary Ann Anderson for her editing ability.

I sincerely hope that you will enjoy *A Patriot's Devotional.*

A Patriot's Devotional

Introduction

As chaplain of the Jeff Davis County Veterans Association, Inc., I was asked by a fellow veteran to write a book of devotions based on those I gave at our meetings. That was more than three years ago. I thought about it deeply, and then took his advice. Now I give you *A Patriot's Devotional*, a collection of devotions not only from our meetings, but also of others I developed along the way.

In additional to daily devotions and Scripture, *A Patriot's Devotional* contains references to history, culture, current events, music, and much more and how each day's reading fits into our lifestyles. Here and there, I've added touches of humor, as life is not all about studying and being serious.

Proverbs 17:22 reads: "A merry heart doeth good like a medicine: but a broken spirit drieth the bones."

And now I give you *A Patriot's Devotional*, with the greatest hope that each day you will be drawn into a deeper relationship with God.

CARROLL WALKER

January 1

On this day we begin a new year. The Holy Bible teaches us that God created all things and spoke the world into being. His son, Jesus, was born of Mary, a virgin. Jesus lived on the earth 33 years, preaching and teaching and then dying on the cross for our sins. After His death, He arose three days later and made a way for us, if we are no longer living, to rise with Him when He comes again. If we are living, then we will meet Him in the air.

But first, you must accept God and His salvation. If you reject Him, then He will reject you.

Romans 1:16 reads: "For I am not ashamed of the gospel of Christ for it is the power of God unto salvation to everyone that believeth to the Jew first and also the Greek."

Romans 3:10 reads: "As it is written, there is none righteous, no, not one."

Romans 3:23 reads: "For all have sinned and come short of the Glory of God."

Romans 6:23 reads: "For the wages of sin is death, but the gift of God is eternal life through Jesus Christ, our Lord."

Romans 10:9 reads: "That if thou confess with thy mouth the Lord Jesus, and shalt believe in thine heart that God hath raised Him from the dead, thou shalt be saved."

Romans 10:10 reads: "For with the heart, man believeth unto righteousness; and with the mouth confession is made unto salvation."

Romans 10:13 reads: "For whosoever shall call upon the name of the Lord shall be saved."

Revelation 3:20 reads: "Behold, I stand at the door, and knock: if any man, hear my voice, and open the door, will come into him, and will sup with him, and he with me."

January 2

On this day in history in 1942, Manila, the capital of the Philippines, was captured by Japanese forces in World War II. The American forces in the Philippines were greatly affected by the Japanese army, and as they advanced the Americans were forced to leave the country, with General Douglas MacArthur proclaiming, "I shall return." He kept his word, and in 1944 went back to free the Philippines from the clutches of Japan.

The Bible records many battles, including the one in which the Children of Israel went to war in the Canaanite city of Ai without asking God. Israel was defeated.

Joshua 7:5 reads: "And the men of Ai smote of them about thirty and six men: for they chased them from before the gate even unto Shebarim, and smote them in the going down: wherefore the hearts of the people melted, and became as water."

Joshua prayed to the Lord, and it was revealed to him about the sin in the camp. After the sin was exposed and dealt with, Israel then was able to defeat Ai.

Is there sin in your camp? You can be like Joshua and confess that sin, and your life will turn around.

January 3

On this day in history in 1959, Alaska became the 49th state. Before that, on March 30, 1867, U.S. Secretary of State William Seward bought Alaska from the Russian Empire, paying $7.2 million or about two cents an acre for the purchase that became known as Seward's Folly or Seward's Icebox.

The passage of 1 Peter 2:15 reads: "For so is the will of God, that with well doing ye may put to silence the ignorance of foolish men."

As is turns out, the Alaska Purchase was neither folly nor foolishness on the part of the United States government in that Alaska is rich in land and natural resources and serves as a military fortress for our nation. As for an "icebox," that is correct since it lies partially in the Arctic Circle.

Are you living in folly or is your heart cold as ice? God will change you if you sincerely ask Him to do so.

January 4

On this day in history in 1809, Louis Braille was born. It is well known that he invented a system that was named for him that allowed blind people to read. Using the dots of the Braille system, each one is arranged in special order to represent letters and words. Braille is still widely used today. Louis Braille died in 1852 at the age of 43.

Luke 7:21-22 reads: "And in that same hour he cured many of their infirmities and plagues, and of evil spirits; and unto many that were blind he gave sight. Then Jesus answering said unto them, Go your way, and tell John what things ye have seen and heard; how that the blind see, the lame walk, the lepers are cleansed, the deaf hear, the dead are raised, to the poor the gospel is preached."

This Scripture tells us that Jesus cares for us. All these things mentioned are examples of Jesus' love for us. He was always willing to help others, but are we willing to do these things?

The actor and comedian Bob Hope once stated, "If you haven't any charity in your heart, you have the worst kind of heart trouble."

Is your heart doing good? Or are you having heart trouble?

January 5

On this day in history in 1781, British Brigadier General Benedict Arnold captured and burned Richmond, Virginia. Arnold, a friend of George Washington, felt that his talents and leadership as a general were ignored by the Americans. When the British offered him money and commanded him to betray the Americans, he accepted and thereafter become known as a traitor. As a matter of fact, his name has become commonly synonymous with the word traitor. After the Revolution, he lived in England until his death in 1801 at the age of 60.

But another more prominent traitor lived before Benedict Arnold, and that was Judas Iscariot.

Luke 6:16 reads: "And Judas the brother of James, and Judas Iscariot, which also was the traitor."

Every time Judas' name is mentioned in the Bible, the word traitor is right behind it. For only 30 pieces of silver, Judas sold his honor and respect when he betrayed Jesus to the Romans. He became so burdened and distressed about what he had done that he hanged himself.

Are we betraying others by our deed and actions? Will we one day be the laughingstock to those around us, much like Benedict Arnold and Judas Iscariot?

January 6

On this day in history in 1945, the Battle of the Bulge ended, with German casualties numbering 130,000 and Allied casualties at 77,000. In December of 1944, Hitler and the Germans attempted to split the Allied armies at an unexpected place in the Ardennes Mountains, where the Germans made their attack. The Allies were not expecting the attack, and the defense lines were greatly bowed by the Germans. A bulge is also called a bow, and the Battle of the Bulge was thus named. While the Allied forces did bend, they were never broken, with General George Patton moving the American 3rd Army in place to successfully hold this position.

King Saul, the first king of Israel, was put in this same type of situation. His army fought David's small army, with both battling in the mountains in the mountains and hiding in caves.

The passage of 1 Samuel 24:4 reads: "And the men of David said unto him, Behold the day of which the Lord said unto thee, Behold, I will deliver thine enemy into thine hand, that thou mayest do to him as it shall seem good unto thee. Then David arose, and cut off the skirt of Saul's robe privily."

But David did not kill King Saul, as King Saul was anointed of the Lord and David respected that.

Do we respect God's men? Are we following God as David did?

January 7

On this day in history in 1789, the electoral college system was put forth. Its members were elected, who in turn later elected George Washington as the first president of the United States.

Each state has the same number of electorates as it does congressmen and senators, although some state laws dictate how an electorate will vote. Some are winner-take-all, others are split on the number of percentage points that each political party has, while still others are called free-for-all.

We choose what we will at any given time: what to eat, what to wear, where to work, and so forth. We even choose our religion or denomination.

Joshua 24:15 urges the Children of Israel to make an important choice. It reads: "And if it seems evil unto you to serve the Lord, choose you this day whom ye will serve; whether the gods which your fathers served that were on the other side of the flood, or the gods of the Amorites in whose land ye dwell: but as for me and my house, we will serve the Lord."

Joshua did not tell anyone whom or how to serve their god. He did, however, tell them whom he would serve.

Who are you serving today? How will others react to your decision? Choose the God that Joshua chose.

uary 8

On this day in history in 1877, Crazy Horse of the Lakota Sioux tribe fought his last battle against the U.S. Cavalry in Montana in a valiant effort to preserve traditions of the Sioux Indians. Crazy Horse was one of the chiefs of the Sioux and Cheyenne to join Sitting Bull at the Battle of the Little Big Horn, where he surrendered but was later killed by federal troops after they heard of his escape plan.

In 1948, building began in the Black Hills of South Dakota near Mount Rushmore of a sculpture of Crazy Horse – it was commissioned by Henry Standing Bear, an Oglala Lakota chief – and when it is completed, it will be the largest sculpture in the world. Construction is still ongoing until this day, and with no estimates of its completion date, it seems as if it will go on forever.

In Matthew 28:18-20, Jesus gives his great commission, "Teaching them to observe all things whatsoever I have commanded you; and lo, I am with you always, even unto the end of the world."

When Jesus gave us the great commission, he wanted us to never surrender or give up. Crazy Horse, never surrendering either, died fighting even in captivity. We should continue the fight to fulfill the great commission.

Are you doing your part to tell others about Christ?

January 9

On this day in history in 1984, Clara Peller appeared in a commercial on television for Wendy's. Standing at a competitor's order counter, she opens a sandwich with a small burger inside, then asks, "Where's the beef?" The commercial was both successful and hilarious and helped put Wendy's on the map as a good place to eat.

Jesus made a statement that cleared up a great deal about his ministry. John 14:6 reads: "Jesus saith unto him, I am the way, the truth, and the life: no man cometh unto the Father, but by me."

With this proclamation, Jesus declares that we must seek Him for salvation.

Are you seeking Jesus today?

January 10

On this day in history in 1946, the first general assembly of the United Nations met in New York City with 51 nations present. It has since grown to presently represent 193 nations. Whatever your opinion is about the UN, it does provide a meeting place for the nations of the world.

Abram did not have a place for him and his descendants to meet and discuss things of the world with their enemies, yet they still had to deal with them, with "them" being the "ites" clans mentioned in Genesis 15:18-21. Oh, so you've never heard of the "ites" clans? Here goes: The Amorites, Kenizzites, Kadmonites, Hittites, Perizites, Canaanites, Girgashites, Jebusites, and Rephaim. Where the Rephaim came from I don't know. All these tribes were against Abram.

Genesis 15:18 reads: "In the same day the Lord made a covenant with Abram, saying, unto thy seed have I given this land, from the river of Egypt unto the great river, the river Euphrates."

The "ites" did not like God's covenant with Abram, but it was God's promise.

Do you like God's promises?

January 11

On this day in history in 1928, the song "Ol' Man River" was recorded by Paul Whiteman and his orchestra with Bing Crosby as the featured vocalist. The song, from the Broadway musical "Showboat," was written by Jerome Kern and Oscar Hammerstein II in the mid-1920s.

David, the second King of Israel, wrote and composed many songs, with some of those listed in the Book of Psalms. If anyone had to choose a favorite passage of the Psalms, it would be difficult, as there are too many great ones. I certainly couldn't select only one.

Probably Psalms 46:1-11 is among the most widely quoted, especially Verse 1: "God is our refuge and strength, a very present help in trouble."

When troubles come our way, we can always turn to God, for He is always with us and will help us in our need.

Do you depend on God to be your helper?

January 12

On this day in history in 1932, Hattie W. Conaway, a Democrat from Arkansas, became the first woman to be elected to the United States Senate. She served for 14 years as a senator. Her election and longevity in the Senate set a trend that allowed women to hold office and in some states the right to vote.

Judges 4:4 begins a story about Deborah, another leader who was a woman: "And Deborah, a prophetess, the wife of Lapidoth, she judged Israel at that time."

Not only was Deborah a prophetess and judge, but also she was a warrior. In Judges 4:8-9, she goes to battle with Barak, the leader of the army of Israel. In fact, Barak would not go without her, and she told him that she would go with him into battle but that a woman would be the heroine.

Are you following God's leadership?

January 13

On this day in history in 1928, Ernst F. W. Alexander gave the first public demonstration of television and the world has not been the same since. Whether it was a good or bad idea, it still has an on and off button so that we can make the choice to either watch it or not. Some people have become so totally captivated by the television that they have even taken guns and shot up perfectly good sets because they did not like certain programming.

Another creation, one made by God and not man, is recorded in Genesis 1:1-5: "In the beginning God created the heaven and the earth. And the earth was without form, and void; and darkness was upon the face of the deep. And the Spirit of God moved upon the face of the waters. And God said; Let there be light: and there was light. And God saw the light, that it was good: and God divided the light from the darkness. And God called the light Day, and the darkness He called Night. And the evening and the morning were the first day."

We all know about television and we also know when God created the Earth. It is indeed a pleasure to have both. While the television has that on and off button, God's creation does not, so let us enjoy the creation of God. It is a lovely place where we can remember the Creator.

Do you have a special place to talk with God?

January 14

On this day in history in 1784, the United States and England ratified a peace treaty that ended the fighting in Revolutionary War and brought freedom for the United States. As we learned in the history books, the Thirteen Colonies won their independence from the British army, one that was far better equipped and trained than they were.

The passage of 1 Samuel 23:1-2 reads: "Then they told David, saying, Behold the Philistines fight against Keilah, and they rob the threshing floors. Therefore, David inquired of the Lord, saying, Shall I go and smite these Philistines? And the Lord said unto David, Go, and smite the Philistines, and save Keilah."

At this time, David's army numbered only 400 men, and he asked for God's permission before going into war. The Lord assured David that the battle was his. The Philistines were robbing the people and taking advantage of them, but that was soon to end as David won the battle.

How are your battles going? Did you ask God to start and finish your battles?

January 15

On this day in history in 1943, the Pentagon was dedicated as the largest office building in the world. The Pentagon covers 34 acres of land and has an astonishing 17 miles of hallways. That makes me tired just writing about it.

The Pentagon houses the main offices of every branch of the military, with all operations going through it and all plans starting there. It is truly the nerve center of the free world.

In 1 Kings 17:1 the passage reads: "And Elijah the Tishbite, who was of the inhabitants of Gilead, said unto Ahab, As the Lord God of Israel liveth, before whom I stand, there shall not be dew nor rain these years, but according to my word."

Elijah the Tishbite was from Gilead, and this is where he began his ministry for the Lord. Gilead was considered the nerve center of Israel, and for most kings and prophets it was an important city. Elijah and the Lord called for no rain to fall on Gilead for three-and-a-half years. During this time, Elijah hid from King Ahab and his wife Queen Jezebel, as the queen had promised to kill Elijah for calling for no rain.

Do you have rain in your life? What about the lifegiving river of salvation? It flows on, and on, and on, and on, and on, and on.

January 16

On this day in history in 1944, General Dwight D. Eisenhower took over command of the Allied forces in London, England, a move that was to speed up the highly secret operations regarding the invasion of France. We now know that invasion as D-Day, an event that took place June 6, 1944. After liberating France, the Allied command had a ready access to Germany. Eisenhower did his duty with great victory.

In 2 Samuel 11:1, the passage reads: "And it came to pass, after the year was expired, at the time when kings go forth to battle, that David sent Joab, and his servants with him, and all Israel; and they destroyed the children of Ammon, and besieged Rabbah. But David tarried still at Jerusalem."

David, as the king of Israel, was to be the leader of the army, with Joab his commanding general. David did not go to war this time, as trouble followed him. He did not do his duty or what was expected of him.

The great Confederate General Robert E. Lee once stated, "Duty is the most sublime word in our language. Do your duty in all things, you cannot do more, you should never wish to do less."

Are you doing your duty to God and to yourself?

January 17

On this day in history in 1945, toward the end of World War II, Warsaw, the capital of Poland, was liberated from the Germans by the Soviet Union and Polish soldiers. Poland had been invaded earlier in the war, and consequently had been under German rule for several years. With Poland back in the hands of the Allies, the way to Germany's defeat was opened wide and the war was nearly finished.

In earlier times, the land of Israel had been captured by the Babylonians, leaving the Children of Israel in bondage for seventy years. Cyrus, the king of Persia, decided to let a remnant of people return to Jerusalem to repair the wall that surrounded the city.

Ezra 1:1-2 reads: "Now in the first year of Cyrus king of Persia, that the word of the Lord by the mouth of Jeremiah might be fulfilled, the Lord stirred up the spirit of Cyrus king of Persia, that he made a proclamation throughout all his kingdom, and put it also in writing, saying, Thus saith Cyrus king of Persia, The Lord God of heaven hath given me all the kingdoms of the earth; and hath charged me to build him a house at Jerusalem, which is in Judah."

This is a strange proclamation from a king of Persia, the sworn enemy of Israel. Today Persia is now called Iran, and Iran is still a sworn enemy of Israel.

Can you even think about these two countries helping one another out of a problem?

January 18

On this day in history in 1993, Martin Luther King Jr.'s birthday, which is January 15, was observed as a national holiday in all 50 states for the first time. Because of the holiday system set up by Congress, most holidays are observed on Monday to allow for a long weekend or a jumpstart on a vacation.

Now these holidays are more about those long weekends than they are about reflecting on or celebrating the person or event, so we must remember that King preached victory through peace. His protests were as nonviolent as much as possible. His "I Have A Dream" speech on August 28, 1963, is considered his greatest of all time in that it urged all races of people to live by peaceful means.

Romans 12:18 reads: "If it be possible, as much as lieth in you, live peaceably with all men."

Throughout the New Testament, the Apostle Paul tells us to live in peace also. By living in peace, we will let Christ's love shine through us.

Are you living in peace?

January 19

On this day in history in 1807, Robert Edward Lee was born, the son of Henry "Light-Horse Harry" Lee III, a Revolutionary War soldier. Robert E. Lee attended West Point Academy in New York, and then spent 32 years in the U.S. Army. He served in the Mexican-American War and was superintendent of West Point Academy.

When Virginia seceded from the Union in 1861, Lee resigned from the U.S. Army and became commander-in-chief of the Army of Northern Virginia and then later became commander-in-chief for all of the Confederate Army. On April 9, 1865, Lee surrendered to General Ulysses S. Grant at Appomattox Court House, Virginia, to end the War Between the States. Lee died October 12, 1870, at age 63.

Acts 16 tells of another man in authority, although his name is not recorded, and he is known only as the Philippians jailer. Verse 25 reads: "And at midnight Paul and Silas prayed, and sang praises unto God: and the prisoners heard them."

Can you imagine singing praises to God if you are in prison?

But God heard them and caused an earthquake and everyone's bonds fell off. After being assured everyone was safe following the quake, the jailer then asked of Paul how he, too, could be saved. Verse 31 gives that answer, "And they said, Believe on the Lord Jesus Christ, and thou shalt be saved, and thy house."

You can also be saved by that same verse. Would you receive Christ today?

January 20

On this day in history in 1958, Elvis Presley was drafted into the U.S. Army, although he received a deferment to finish "King Creole," a movie in which he was starring. Afterward, Elvis honored his duty and served into the military.

Luke 17:7-10 gives us Scripture stating that we should be of service to others, and it also tells us how we are to treat our servants. Verse 10 reads: "So likewise ye, when ye shall have done all those things which are commanded you, say, we are unprofitable servants: we have done that which was our duty to do."

Sometimes we just have to do our duty. We have all done things that were hard, complicated or out of the normal, but still we did them because it was our duty, things like getting drafted, leaving home, or getting married. We do our duty just as Elvis did.

Are you doing yours in your life?

January 21

On this day in history in 1824, Thomas J. Jackson was born. He came from a poor family and didn't have much education. His father had died of typhoid fever shortly after his birth, and his mother later remarried to a man who did not like her children, so they were often sent to live with relatives.

In 1842, Jackson enrolled in the military at West Point Academy. After graduating he served with the 1st U.S. Artillery in the Mexican-American War. Then after the war ended, he settled in Lexington, Virginia, to teach at Virginia Military Institute. But the War Between the States began, where he served under Confederate Generals Joseph E. Johnston and Robert E. Lee to become commander of the army of the Shenandoah. Jackson earned his nickname "Stonewall" from a fellow officer at the First Battle of Bull Run, also known as Manassas. Later he was wounded by friendly fire at the Battle of Chancellorsville and died ten days later of pneumonia.

While Jackson lived a short life, we can read about a king who lived a long life. In 2 Kings 19, the story is told about King Hezekiah who started his reign by following the Lord. All during his reign, King Hezekiah went to the Temple of the Lord to worship and asked God for advice and help.

Verse 20:6 tells of the way the Lord rewarded King Hezekiah when he became sick and asked the Lord to not let him die: "And I will add unto thy days fifteen years; and I will deliver thee and this city out of the hand of the king of Assyria [modern day Syria]; and I will defend this city for mine own sake, and for my servant David's sake."

Do you follow the Lord the way King Hezekiah did? Are you listening to his word today in the things you do?

January 22

On this day in history in 1973, the Supreme Court decided the infamous court ruling of *Roe v. Wade*, which struck down all state laws against abortion during the first six months of pregnancy. In making the ruling, the Supreme Court voted 7-2 to overturn a Texas law that prevented abortions. The ruling was based on the 9th and 14th amendments to the Constitution and focused on a woman's right to privacy. Even today, *Roe v. Wade* is still as hard fought over as it was in 1973, with both pro and con sides of the issue refusing to give even one inch.

Job 31:15 reads: "Did not he that made me in the womb make him? and did not one fashion us in the womb?"

Psalms 22:10 reads: "I was cast upon thee from the womb: thou art my God from my mother's belly."

Isaiah 49:15 reads: "Can a woman forget her sucking child, that she should not have compassion on the son of her womb? yea, they may forget, yet will I not forget thee."

Exodus 20:13 reads: "Thou shalt not kill."

These are a few of the Scriptures regarding a child's life. We are created in God's image. He knows everything we do, and we cannot fool Him. Some of the verses of the song "Jesus Loves the Little Children" are "Red and yellow, black and white, they are precious in his sight" also includes the unborn.

Are you being protective of life?

January 23

On this day in history in 1964, the 24th amendment to the Constitution was repealed to end the poll tax in America. The poll tax was one that had to be paid before an individual could vote and was mostly aimed at African-American voters. It also hurt the poor and uneducated of all races in that it was meant to create a superior race and make discrimination easier. Efforts to repeal it had begun in 1939 and then really began to roll after World War II ended in 1945.

When we hear the word tax, we can think about Joseph and Mary. Luke 2:1-3 reads: "And it came to pass in those days, that there went out a decree from Caesar Augustus, that all the world should be taxed. (And this taxing was first made when Cyrenius was governor of Syria.) And all went to be taxed, everyone into his own city."

Taxes have always been a way to control people and their actions, and the poll tax in particular allowed only the elite to vote. A tax decree from the president seems to only collect money for more wasteful spending.

Do you have to pay taxes? How are they beneficial to you? Does God approve of your actions?

January 24

On this day in history in 1848, James W. Marshall discovered gold at Sutter's Mill in an area now northeast of Sacramento, California. The event led to the gold rush of 1849 and became quite popular with prospectors who came from everywhere. All types of people flocked into California: the good and bad, the rich and poor, and the criminals and crooks. It was a lawless land, as gold has a way of changing people and not always for the better.

Now consider this story told in Acts 3:1-11. The Apostles Peter and John went to pray in the temple, where they met a crippled man who was begging for money so that he could afford to live. He asked Peter and John for a handout. Verse 6 reads: "Then Peter said, Silver and gold have I none; but such as I have, give, I thee: in the name of Jesus Christ of Nazareth rise up and walk."

Healing is better than gold. Can you imagine how the crippled man felt when he arose to walk? The Bible further records that he left jumping, leaping and praising God.

What is the value of our gold today? Would healing be better? Talk with someone who has been healed from a devastating illness. Are they full of joy and happiness?

January 25

On this day in history in 1915, Alexander Graham Bell, who was in New York City, spoke by telephone to his assistant in San Francisco, California, in history's first transcontinental call.

The telephone is something we take for granted today, as we can call almost anywhere in the world in only a few seconds. Even cell phones are something still hard for me to imagine. Everything imaginable is on a cell phone – the Internet, maps, news, games, gossip – name it, and the cell phone has it. What would we do without it?

The only communication we have better than the phone is prayer. In Psalms 143:1, David asks the Lord to hear his prayer: "Hear my prayer, O Lord, give ear to my supplications: in thy faithfulness answer me, and in thy righteousness."

Does God hear our prayers? Yes. The answer He gives, though, is not always the one we want to hear. He answers with either yes, no, maybe, or not now. In any case, you have an answer. And prayer is faster than the telephone.

Do you have a problem that needs a solution? Ask God and not the phone for guidance

January 26

On this day in history in 1970, Navy Lt. Everett Alvarez Jr., was the first American aviator to be shot down over North Vietnam during the Vietnam Conflict and captured as a prisoner of war. He was held for 8-1/2 years, making him the longest known POW in American history.

I'm sure Alvarez was happy when he was released and returned home as a free man. Think how happy you would be to return home after being held captive for so long.

In John 8:36, Jesus said, "If the Son therefore shall make you free, ye shall be free indeed."

Jesus, the Son of God, can release you from your aches, concerns, and heart troubles if you let Him. He can release you from your burdens of sin so that you can spend eternity with Him.

Will you accept Him today?

January 27

On this day in history in 1785, Georgia became the first state to charter a higher institution of learning, and that school is the University of Georgia. At the time, UGA was primarily to educate mostly young farm boys in the study of agriculture. But as we know now, education of any kind is always a good thing.

In his second letter to Timothy, the Apostle Paul wrote in Chapter 2:15-16: "Study to show thyself approved unto God, a workman that needeth not to be ashamed, rightly dividing the word of truth. But shun profane and vain babblings: for they will increase unto more ungodliness."

When we study God's Word, then we will be better students of what He is teaching us. Study to be wiser and do not study ungodliness.

What are you studying?

January 28

On this day in history in 1915, Congress created the U.S. Coast Guard. Its main duty was to rescue ships in distress off the coast of America and to intercept contraband from coming into the country. The creation of the Coast Guard freed the U.S. Navy to allow for other things in any upcoming war efforts. Further, in times of war, the Coast Guard may be transferred to the Navy, an occurrence that has happened only twice in our history, once in World War I and the other in World War II.

King Solomon, the son of David, was the first power to use a navy. His navy did not go to war, so it in essence served the purpose of a coast guard.

In 1 Kings 9:26-28, the passages read: "And King Solomon made a navy of ships in Ezion-geber, which is beside Eloth, on the shore of the Red Sea, in the Land of Edom. And Hiram sent in the navy his servants, shipmen that had knowledge of the sea, with the servants of Solomon. And they came to Ophir, and fetched from thence gold, four hundred and twenty talents, and brought it to king Solomon."

King Solomon used his coast guard to carry gold and other valuables.

Our Coast Guard was made to protect our ships with their valuables and gold.

Are you protecting the valuables in your life? If you aren't, then call upon God to help you become better prepared.

January 29

One of the more well-known phrases that came from World War I was, "The only thing we have to fear is fear itself."

These words were originally spoken by Franklin D. Roosevelt, our 32nd president who was born January 30, 1882. Roosevelt's words still hold true, and maybe we should have this statement read in the White House, Senate, and House of Representatives today.

Fear is mentioned several times in the Bible, including in Luke 2:10 when the angel of the Lord tells the shepherds, "Fear not: for, behold, I bring you good tidings of great joy, which shall be to all people."

Furthermore, in Luke 12:7, Jesus said, "But even the very hairs of your head are all numbered. Fear not therefore: ye are of more value than many sparrows."

When Roosevelt first uttered those famous words regarding fear in his first inaugural address, he was the leader of the free country and encouraging us to be faithful and not fearful.

What are you doing to remain faithful and unafraid?

January 30

On this winter in history in 1777-78, the Constitutional Army was encamped at Valley Forge, Pennsylvania, already two years into the Revolutionary War. General George Washington's men were ill-equipped for that frigid winter. Some had no shoes, and many starved or froze to death. The winter started with eight thousand men, and by spring only six thousand remained alive. Even the British nicknamed them "Washington's Ragtag Army."

One day during this time, a Quaker farmer named Isaac Potts was in the woods near Valley Forge when he heard a man's soft voice. When he approached, he saw that the man was Washington, who was on his knees in the snow in prayer for his men. Potts told his wife later that night, "All will be well because General Washington was praying for his men," and that because of it, he continued, "Our independence is certain,"

In Matthew 6:33, Jesus tells us to seek him first: "But seek ye first the kingdom of God and his righteousness; and all these things shall be added unto you."

Let us be like Washington and pray and seek God's favor on the things we need.

Are you praying for what you need?

January 31

In January 1946, the U.S. Mint began making the Roosevelt dime. It had Franklin D. Roosevelt's image on one side and three emblems on the other. The first or left emblem is an olive tree branch for peace. The middle is a torch, which stands for freedom. And the third or right emblem is an oak tree, which stands for strength.

During his lifetime, Roosevelt asked children to send dimes for the National Foundation for Infantile Paralysis, which became the March of Dimes. Because of efforts of so many, the disease of infantile paralysis has been stopped in America today.

As January comes to an end, we all turn our minds to tax forms, including W-2s, 1099s, charitable giving statements, interest statements, and more as we prepare our returns.

The passage of Matthew 22:21 reads: "They say unto him, Caesar's. Then saith he unto them, Render therefore unto Caesar the things which are Caesar's; and unto God the things that are God's."

Jesus' disciples wanted to know if they had to pay taxes, and He told them to give their due. Essentially, he said to pay your taxes and give to God.

Are you being faithful with God's money?

February 1

On this day in history 1862, Julia Ward Howe first published "The Battle Hymn of the Republic" in the *Atlantic Monthly*, a song that would become one of the most popular patriotic hymns in United States history. It is classified as both a patriot's song and a religious hymn. During the War Between the States, it became more associated with Union soldiers than the Confederacy, although today it is loved by everyone.

Songs have been an important part of wars and battles for years. We as veterans were trained by songs from the time we entered the service, although the words for some should not be repeated. During basic training, we were also taught to march by rhythm and song.

In 1 Samuel 18:6, the passage reads: "And it came to pass as they came, when David was returned from the slaughter on the Philistine, that the women came out of all cities of Israel, singing and dancing, to meet king Saul with tablets, with joy, and with instruments of music."

King Saul and David returned home from battle with songs and music.

Do you have music and a song in your heart today?

February 2

On this day in history in 1887, a new tradition began in America when Punxsutawney Phil of Pennsylvania became known as a weather forecaster with the first Groundhog Day. Later General Beauregard Lee, another groundhog from Jackson, Georgia, became the prognosticator for the South.

Sometimes Punxsutawney Phil and General Beauregard Lee disagree with each other's forecast, just as the North and South disagreed with one another in the 1860s in the War Between the States. With the groundhogs, though, we just wait and see which one is correct in its forecast, because there's no use in fighting over a little snow. In South Georgia, where I live, six more weeks of winter don't affect us that much anyway. But I won't speak for the people in Pennsylvania in that regard. Besides, it's the hot and humid summers that give us a fit in the South.

The Pharisees and Sadducees were always trying to trick Jesus into something or another. Matthew 16:1-5 tells of another way to lead to trickery, with Verses 2-4 reading: "He answered and said unto them When it is evening, ye say, it will be fair weather: for the sky is red. And in the morning, it will be foul weather today: for the sky is red and lowering. O ye hypocrites, ye can discern the face of the sky; but can ye not discern the signs of the times? A wicked and adulterous generation seeketh after a sign and there shall no sign be given unto it, but the sign of the prophet Jonah. And he left them and departed."

Whether the two groundhogs know what they are doing, I don't know. When I need a weather forecast, I talk to the ultimate weather maker. Whether it's cold, hot, warm, dry, or rainy, God will provide and answer our prayers.

Do you trust Him?

February 3

On this day in history in 1913, the 13th amendment to the Constitution was ratified. While it is known by names I won't repeat, it is also called the Income Tax Amendment and it gives the federal government the right to levy and collect income taxes. It is a good and bad deal for the American people in many respects. While I'm sure that many who work with the Internal Revenue Service are good people, they are not generally liked because of their employer.

Luke 5:27 reads: "And after these things he went forth, and saw a publican, named Levi, sitting at the receipt at custom: and he said unto him, Follow me."

Levi and Matthew are the same person. In our own lives, we often call a person by different names, perhaps either their first or middle name. In any case, Matthew was a tax collector. No one liked him very much, but he had a job to do. Many Jews even called him a sinner and a publican—it's not the same as Republican. But soon Matthew gave up his job to follow Jesus.

Have you given up anything to follow Jesus? How about a good government job and the retirement that came with it?

Are you serving Jesus? Think about your retirement. It's heavenly.

February 4

On this day in history in 1789, the Electoral College chose George Washington as the first president of the United States of America. Six years earlier, the American War of Independence, or the Revolutionary War, was finally over – it had begun in 1775 – and all hostilities stopped. The presiding officer of Congress was in effect the leader for those six years while the Constitution was being written.

The process of choosing a president is much like today. Candidates choose to run or are drafted to run. A popular vote is held only as a preference vote. Delegates pledge to the particular candidate to then become the Electoral College. They meet and vote in January and the president is then selected. A candidate may get more popular votes and still lose the election because of the electoral vote.

In Deuteronomy, Moses gave a parting lesson to the younger generation. (We should be doing likewise.) A quick history of Israel shows us how the Lord protected them as they wandered in the wilderness. Deuteronomy 4:37 reads: "And because he loved thy fathers, therefore he chose their seed after them, and brought thee out in his sight with his mighty power out of Egypt."

God chose the Children of Israel to be His people. He also chose you as one of His people if you believe that His son Jesus died for you.

Do you believe? Choose Him.

February 5

On this day in history in 1934, Henry Louis "Hank" Aaron was born in Mobile, Alabama. As a professional baseball player, he became known as Hammer or Hammering Hank. He played baseball for the Milwaukee Braves and then the Atlanta Braves for 21 years. He also played two seasons for the Milwaukee Brewers of the American League. Hammering Hank held the career homerun title for 33 years and still holds other records as well. Now in his retirement from the field, he currently works in the front office of the Atlanta Braves. Those of us who are Braves fans hope that his records last a long time.

Numbers 9:3 reads: "In the fourteenth day of the month, at even, ye shall keep it in his appointed season: according to all rites of it and according to all the ceremonies thereof, shall ye keep it."

In these verses, the Lord is talking about the Passover. Let us also apply these words to baseball. Hank Aaron wants his records to stand forever, and that is his right. Others want to break his records, and it is their right.

Will your life and its accomplishments stand forever? Is what you are doing being preserved in God's Kingdom?

February 6

Two things happened on this day in history. In 1987 President Ronald Reagan turned 76 years old and became the oldest person to serve as president. Also in 1998, the name of one of Washington, D.C.'s airports was changed to Reagan National in Reagan's honor (the other Washington airport is Dulles International). The name change bill was signed by President Bill Clinton. What an honor it must have been to become the oldest American president and to also have an airport named after him.

Methuselah also lived to be an old man. At age 187 he became a father, and then he lived for another 782 years. Methuselah, the longest living person on earth, lived to be 969 years old. His story is told in Genesis 5:6-32.

Methuselah lived in the time before Moses wrote the Ten Commandments, but he must have had a foresight into this, as Exodus 20:12 reads: "Honor thy father and thy mother: that thy days may be long upon the land which the Lord thy God giveth thee."

Are you living so that you can be an old person? Do you honor your father and mother? Do you honor God?

February 7

On this day in history in 1804, John Deere was born in Vermont. He helped raise his siblings after his father abandoned them in 1808. At age 17, he became a blacksmith, and then at age 33 he left Vermont for Grand Detour, Illinois. Soon after that, he moved to Moline, an Illinois town on the Mississippi River, to be close to shipping and waterways so that he could ship his products. At one point, Deere had a problem getting steel for his farming implements. Deere had nine children, and when his wife died in 1865, he married her sister. He died May 17, 1886, at his home in Moline.

Isaiah 2:4 reads: "And he shall judge among the nations, and shall rebuke many people: and they shall beat their swords into plowshares, and their spears into pruninghooks: nation shall not lift up sword against nation, neither shall they learn war anymore."

In the end times, as Isaiah writes in Verse 4, this will not be a problem.

Are you ready to make plows and a harvest? Are you harvesting souls for Jesus now?

February 8

On this day in history in 1820, William Tecumseh Sherman was born in Lancaster, Ohio. His father died when he was still a boy, so he was then brought up by Thomas Ewing, a family friend. Sherman later married Eleanor Boyle in 1850.

Sherman's military career began as a colonel, and his first action was at the Battle of Bull Run, also known as Manassas. His military career was shaky at best before he joined General Ulysses S. Grant in Mississippi. After the fall of Vicksburg, Sherman then headed to Chattanooga, Tennessee, to further attempt to cut the Confederacy in half. After the fall of Chattanooga, Sherman next set his sights on Atlanta, and after victory there went toward the Georgia coast in his now infamous March to the Sea.

Sherman's scorched earth policy of burning everything in his path stayed with him from Vicksburg until the end of the war, and kill and burn everyone and everything became the order of the day. Sherman's belief was that people had to feel the effects of the war, which is why he destroyed everything in his path.

One of Sherman's well-known quotes was given after he was asked to run for president. His answer? "If nominated, I will not accept. If elected, I will not serve." He would not rise to the challenge.

The passages of 2 Samuel 23:22-23 read: "These things did Benaiah the son of Jehoiada, and had the name among three mighty men. He was more honorable than the thirty, but he attained not to the first three. And David set him over his guard."

Benaiah rose to the command and was counted as a mighty warrior in King David's Army.

Are you being called of God? Do you answer the way Benaiah did or the way General Sherman did?

February 9

On this day in history in 1943, the Battle of Guadalcanal was won by American forces. The battle began in August of 1942 when Japanese troops began constructing an airfield there. But U.S. Marines made a surprise attack and captured the airbase that was still under construction, a battle that involved air, land, and sea. The heaviest losses were for the Japanese, who lost most of their air power, although both sides lost ships in the battle. Guadalcanal is in the Solomon Islands in the Pacific Ocean and strategically located for Australia, Hawaii and Japan.

Acts 27:16 reads: "And running under a certain island which is called Clauda, we had much work to come by the boat."

Here the Apostle Paul is headed to Rome. He is on a ship that is caught up in a storm. The ship is heavily damaged, and its crew is tired as they land on an island.

Think of how the Marines felt on the Solomon Islands, almost cut off from everything in the world. The Japanese troops probably felt the same way. Being all alone except for your service buddies is a bad feeling.

How can we help others in their time of loss and despondency? How do we tell them about Christ? Just as the Marines had victory, we will, too, when we trust God.

February 10

On this day in history in 1779, militias from South Carolina and Georgia fought the battle of Carr's Fort in Wilkes County, Georgia. The Patriots quickly got the upper hand in the battle, and before it was over the Patriots learned that Loyalist replacements from North Carolina were coming their way. The Patriots decided to leave the battle and meet the Loyalists who were under the command of Colonel John Boyd. Four days later they met at the Battle of Kettle Creek, where the Patriots surprised the Loyalists and defeated them in the ongoing battle.

Jeremiah 51:12 reads: "Set up the standard upon the walls of Babylon, make the watch strong, set up the watchmen, prepare the ambushes: for the Lord hath both devised and done that which he spoke against the inhabitants of Babylon."

Jeremiah is prophesying against Babylon and telling Israel how to prepare for battle and to make sure they were covered.

Make sure you are covered in all you do in case of ambush and make sure that everyone is informed and knows what to do. The South Carolina and Georgia Militia were ready and prepared to do battle, and the outcome was victory for the Patriots.

Are you ready to do battle against Satan? He is prepared to battle for your soul, but are you prepared to fight against him?

February 11

On this day in history in 1751, the Pennsylvania Hospital, founded by Benjamin Franklin and Dr. Thomas Bond, became the first hospital to open in America. It is still in existence today, its main building dating to 1756, and is also listed as a National Historic Landmark. Today, the nonprofit teaching hospital is part of the University of Pennsylvania School of Medicine. It also has the first medical library and a surgical amphitheater in America.

When you think of physicians of the Bible, your mind will probably drift toward two people. The first is Luke, the author of the Book of Luke and who was a physician. The second is a woman whose story is told in Luke 8:43: "And a woman having an issue of blood twelve years, which had spent all her living upon physicians, neither could be healed of any."

The Bible does not mention what sickness the woman had, but it does say she spent all her money on doctors. She then turned to Jesus for help. Her faith was such that only a touch of the Master's garment was good enough for her.

Have you lived your life so that your faith will make you whole? Have you touched the Master?

February 12

On this day in history, two events happened regarding Abraham Lincoln. In 1892, Lincoln's birthday became a national holiday, and then in 1915, the cornerstone for the Lincoln Memorial was laid. Lincoln was born in 1809 and later would become the 16th president of the United States. This actual date of Lincoln's birthday as a national holiday was dropped in 1971 with the passage of the Uniform Federal Holidays Act and is now celebrated along with George Washington's birthday on the third Monday in February and is known as President's Day.

When we speak of birthdays in the Bible, most of us think of Jesus' birth, which we celebrate on December 25.

Herod's birthday turned out to be a very bad one for John the Baptist. Matthew 14:1-14 tells that story. John the Baptist preached about adultery, with Verse 6 reading: "But when Herod's birthday was kept, the daughter of Herodias danced before them and pleased Herod."

And Herod and his sister-in-law Herodias were guilty of adultery. They were both mad at John the Baptist because he spoke against the relationship, her more so than him. On Herod's birthday, his niece danced before him, much to his delight. He then told her he would give her anything she wanted. The young woman then asked for the head of John the Baptist and was even urged on by her mother.

What does this story have to do with President Lincoln? A lot, really. Lincoln has a holiday and a monument named after him and is honored by his country. But this can't be said of Herod. Lincoln was a leader and Herod was a wimp for following the wishes of his wife.

What will you be? Is God making you a leader today?

February 13

Two things happened on this day in history in 1945 that both involved Germany when the United States was still in World War II. The first thing that happened is that the Russians captured Budapest, Hungary, from the Germans and pushed the Nazis back to Germany. The second is that Allied aircraft began bombing the German city of Dresden. With Germany losing ground on two fronts, the war would soon be over.

Psalms 18:39 reads: "For thou hast girdest me with strength unto the battle: thou hast subdued under me those that rose up against me."

Here David gives God the glory for a victory. Much like the Soviets and Allies, David put his enemies under his feet. Germany was soon to be under the feet of the Allies.

The Germans were the enemy and rose up against the world. But their uprising was short-lived as compared to the history of the world.

Where are your enemies today? Have you put them under your feet? Have you asked God for a victory over a problem you have?

February 14

Today in history is Valentine's Day, the perfect opportunity to tell you about three people and their hearts. On this day in history in 1984, six-year-old Stormy Jones of Fort Worth, Texas, became the first person to receive a heart and liver transplant at the same time. This type of operation had never been done before. Stormy lived for six more years before her body rejected the heart and liver. She died at a Pennsylvania hospital where her surgery was first performed.

The second person was the donor. We don't know who that was, but obviously he or she came from a great family who was willing to help others have a better life. With the loss of a loved one who has just passed into eternity, it is especially challenging to offer a part of that body to someone you don't know, and this family did and should be thanked.

Jesus is the third person. Ephesians 3:17 reads: "That Christ may dwell in your hearts by faith; that ye, being rooted and grounded in love."

Whether you are the donor or recipient, Jesus can still abide in your heart when you ask Him. This verse tells us that Christ may dwell in you because of faith and that Jesus has enough love for everyone.

Today, on Valentine's Day, where is your heart? Who abides in your heart? Why not let Jesus?

February 15

On this day in history in 1942, the British stronghold of Singapore fell to the Japanese. On December 6, 1941, the Japanese landed more than twenty thousand troops near Singapore in a surprise attack. Poor communications and overwhelming manpower stopped the British defense and it lost its foothold in the Far East.

One of the strongholds we can read about in the Bible is called Nineveh. The prophet Nahum prophesied against the people of Nineveh for their sin against God. If you recall, Nineveh was the city that Jonah prophesied against, and its people repented and came back to the Lord. Then about 150 years later, Nineveh is facing the same problem.

Nahum 3:14 reads: "Draw thee waters for the siege, fortify thy strongholds: go into clay, and tread the mortar, make strong the brickkiln."

Nahum is telling the people to build, fortify, and supply and get everything ready.

When some people hear about what God does to you, they may cover their ears.

Are you living against God? Have you realized that it is hopeless to fight God? Trust God, He will protect you and save you.

February 16

On this day in history in 1862, Fort Donaldson, Tennessee, and Fort Heiman, Kentucky, fell to General Ulysses S. Grant and the Union Army. This battle was very important because it opened the Tennessee and Cumberland rivers to Union shipping and control. Shortly after that, Nashville, Tennessee, also fell, and the western territory was now in Union hands. The Union then turned their attention toward Memphis, Tennessee, and Vicksburg, Mississippi, as part of a major plan to split the Confederacy in half.

Nebuchadnezzar was the King of Babylon, and the Babylonians had taken the Children of Israel captive. Nebuchadnezzar was wicked and always punishing the Jews. But then one night he had a dream, with David interpreting it for him through God after he told the king that only God can interpret dreams.

Daniel 5:28 reads: "PERES; Thy kingdom is divided, and given to the Medes and Persians."

Nebuchadnezzar's kingdom was now divided. Just like the Confederacy, their nation was divided, and the Rebels couldn't get their supplies from the west.

In the passage from Daniel, Nebuchadnezzar's supply line had been cut.

What kind of a nation do you have? Is it divided? Why not let God reunite your nation? Trust Him and believe.

February 17

On this day in history in 1933, Blondie Boopadoop married Dagwood Bumstead, an event that happened three years after the debut of the strip "Dagwood" by Chic Young. In its time, and even today, it is a popular comic strip. Dagwood and Blondie had a running script about living life, raising kids, spending money, and participating in other general happenings. Dagwood is also known for his enormous Dagwood sandwich that included just about everything edible in the kitchen, often with several layers. Whatever he had in the refrigerator went into the sandwich.

Speaking of hunger, Matthew 5:6 reads: "Blessed are they which do hunger and thirst after righteousness: for they shall be filled."

Being hungry and thirsty for righteousness' sake is a different hunger from that you would get thinking of a Dagwood sandwich. When we seek righteousness, that is the part for which our hunger yearns – and it's food for the heart and soul. When you're hungry, you want more.

Are you hungry for God's word? Do you search after righteousness? Why not begin now?

February 18

On this day in history in 2001, Dale Earnhardt Jr. was killed in a racecar accident in the Daytona 500. While he was a popular driver, he won the Daytona 500 only once. The race is the first of the season of the National Association for Stock Car Racing, which we know as NASCAR, and it presents opportunities to identify and place safety measures into racing. After Earnhardt's death, even more safety measures were put into place.

Most men at some phase in their lives enjoy NASCAR and racing, and for some the passion lasts longer than for others.

The Apostle Paul also loved to run the course. The passages in 2 Timothy 4:7-8 read: "I have fought a good fight, I have finished my course, I have kept the faith: Henceforth there is laid up for me a crown of righteousness, which the Lord, the righteous judge, shall give me at that day: and not to me only, but unto all them also that love his appearing."

Earnhardt loved racing, and he gave his best in every race he entered. The Apostle Paul here states that his life is over, and he is on his last course and looking forward to his reward. Paul's reward was a crown of righteousness.

Will you receive a crown of righteousness? Are you on your last course? Do you know when you race will be over? Put your trust in God.

February 19

On this day in history in 1945, some 30,000 U.S. Marines began their invasion of Iwo Jima, an island close to Japan that is useful for its defensive and offensive position. The island was defended by 23,000 Japanese through an elaborate network of caves and tunnels.

America wanted the base for offensive reasons, as it had three landing strips on it. Being close to Japan, it provided a base of operations for aircraft coming and going after the bombing of Japan.

Iwo Jima is also known for the famous photograph of the American flag being raised on top of Mount Suribachi, and a memorial depicting the event was later dedicated.

Psalms 20:5 reads: "We will rejoice in thy salvation, and in the name of our God we will set up our banners: The Lord fulfill all thy petitions."

We rejoice in salvation, just as the Marines rejoiced when the flag was raised at Mount Suribachi.

What kind of banner will you lift up? A joyful life is a great banner to lift up. Is your banner a God-filled banner?

February 20

On this day in history in 1944, Operation Big Week began. Allied forces were getting better all the time, and the war machines and the people who operated them were learning fast how to use them. With longer range bombers and faster escorts, targets became easier to make. Operation Big Week started with the Allies bombing aircraft manufacturers in Germany with the notion that if the supply were cut off, a win could be within reach. As a matter of fact, most German aircraft factories were destroyed. Fighting could also be brought to the home front. As with Union General William T. Sherman's scorched earth policy, it could also cut off morale.

Numbers 21:2 reads: "And Israel vowed a vow unto the Lord, and said, if thou wilt indeed deliver this people into my hand, then I will utterly destroy their cities."

Here Israel is at war with the Canaanite King Arad, and the Canaanites had captured some spies for Israel. Israel wanted to completely destroy them and asked for God to let them do it.

Just like the Allies who wanted to destroy Germany's cities and aircraft factories, Israel wanted to destroy the land of the Canaanites.

How well are you facing your enemies? Are you being destroyed? God will help you to be delivered from your problems.

February 21

On this day in history in 1948, NASCAR was officially incorporated with William "Bill" France Sr., as the driving force behind its success. France was an auto mechanic from Washington, D.C., who moved to Daytona, Florida, and began working on cars for NASCAR owners. Because of the difference in rules for stock car racing, he wanted an association that had only one set of rules. Soon NASCAR began building racetracks across the South as the sport became more popular. In 1972, France took over as president of NASCAR, and through his leadership, the organization became known worldwide.

The passage of 1 Corinthians 9:24 reads: "Know ye not that they which run in a race run all, but one receiveth the prize? So, run, that ye may obtain."

There are 43 cars at the start of every NASCAR race, but only one winner can claim the top prize. The Apostle Paul tells us that we also need to run for the top prize. The difference between Paul's race and NASCAR's is that by believing in Christ, everyone can win the prize, but as we know NASCAR has only one winner.

How are you running? Will you receive the prize of the high calling of Jesus?

February 22

On this day in history George Washington was born in 1732. During his lifetime, he became commander of the Continental Army and was also a farmer, surveyor, and landowner. He also served two years at the Constitutional Convention, during which he became the first president of the then-young United States of America.

After a long and lustrous career, Washington died at the age of 67 at his home in Mount Vernon, Virginia, just a few miles south of Washington, D.C. In 1960, his estate became a national monument.

Another man in earlier times who became a great leader was David. David was the youngest of eight sons born of Jesse, and his first claim to fame was that he fought the giant Goliath and won in what was probably the first rock party in recorded history. From his beginnings as a poor shepherd boy to becoming the king of Israel, David fit in, living a life that was rife with both good and bad but always in the spirit of repentance.

Acts 13:22 reads: "And when he had removed him, he raised up unto them David to be their king; to whom also he gave testimony, and said, I have found David the son of Jesse, a man after mine own heart, which shall fulfill all my will."

Are you a man after God's own heart? Are you just getting by? Are you doing God's commands? Trust God to make you a leader.

February 23

On this day in history in 1945, U.S. Marines serving on Sulfur Island looked up to Mount Suribachi on Iwo Jima to see a small American flag waving in the wind. After four days of fighting on Iwo Jima, the Marines finally crested the summit of the volcanic mountain that covered the island. With the win, American planes could now attack the Japanese homeland with no danger. Later that afternoon, the Marines raised another larger flag that was even more visible. Five Marines and a lone Navy companion raised that second flag for a photo opportunity that became a symbol of the end of World War II.

In Psalms 121:1-2, David says: "I will lift up mine eyes unto the hills, from whence cometh my help. My help cometh from the Lord, which mad heaven and earth."

Just like David, I'm sure the Marines on Iwo Jima saw our national banner and thus raised not only their spirits, but also for those across the earth.

Do you lift up God's banner?

February 24

On this day in history in 1942, the U.S. government diverted all 12-gauge shotguns to be used in the military. Yahooooo! That was a country boy veteran's dream. Previously the 12-gauge shotgun was – and still is – used for sporting or hunting. Can you imagine how a country boy would feel if he could use a 12-gauge shotgun while in battle? Those shotguns don't hold as much ammunition as a rifle, but its blast scatters – and so does everyone who may be within reach of its pellets.

The passage in 2 Kings 25:5 reads: "And the army of the Chaldees pursued after the king, and overtook him in the plains of Jericho: and all his army were scattered from him."

The Chaldees Army from Babylon had just defeated Israel, and the King of Israel was fleeing to avoid capture. Although he was caught, his men scattered like the pellets of a shotgun blast.

Whether an army is armed with rifles, pistols or shotguns, its men still could be scattered; and the more disturbance that you caused, the easier it became to scatter others. We should be trained to hold fast instead of to scatter.

Are you being scattered? Can God depend on you?

February 25

On February 6, 1986, President Ronald Reagan addressed the nation, saying, "To preserve our blessed land we must look to God, it is time to realize we need God more than He needs us."

How true that is today. In 1 Timothy 2:1-3, the Apostle Paul writes: "I exhort therefore, that, first of all, supplications, prayers, intercessions, and giving of thanks, be made for all men; For kings and for all that are in authority; that we may lead a quiet and peaceable life in all godliness and honesty. For this is good and acceptable in the sight of God our Savior."

Yes, that does include our nation's current leaders, and not only them, but also all leaders of the church, community, county, city, state, and even civic club leaders. Let's remember our leaders as we pray.

Can you ask God to protect our leaders?

February 26

On this day in history in 1968, the American and South Vietnamese troops recaptured the city of Hue from the defenders of the Viet Cong and North Vietnamese soldiers. Later a mass grave was found that contained the remains of 2,800 men, women and children, with estimates that upwards of 5,700 died there. Regardless of the number of those killed, they were believed to be loyalists of the government in Saigon. And it should be noted that the Tet Offensive of 1968 was also the worst time for Americans in Vietnam, as from January 30 until February 26 of that year, most of the gains made by the Communists were at the heavy cost of lives on both sides.

Luke 9:24 reads: "For whosoever will save his life shall lose it: but whosoever will lose his life for my sake, the same shall save it."

During the Vietnam Conflict, the Allies and Communists alike were winners and losers. The Communists won when they captured Hue, and the Allies won when they retook the same city.

This verse in Luke tells us that if we save our lives on earth, they will be lost in eternity. Thinking and acting for one's self only is a life gone bad. This verse also tells us that when we lose our lives on this earth for the sake of the Gospel, we will win in eternity.

Are you saving your life on this earth? If we stand for Christ and lose our life, the eternity in Heaven is our goal. Are you reaching your goal? And if you are, for which one are you reaching?

February 27

On this day in history in 1776, the Continental Navy began its first operation, which was to go to the Bahamas and capture much-needed munitions. Onboard was the first Navy Jack flag designed by Christopher Gadsden of South Carolina and included a yellow banner with a coiled rattlesnake. Underneath the rattlesnake were the words "Don't Tread On Me."

Ephesians 6:11 reads: "Put on the whole armor of God, that they may be able to stand against the wiles of the devil."

Gaining the needed munitions to supply our Navy helped us to use our armor more effectively.

Are you using the armor called peace of mind that God gave you? Do you have His peace of mind for your life?

February 28

On this day in history in 1969, Airman First Class John Levitow was in a hospital in Japan. Four days earlier, he had been on a combat mission in Vietnam, and the AC 47 gunship known within the ranks as Puff the Magic Dragon was hit by a Viet Cong mortar shell. Levitow pulled a wounded airman to safety from the rear hatch of the plane and then saw a live flare rolling on the floor. He threw himself on the flare and slid to the rear hatch. Next he half-pushed, half-tossed the flare out of the rear hatch of the plane, where it ignited a split second later. Before it was over, Levitow ended up with forty shrapnel wounds – although all eight people on the plane lived.

On Armed Forces Day in 1970, President Richard M. Nixon awarded Levitow the Medal of Honor for his heroic efforts. Levitow later served as a representative of the Connecticut Department of Veterans Affairs until his death from cancer in October of 2000.

Matthew 5:15 reads: "Neither do men light a candle, and put it under a bushel, but on a candlestick; and it giveth light unto all that are in the house."

How is your light shining for Jesus?

February 29

On this day in history in 1940, Hattie McDaniel became the first African-American to win an Oscar for Best Supporting Actress for her portrayal of Mammy in "Gone With the Wind," the epic Southern romance movie. In her early life, the very talented McDaniel dropped out of high school and joined several traveling minstrel shows. She also became the first African-American to sing on the radio. During the Great Depression, she lived in Milwaukee, Wisconsin, where she worked as a ladies' room attendant in a club, as only white singers were allowed to perform at the club. Later, the club later changed its policy and agreed to let her sing.

Matthew 25:21 reads: "His lord said unto him, Well done, thou good and faithful servant: thou hast been faithful over a few things, I will make thee ruler over many things: enter thou into the joy of thy lord."

You have two choices when you have a talent, and those are to use it or lose it. When you use your talent, God will bless you with more talent, but if you lose it, you will be most miserable. I don't profess to know McDaniel's faith or belief, but I do know about the use of talent, and I believe that she used hers.

Are you using your talent? What would God have you to do?

March 1

On this day in history in 1912, Army Captain Albert Berry made the first recorded parachute jump from a moving airplane. He became one of two men to be the first parachute jumpers. The other was a man named Grant Morgan, who jumped in 1911. While that is a year earlier than Berry's jump, Morgan's jump could not be verified, so Berry's record stands.

This reminds me of a story-joke that I once heard. A young army parachutist was about to make his first jump. As he waited for his turn, he asked the pilot if he had ever jumped from a plane. The pilot's answer? "Not from a perfectly good one." These are my feelings exactly.

We sometimes do things that are equally as crazy as jumping from a plane, and sometimes we simply enjoy being a daredevil. Stop for a minute and think of all the occupations that are dangerous. Most of the time, we don't even consider the dangers behind what we do.

James 1:5 reads: "If any of you lack wisdom, let him ask of God, that giveth to all men liberally, and upbraideth not; and it shall be given him."

James tells us to ask God for wisdom. Some may believe jumping from an airplane is okay and safe, while some of us would rather ask God to show us what is dangerous.

What are you asking God for today? Is it something dangerous or wise?

March 2

On this day in history in 1877, Rutherford B. Hayes was declared by Congress to be president of the United States. Samuel J. Tilden was Hayes's Democratic opponent, and he had won the popular vote with one electoral vote ahead of Hayes. Disputed votes had come from Oregon, with the rest from the South, including Florida, Louisiana, and South Carolina. To settle the controversy, an electoral commission was created by Congress. After a bitter fight, Hayes was finally declared the winner.

Matthew 6:20 reads: "But lay up for yourselves treasures in heaven, where neither moth nor rust doth corrupt, and where thieves break through and steal."

The election between Hayes and Tilden was controversial, and I don't know that it was won fair and square. Tilden told his supporters that the nation had enough war problems and to accept the ruling of Congress making Hayes president; thus, another war so close on the heels of the War Between the States was possibly avoided.

Matthew tells us to lay up our treasures in Heaven. By doing this we assure ourselves that Heaven is our goal. Doing the right thing is having a good treasure.

With God, whom do you support? Are you voting for His will in your life?

March 3

On this day in history in 1931, "The Star-Spangled Banner" officially became our national anthem. The song was adopted from the poem "Defense of Fort McHenry" by Francis Scott Key. He wrote the poem while on a ship in the Baltimore's harbor. After a night at battle fighting for America's independence, he saw that our flag was still flying after the melee.

Psalms 69:30 reads: "I will praise the name of God with a song, and will magnify him with thanksgiving."

This verse tells us that David praised God with a song, just as Francis Scott Key praised God with a song.

What better time to sing praises to God than on a battlefield? Think about how you praise Him on your own personal battlefield. You could be praying, or humming, or singing songs of assurance. I once heard that the only thing to do on a battlefield is pray, pray, pray, and then pray some more.

While Francis Scott Key's poem and song may not be considered religious, it does seem to become more religious as we time passes. Let us honor our national anthem, and let us also honor God for His protection on this land.

In the fourth verse of "Defense of Fort McHenry," a line reads, "And this be our motto: In God is Our Trust."

Is your trust in God?

March 4

On this day in history in 1933, President Franklin Delano Roosevelt said in his inauguration speech, "We have nothing to fear but fear itself." America and the world were coming out of the Great Depression, and almost everyone had a fear of something, and perhaps their current, past and future living conditions were all based on fear.

Today both political parties make a good living selling fear. Yes, I said *both* political parties. Whoever sells fear the best gets elected. I wonder what would happen if just one politician said, "Do not fear." His entire party could die a fast death and he could be banished from the world and talked about like no one else.

The Bible has a lot to say about fear. Romans 8:15 reads: "For ye have not received a spirit of bondage again to fear; but ye have received the Spirit of adoption, whereby we cry, Abba, Father."

I am allergic to wasps and other insects. A wasp scares me greatly because of reactions I have to their stings; therefore, I fear wasps.

God has also adopted me, and I can call on Him and will be okay. I will not fear.

What is your fear today? Does it have control of your life? Has God adopted you and made you His child and follower?

March 5

On this day in history in 1960, Elvis Presley was discharged from the U.S. Army, after having been drafted in 1968 and then later serving in Germany. Those who were close to him say that he was just a regular guy. During his military service, he continued to sing for audiences. After his discharge, he spoke of his time in the army with happiness and fondness.

The Holy Bible is full of accounts of singing. In fact, the Book of Psalms is a collection of songs that were written by King David of Israel. Most of us cannot imagine going to church or a place of worship that has no singing, as music sets the pace for worship.

Psalms 100:1 reads: "Make a joyful noise unto the Lord, all ye lands."

Psalms 101:1 reads: "I will sing of mercy and judgment: unto thee, O Lord, will I sing.

Psalms 95:1 reads: "O come, let us sing unto the Lord: let us make a joyful noise to the rock of our salvation."

These few Psalms are about singing, giving praise, and worshipping the Lord through song.

What songs do you sing? Do they bring honor and praise to God?

March 6

On this day in history in 1836, the 13-day siege of the Alamo ended during the Texas Revolution. General Antonio Lopez de Santa Anna with his army of three thousand men finally overran 189 volunteers who had been defending the Alamo and southern Texas against Mexico.

The Alamo is a small Catholic mission in San Antonio, and today it is open to the public and still used as a place of worship. The battle gave rise to the famous war cry of "Remember the Alamo!" Later that year, Texas gained its independence by defeating Santa Anna and his army.

The passage of 1 Corinthians 16:12 reads: "Remember his marvelous works that he hath done, his wonders, and the judgments of his mouth."

As we think of the Alamo, let us also think of God's marvelous deeds in defense of the Alamo. So few withstood so many for so long, and its defenders took refuge in a mission house because it was the strongest fortress around. I believe it was God's leadership and faithfulness. The call of "Remember the Alamo!" was a judgment out of freedom's mouth used by God to inspire others to fight.

How are we being inspired to fight for God and resist Satan today? What is our rallying cry? Do we even have one?

March 7

On this day in history in 1876, Alexander Graham Bell received a patent for his new contraption, the telephone, so we can blame him for those interruptions from friends, family, and telemarketers during suppertime.

All joking aside, telephones have greatly improved since 1876. We've seen them all, from the old wall-hanging phones, to the battery-operated ones that could weigh several pounds, to the bag phone, to the cell phone, to the handheld smartphone. Most of us laughed at the comic character Dick Tracy's watchphone, but that day has arrived with the Apple Watch.

Communications have improved since the first telephone, and now we can call anyone in the world in just a matter of seconds or minutes.

Matthew 6:8 reads: "Be not ye therefore like unto them: for your Father knoweth what things ye have need of, before ye ask him."

Matthew tells us in this verse that communication is fast with God. It's so fast that even before we ask God what we need, He already knows our prayers. Think about that for a moment. Before we realize that we're hungry, God already knows that. Even before we get a new suit of clothes, a car, tools, or anything, God knows our needs. He is like an earthly father, as we can ask for or tell Him our problems. He is ready to hear from his children.

Have you talked to God lately? How often do you talk to God? Now is the time.

March 8

On this day in history in 1965, about 3,500 U.S. Marines were deployed to South Vietnam, the first group of combat troops to land there. Several more were to follow. These troops were to escalate the war and defeat Communism, but it served only to make the war more despised on the home front.

David, King of Israel, did not have Marines in his military, but he did have troops as outlined in 2 Samuel. One of David's mighty men was Uriah. The passage of 2 Samuel 11:15-17 tells of the honor and bravery of Uriah. King David had used trickery to cover his great sin of adultery with Uriah's wife Bathsheba, and he had ordered Uriah killed when the army withdrew from battle. Now King David was guilty of murder, too. Verse 17 reads: "And the men of the city went out, and fought with Joab: and there fell some of the people of the servants of David; and Uriah the Hittite died also."

David thought that one sin would hide another. He was wrong. Instead of hiding a sin, it only added to his guilt.

Do we try to hide our sin? Are the troops mentioned above covering a sin for someone else? Who or what is covering your sin?

March 9

On this day in history in 1862, the Battle of Hampton Roads, Virginia, was fought. How it got its name is still a mystery to me. The battle was the first at sea featuring two ironclad ships, the Union ship the *USS Monitor* and the Confederate ship the *CSS Virginia* (formerly the *USS Merrimac*). The battle lasted for five hours but produced no victor. Until this time all ships were wooden, and many of them were several layers thick. This battle changed the way naval battles were fought, as many believed that iron would not float. It was proved here that it would.

In 2 Kings, the prophet Elisha recovered an ax head and proved it could float. The passage of 2 Kings 6:5 reads: "But as one was felling a beam, the ax head fell into the water: and he cried, and said, Alas, master! for it was borrowed."

The man had lost an ax head, and now he was upset about what to do about it. Elisha then made the ax head to swim, proving iron could float.

Some of the things we hear about today are just as strange. Is it impossible? Do you have the faith to believe?

March 10

On this day in history in 1903, Clare Boothe Luce was born. Luce was her married name. She was a playwright, journalist, and U.S. ambassador to Italy. She was also the first lady elected to Congress from Connecticut as a conservative.

Luce accomplished many firsts, including writing one of her plays that would feature an all-female cast. She was the first woman to serve as ambassador to a major country and the first to become a congresswoman.

The passage of 1 Samuel 25:3 reads: "Now the name of the man was Nabal, and the name of his wife Abigail; and she was a woman of good understanding, and of a beautiful countenance: but the man was churlish and evil in his doings; and he was of the house of Caleb."

King David needed a little food from Nabal. He was going to pay for it, but Nabal refused. Abigail heard about this, so she took supplies and went to see David. She asked for mercy for Nabal, her husband. After Nabal's death, Abigail became a wife to David, and bore him a son named Chileab.

Luce and Abigail had a great deal in common: They were resourceful, leaders in their communities and dedicated to their husbands.

Are you like Luce and Abigail? Do you trust God for the things you need?

March 11

On this day in history in 1955, the gifted singer and songwriter Jimmy Fortune was born in Williamsburg, Virginia. For 21 years, he sang tenor with the Statler Brothers, and even wrote the song "Elizabeth," a hit that the group recorded. After the Statlers retired, Fortune became a solo artist and now sings both country and gospel. Probably one of his best-known songs today is "More Than a Name on the Wall," which he co-wrote with John Rimel.

The Psalmist David wrote many Psalms (or songs, as the word translates). One of my favorites is Psalms 91, and Verse 1 reads: "He that dwelleth in the secret place of the most, high shall abide under the shadow of the Almighty."

Jimmy Fortune's "More Than a Name on the Wall," which is about the Vietnam Wall, has a special meaning to many of us veterans. And the verse from Psalms also has a special meaning to those of us who need to hide in a place of comfort.

Why not hide under the shadow of the Almighty? It is close to God, and there is room for all.

March 12

On this day in history in 1989, about 2,500 veterans and supporters protested an art display at the Art Institute of Chicago because it portrayed the American flag spread across the floor. The veterans wanted the display removed. This case is only one of many where "Ole Glory" has been disrespected. When the flag is disrespected, then its entire nation is disrespected, especially for those veterans who paid the ultimate price for our freedoms.

Jeremiah 14:21 reads: "Do not abhor us, for thy name's sake: do not disgrace the throne of thy glory: remember, break not thy covenant with us."

Jeremiah is asking the Lord to forgive Israel of its sins and he wants to respect the Lord's house. He is asking God not to destroy the Children of Israel because it would bring dishonor to Him, the Lord. God had made a covenant with Israel that their people would always be here, and he asked them to not break that covenant.

Do you treat the flag and God's house and its people with respect? Could or would anyone protest your life and the way you live it? God will establish His covenant with you if you will let Him.

March 13

On this day in history in 1868, the impeachment trial of President Andrew Johnson began, and it would only prove true the adage that every vote counts.

Johnson was Abraham Lincoln's vice-president. When Lincoln was assassinated, Johnson then became president.

Johnson's years as president were lackluster as he favored admitting Southern states back into the Union. He also didn't support any freedoms for the slaves. Most historians say that the only good thing about Johnson's administration was that Secretary of State William Seward negotiated the Alaska Purchase from Russia in 1867.

Johnson was impeached by the House of Representatives, but the Senate refused to remove him from office by only one vote.

One is an important number. Consider the parable about the lost sheep.

Luke 15:4 reads: "What man of you, having an hundred sheep, if he lose one of them, doth not leave the ninety and nine in the wilderness and go after that which is lost, until he find it."

The lost sheep was important for the shepherd to go look for it. You are important enough for Christ to die for, and He did just that.

Will you put your trust in Him?

March 14

On this day in history in 1945, the Royal Air Force's Dumbuster squad dropped a 22,000-pound bomb on the Bielefeld Railway viaduct in Germany. The Grand Slam, as the bomb was called, was the largest to be used in World War II.

Ever since the beginning of time weapons have been getting bigger and better at killing people. All through the Bible, we read accounts of murder and killing, all the way back from Cain and Abel to reports of what will happen in the end times in Revelation.

Ecclesiastes 3:1-3 reads: "To everything there is a season, and a time to every purpose under the heaven: A time to be born, and a time to die; a time to plant, and a time to pluck up that which is planted; A time to kill, and a time to heal; a time to break down, and a time to build up."

Ecclesiastes was written by Solomon, the son of David. He writes about everything under the sun. In these verses, Solomon tells us there is a time for everything. All of these things are not bad but a few are. Killing is followed by healing; this applies to the family of the deceased and the killer. Killing can come in different forms: by words, deeds and weapons.

Are you killing anyone today? Are you asking for God's forgiveness for your past killings?

March 15

On this day in history in 1781, it was one that was very dark during the American Revolution. British General Charles Cornwallis and his force of 1,900 soldiers defeated an American force of 4,400, an event that became known as the Battle of Guilford Courthouse in North Carolina. During most wars, it seems, there is almost always a dark period just before a final victory.

Exodus 17:11 reads: "And it came to pass, when Moses held up his hand, that Israel prevailed: and when he let down his hand, Amalek prevailed."

Israel and the army of Amalek were at war. While Moses gave the plan of battle, Joshua was to carry it out. When Moses' hands were raised, Israel was winning. When Moses' hands became tired and he let them down to rest, then Amalek won. This went back and forth for a while. Moses then sat on a stone, and then Aaron, his brother, and Hur, a companion to the two, held his hands up until dark. Israel won a hard-fought battle. I don't know whose army was the largest, but it really doesn't matter. God was with Moses and the Children of Israel.

Will God be with you now and forever? He will help you win your battles. Believe in Him and trust His leadership.

March 16

On this day in history in 1945, the Japanese island of Iwo Jima was secured by the U.S. Marines. A few small pockets of resistance of the Japanese remained but most of the fighting was over. The epic attack on Iwo Jima, an island filled with caves, tunnels, dugouts, and underground installations, started February 19, 1945. So complex were these passageways that two Japanese defenders did not surrender until 1951, as they had remained hidden and didn't know the war had been over for years. History would prove that a harder-fought battle would be difficult to find.

Hundreds of years before, another war raged, with King David and his son Absalom. Ahithophel was a prophet of Israel, and he gave bad advice to Absalom and his men. Ahithophel wanted Absalom to win the battle with David and kill him. During World War II, a popular saying was, "Loose lips sinks ships." This could be true here also, as King David's war, too, was filled with spies and counterspies.

The passage in 2 Samuel 18:4 reads, "And the king said unto them, What seemeth you best I will do. And the king stood by the gate-side, and all the people came out by hundreds and by thousands."

David then commanded the leaders of his army to be kind to Absalom. A father will always love his son even if the son is doing wrong. In the end, battle belonged to King David and his men.

Whose advice are you taking? Does it match up with God's Word?

March 17

On this day in history in 1942, General Douglas MacArthur was named commander of all Allied forces in the southwest Pacific, which included the Philippines. His headquarters were in Manila. When the Japanese invaded the islands, MacArthur was forced to leave the Philippines, famously declaring, "I shall return!" MacArthur, being a man of character, during the war later returned to the Philippines as he had promised and forced the Japanese to leave.

Jesus, another man, one of perfect character, left His place on earth and also promised to return.

Acts 1:9 reads: "And when he had spoken these things, while they beheld, he was taken up; and a cloud received him out of their sight."

Jesus then ascended unto Heaven, His disciples watching Him as He rose up into the sky. Then two men wearing white robes joined the disciples, saying, "He is gone, but He will return the same way He left. He went up in a cloud and will come down in a cloud."

What kind of character do you have? When you say something, do you do it? Are you ready for Jesus Christ to return?

March 18

On this date in history in 1975, the government of South Vietnam surrendered most of the Central Highlands of their country to the North Vietnam government in Hanoi, marking the beginning of the end for the separate country of South Vietnam. From the Central Highlands and then following north along the Demilitarized Zone, the DMZ, South Vietnam began falling like dominoes, one piece of it after another. American soldiers were immediately evacuated as Saigon fell to the Communists, signaling the war in Vietnam was over, at least for the Americans. Its remnants today include health complications from Agent Orange as well as Post Traumatic Stress Disorder (PTSD).

Matthew 25:31-46 tells of two sets of people and how they treated God. The first group Jesus said were to enter into the throne of his glory (Verse 31), and the second group Jesus told to depart.

Matthew 25:41 reads: "Then shall he say also unto them on the left hand, Depart, from me, ye cursed, into everlasting fire, prepared for the devil and his angels."

In this verse, Jesus tells us what will happen when we don't treat others the way we should. The way we treat others is the way we would want to be treated. But there is help for those who are sick and stressed.

How do you treat others, especially the sick and stressed? It is hard to follow God's Will, but for our sake, we must.

March 19

On this day in history in 1945, Adolf Hitler issued the Nero Decree. With the Allies moving toward victory, the Germans were retreating and World War II was drawing to a close in Europe. The Nero Decree stated that all retreating German armies were to burn anything that the Allies could use for the war effort. In effect, it told the Allies that they were winning the war. Even if Germany could turn things around and counterattack, they would have no supplies.

The verse of 1 Samuel 30 tells of David and how he avenged the burning of a city in Israel called Ziklag. The Amalekites had invaded Ziklag when David was away, taking its women and children captive and then burning the city. When David and his men returned, everyone was gone and the city in ashes. David then asked God if he should pursue the Amalekites, and God answered a resounding yes. When David captured them, he slew them all except four hundred men who had escaped on camels.

The verse of 1 Samuel 30:18 reads: "And David recovered all that the Amalekites had carried away: and David rescued his two wives."

Just as Hitler ordered everything burned in the Nero Decree, the Amalekites burned Ziklag in hopes of stopping the victors from advancing. In the end, neither Hitler nor the Amalekites were victorious.

Are you burning the ground behind you? Are you living a victorious life?

March 20

On this day in history in 1922, the U.S. Navy commissioned its first aircraft carrier, the *USS Langley*. At one time the *Langley* was a coal-carrying ship called the *USS Jupiter*. It was converted as an aircraft carrier from 1920-22, and then served in World War II alongside two other ships until the Japanese successfully bombed it on February 27, 1942. The captain gave the order to abandon ship, and then around 1:30 that afternoon the *USS Whipple* and the *USS Edsall* shelled the *Langley* to sink and keep her from Japanese hands.

The verse of 2 Chronicles 20:37 reads: "Then Eliezer the son of Dodavah of Mareshah prophesied against Jehoshaphat, saying, Because, thou hast joined thyself with Ahaziah, the Lord hath broken thy works. And the ships were broken, that they were not able to go to Tarshish."

This verse has nothing to do with a ship being hit in battle, but it does say that the ships would not sail. Both types of ships are worthless, one hit by the enemy and the other by God who did not give His approval for the other ship.

How does your ship sail? Is your ship in God's Will? Is your ship just getting by and not sailing?

March 21

On this day in history in 1939, Kate Smith recorded "God Bless America." She had asked Irvin Berlin to compose a patriotic song for her to sing and record. World War II was just beginning, and soon she sang it in the 1943 movie "This is the Army," a comedy-musical that Berlin also wrote. While many artists have recorded the song, the general consensus is that no other versions have been better than Kate Smith's.

Psalms 33:12 reads: "Blessed is the nation whose God is the Lord; and the people whom he hath chosen for his own inheritance."

"God Bless America" could have been taken from this passage of Scripture, because its words are more truthful today. By asking God to bless America, it also means that we must let God be our Lord. When we bless God, He will bless us. We will then inherit His Kingdom.

Do you bless the Lord? Are you a part of His chosen people who will one day inherit His Kingdom?

March 22

On this day in history in 1965, the United States confirmed that its troops used chemical weapons against the Viet Cong, but what they did not say was that American troops were also exposed to those same chemical weapons. We know that weapon today as Agent Orange, and its effects include, among other maladies, diabetes, heart disease, all types of cancers, memory loss, and increased Post Traumatic Stress Disorder (PTSD).

Matthew 9:35 reads: "And Jesus went about all the cities and villages, teaching in their synagogues, and preaching the gospel of the kingdom, and healing every sickness and every disease among the people."

This Scripture gives us hope that Jesus will heal all of our diseases, whether from Agent Orange and or others if you ask Him to heal. He will, according to His will and in His own time. It brings a real-life blessing for someone to pray for your healing.

Have you asked God to forgive you of your sins? Have you asked God to heal your body?

March 23

This day in history in 1942 was a dark day for America. The United States began relocating Japanese-Americans from the West Coast to detention centers in the central part of the country. Our government feared that some of the Japanese-Americans were spies for Japan and took them, at least most of the time, without warning in snatch-and-grab scenarios.

The passage of 2 Kings 24:14 reads: "And he carried away all Jerusalem, and all the princes, and all the mighty men of valor, even ten thousand captives, and all the craftsmen and smiths: none remained, save the poorest sort of the people of the land."

The "he" in this verse is King Nebuchadnezzar of Babylon. The Children of Israel were not expecting to be captured and deported against their will. Much like the Japanese-Americans, they were forcefully moved, followed by much hardship among their numbers.

How do we treat our enemies today? Do we punish them because we're mad or just going to get even? Before we go against our enemies, do we really think and pray about it? Next time the shoe may be on the other foot, and it may not fit as well as we think.

March 24

On this day in history in 1765, Britain passed the Quartering Act, which required Americans to house ten thousand British troops in private and public buildings. With tensions already high with Great Britain, the act made things only worse. Americans may have been under British rule, but that didn't mean they had to like it, much less have to feed them. The Quartering Act stayed into effect until the War of Independence was won; however, it was rarely enforced and when it was, there was always the possibility of bloodshed.

Acts 28:7-8 reads: "In the same quarters were possessions of the chief man of the island, whose name was Publius; who received us, and lodged us three days courteously. And it came to pass, that the father of Publius lay sick of a fever and of a bloody flux: to whom Paul entered in, and prayed, and laid his hands on him, and healed him."

On the island of Melita, the Apostle Paul needed a place to stay as he wandered and preached. The chief of the island welcomed him in a way that we would call with great Southern hospitality. The chief's father was sick, but Paul healed him, which no doubt made the chief even happier. Unlike the British whom no one wanted to house, the Apostle Paul was welcomed with open arms.

How do you treat strangers today? Do you treat them like the British or like the chief of Melita? The Bible tells us that we may treat angels unaware, so treat everyone as if he or she were an angel.

March 25

In March of 1775, Patrick Henry addressed the Second Virginia Convention. We all know the last line of his speech: "Give me liberty or give me death."

What about Henry's next-to-the-last line, "Is life so dear or peace so sweet, as to be purchased at the price of chains and slavery? Forbid it, Almighty God."

This passage is probably more important for us to learn than the first one.

The prophet Jeremiah, while in captivity in Babylon, writes the words God gave him.

Jeremiah 29:11-13 reads: "For I know the thoughts that I think toward you, saith the Lord, thoughts of peace and not of evil, to give you an expected end. Then shall ye call upon me, and ye shall go and pray unto me, and I will hearken unto you. And ye shall seek me, and find me, when ye shall search for me with all your heart."

Do we seek peace today?

March 26

On this day in history in 1953, Dr. Jonas Salk announced that he had discovered a cure for polio, a crippling disease that anyone could get, even presidents, as evidenced by Franklin Delano Roosevelt. Most of us today can remember when we took the polio vaccine; it resembled a sugar cube. Salk, the son of a Polish immigrant, could have been rich for finding the cure but he refused to patent the formula. Within a few months of getting the vaccine to the public, the disease began to fade away.

Exodus 15:26 reads: "And said, if thou wilt diligently harken to the voice of the Lord thy God, and wilt do that which is right in His sight and wilt give ear to His commandments, and keep all His statutes, I will put none of these diseases upon thee, which I have brought upon the Egyptians: for I am the Lord that healeth thee."

The Children of Israel had left captivity in Egypt and crossed the Red Sea, headed to the Promised Land. They were out of the water and cried to the Lord, who told them to follow Him and trust Him and seek His voice. Only then would He heal them.

Salk invented the cure for polio, but it was up to us and our parents to accept and take the vaccine. After that, we never again became ill from polio.

Are you following God's voice today?

March 27

In March of 1953, Dr. Jonas Salk announced that he had discovered a cure for polio. I know that this same topic was also in yesterday's devotion. Life expectancy for those born around 1900 was 46.3 years for men and 48.3 for women. In 1950, the life expectancy was 65.6 for men and 71.1 for women. The discovery of the polio vaccine and other medical breakthroughs helped these numbers to rise. In the year 2000, the life expectancy was 75 for men and 80 for women.

John 10:10 reads: "The thief cometh not, but for to steal, and to kill, and to destroy: I am come that they might have it more abundantly."

The word abundantly means simply "more than enough." Jesus is telling his disciples that through Him, we will have more than enough.

The lifespan is eternity for both men and women. Are you living an abundant life today?

March 28

On this day in history in 1797, Nathaniel Briggs was awarded a patent for a washing machine – and all of our clothes have been cleaner since. What a joy it is to have clean clothes.

The passage of 1 John 1:7 reads: "But if we walk in the light, as he is in the light, we have fellowship one with another, and the blood of Jesus Christ his Son cleanseth us from all sin."

This verse tells us that we can always walk in the light, that we can have good fellowship with others, and that Jesus Christ cleanseth us of our sins.

How is your walk today? Is it clean?

March 29

On this day in history in 1927, Major Henry O'Neil de Hane Segrave become the first man to drive more than 200 miles per hour, achieving this feat at Daytona Beach, on Florida's Atlantic coast. Ever since then, man seems to have a need for speed. Maybe not 200 miles per hour fast, but fast, nonetheless.

David writes in Psalms 46:10; "Be still, and know that I am God: I will be exalted among the heathen, I will be exalted in the earth."

While we may have a need for speed, God's Word tells us to slow down and listen to him.

Have you heard God talk lately?

March 30

On this day in history in 1842, Dr. Crawford W. Long performed the first operation with the use of ether. As for his background, Long was born in Danielsville, Georgia, just outside of Athens. At the age of 14, he entered Franklin College, which later became the University of Georgia.

Upon graduation five years later, Long studied under Dr. George Grant of nearby Jefferson, a town northwest of Atlanta. He then attended medical school at Transylvania College in Kentucky and the University of Pennsylvania in Philadelphia. It was in Pennsylvania where he received his surgical training. He then worked in New York City for a year before returning to Jefferson to buy Grant's practice.

Long noticed that men taking ether for a recreational drug suffered no pain from their follies. For example, his patient, James Venable, had a cyst removed while under ether with three witnesses present for the procedure and saw that he felt no pain during the surgery. That type of anesthesia works wonders to this day.

Revelation 21:4 reads: "And God shall wipe away all tears from their eyes; and there shall be no more death, neither sorrow, nor crying, neither shall there be any more pain: for the former things are passed away."

Imagine a time when we will not need ether anymore. We will all be new people in a place called Heaven. God will wipe our eyes and there will be no more pain. What a glorious time that will be.

Are you ready for God to remove your pain? Trust and believe and He will handle your pain.

March 31

On this day in history, the town of Wabash, Indiana, became the first in the United States to have a complete electrical light system. The lights were powered by a steam engine that generated electricity. Today electricity is one of the resources that we take for granted, and it is plentiful and relatively inexpensive.

In John 8:12, Jesus said; "I am the light of the world: he that followeth me shall not walk in darkness, but shall have the light of life."

Just as the streetlights of Wabash provide light, Jesus provides us light to follow Him in everything we do.

Are you following Jesus?

April 1

On this day in history in 1789, John Adams took the oath of office of vice-president of the United States of America. This had never happened before. America was experimenting with a new form of government, but at that time no one had heard of peaceful change of government. Maybe if you were a king and had a son or daughter to follow you, that would have been peaceful. But some changes of government were not peaceful at all.

The passage of II Kings 19:37 reads: "And it came to pass, as he was worshipping in the house of Nisroch, his god, that Adrammelech and Sharezer, his sons, smote him with a sword: and they escaped into the land of Armenia. And Esar-haddon, his son, reigned in his stead."

You could say that this was not a peaceful change in government. Several times in American history, the vice-president has had to take over as president. No war ever started from that change, though, and to my knowledge no one was killed.

We are a nation of laws. We must follow our laws. But God has His laws, too. Do you follow God's laws?

April 2

On this day in history in 1865, Jefferson Davis, president of the Confederacy, and most of his cabinet fled Richmond, Virginia, which was at the time the capital of the Confederacy. General Robert E. Lee surrendered his Army of Northern Virginia to Union General Ulysses S. Grant a week later at Appomattox Courthouse in Virginia, an act that brought about the end of the War Between the States.

The prophet Isaiah said in the book of Isaiah 2:4; "And he shall judge among the nations, and shall rebuke many people: and they shall beat their swords into plowshares, and their spears into pruninghooks: nation shall not lift up sword against nation, neither shall they learn war anymore."

We are still studying the War Between the States even until this day. Even in the presence of war, we need to pray for peace.

Are you seeking peace?

April 3

On this day in history, two separate but related events happened, even though they are four years apart.

In 1942, the Japanese launched an all-out assault against the United States and Filipino forces at Bataan. Then in 1946, Lieutenant General Masahaw Homma, the Japanese commander for the 1942 event, was executed in the Philippines for his actions in that the Bataan Death March was one of the cruelest events in history. Troops were beaten, starved, and deprived of water while Japanese forces lived it up around him.

The prophet Isaiah was in captivity in Babylon. He was prophesying on the punishment the Lord would render not only to Babylon, but also to the entire world for their treatment of Israel.

Isaiah 13:9 reads: "Behold, the day of the Lord cometh, cruel both with wrath and fierce anger, to lay the land desolate: and he shall destroy the sinners thereof out of it."

The Lord will protect His people. When you trust Christ, you will be saved and protected also.

Are you being protected?

April 4

On this date in history in 1841, President William Henry Harrison became the first president to die while in office. He had been in office for only a month when he died from pneumonia. Historians tell us that at his inaugural address, he refused to wear a coat and hat in spite of bad weather, and as a result of being exposed to such harsh conditions, Harrison then came down with pneumonia.

The passage of 2 Kings 20:1 reads: "In those days was King Hezekiah sick unto death. And the Prophet Isaiah the son of Amoz came to him and said unto him, Thus saith the Lord, set thine house in order; for thy shalt die and not live."

Sometimes we ask God for things that are not in our best interests. This is what King Hezekiah did. He served God all of his life, and then asked for more time. God gave him fifteen more years, but in that time, he didn't serve the Lord. All of Israel had to pay, and they were taken into captivity.

What are you asking God for? Is it in his will or just yours? Hezekiah is remembered for not following God. What will you be remembered for?

April 5

On this day in history in 1869, Daniel Bakeman, the last survivor of the Revolutionary War, died at the age of 109. Bakeman fought for our country's independence, and then lived to see our country torn apart and then reunited again by the War Between the States. Amazingly, Bakeman was only 16 years old when he joined the war effort in 1777.

Proverbs 20:29 reads: "The glory of the young men is their strength: and the beauty of the old men is the grey head."

Bakeman lived this verse. At one time in his life he was a strong man. As we grow older, we all probably say at one time or another, "I used to be able to do that." Bakeman also lived in the gray-haired side of life, where wisdom comes with age.

Whether your life now is young or old, what is it saying about you? How are you living your life?

April 6

On this day in history in 1965, President Lyndon B. Johnson authorized the use of ground troops in combat operations in Vietnam. Before this time, and before 1959, all other troops were advisers.

The first American killed in Vietnam was Lt. Col. Peter Dewey, an American Army officer stationed in Saigon. Dewey was reported killed in South Vietnam in 1945 while he was on a mission during World War II. In 1959, the official start of the Vietnam War, Major Dale R. Ruis and Master Sergeant Chester M. Ovnand died at Bien Hoa to become the first of those killed in action since the official start of the conflict.

John 15:13 it reads "Greater love hath no man than this, that a man lay down his life for his friends."

Dewey, Ruis and Ovnand are probably known only to a very few, but we must honor them for their service and sacrifice, for as veterans they are our brothers. Their love was great for us and their country.

Is your love that great? How has God blessed you because of your sacrifice to others?

pril 7

On this day in history in 1971, President Richard M. Nixon pledged to withdraw a hundred thousand troops from Vietnam by December, a pledge that is considered the beginning of the end for the Vietnam War. America was just at the threshold of winning that unpopular war or getting out. Nixon chose for the United States to cut and run.

Genesis 15:1 reads: "After these things the word of the Lord came unto Abram in a vision, saying, Fear not, Abram: I am thy shield, and thy exceeding great reward."

God uses His word in the Holy Bible to teach us things that we face today. One of those things is fear. God tells us that He will be our shield, and the stand we take for Him lets us know that he will protect us.

Do we stand for God and His protection?

April 8

On this day in history in 1832, three hundred troops of the U.S. 6th Infantry Division left Jefferson Barracks at St. Louis during the Black Hawk War. In the 1830s, the process of removing Native Americans from their ancestral lands began. Most of the process was peaceful because of America's growth and power.

In 1830 the Sauk and Fox tribes were moved west of the Mississippi River, which meant they had to leave their tribal grounds. Black Hawk, the chief of the Sauk, returned to better lands east of the Mississippi. But the Illinois governor called for the U.S. Army to remove them to the West. During the conflict, now known as the Black Hawk War, and which lasted just fifteen weeks, more than half of the Sauk warriors were killed but very few Americans died.

In 1 Samuel 28:1 reads: "And it came to pass in those days, that the Philistines gathered their armies together for warfare, to fight with Israel. And Achish said unto David, Know, thou assuredly, that thou shalt go out with me to battle, thou and thy men."

Just like the troops from Jefferson Barracks, David and his men had to go out and fight.

Battles will not be won by staying home. When we spread the Gospel of Christ, we must go out to reach others.

Have you gone out to reach someone lately?

April 9

On this day in history in 1998, the National Prisoner of War Museum opened in Andersonville, Georgia, the site of the infamous prisoner of war encampment during the War Between the States. Camp Sumter was the official name of Andersonville prison, and it housed Union soldiers. Between February 24, 1864, and April 9, 1865, more than 13,000 men died from disease and hunger at the camp. Many of the Confederate soldiers guarding the camp also died from the same diseases.

Many Biblical people were sent to prison for one reason or another, but mostly for preaching the Gospel of Jesus Christ.

Acts 16:25-34 tell of the Philippian jailer and his conversion, with Verse 25 reading, "And at midnight Paul and Silas prayed, and sang praises unto God: and the prisoners heard them."

The Apostle Paul and his missionary companion were put into jail. While in prison, they prayed and sang praises unto God. Other prisoners heard them. I can only guess how this felt to those other prisoners. Even the main prison guard was saved, and then he helped clean and bandage the disciples' wounds.

Put yourself in the place of the disciples. How about the jailer? Would you be able to sing praises to God? What about a small silent prayer?

April 10

On this day in history in 1865, Confederate General Robert E. Lee issued his last general order, number 9. He acknowledged defeat to the better-supplied and more well-fed Union army. He gave thanks to his men and asked that God would bless them for the rest of their lives.

The Bible teaches that we should always be thankful for our blessings. We must have wisdom to always be thankful. General Lee once said, "Wisdom is nothing more than healed pain." With wisdom we give thanks.

Psalms 136:1-3 reads: "O give thanks unto the Lord; for he is good: for his mercy endureth forever. O give thanks unto the God of gods: for his mercy endureth forever. O give thanks to the Lord of lords: for his mercy endureth forever."

Do you give thanks for the things we have? Do you give thanks for the sufferings we have suffered to make us a better person?

The late Edna Rowell, who lived in a small South Georgia town, once said, "God blesses you with everyone you meet. Some He blesses you when they enter the room, while others bless you when they leave the room."

Let us be a people who bless others and make them thankful for the thing they have. What kind of blessing will you be?

April 11

On this day in history in 1945, American soldiers liberated the prisoners held at Buchenwald, a Nazi concentration camp in Germany. Buchenwald was on the largest of the Nazi camps. In its eight years of its existence, more than 238,000 people from thirty countries were housed there. The prisoners endured forced labor, severe punishment, hangings and medical experiments. When American troops liberated the camp, more than eleven thousand prisoners were still held there.

In Genesis 39:40, the Bible tells us the story of another prisoner named Joseph. After being falsely accused of trying to seduce Potiphar's wife, he was imprisoned. But God protected him, and he gained favor with the leaders of the prison. After several years in prison, he came to interpret Pharaoh's dreams and was released. Joseph served Pharaoh faithfully for the rest of his life, all the while praising God.

Genesis 40:8 reads, "And they said unto him, we have dreamed a dream, and there is no interpreter of it. And Joseph said unto them, do not interpretations belong to God? tell me them, I pray you."

Do you have dreams? Let God interpret them for you as you seek Him now and forever.

April 12

In this season of history, Easter or the Passover is celebrated each year. The dates change from year to year depending on the Jewish calendar. Easter can fall on any given Sunday between March 21 and April 25, depending on when the full moon occurs. Passover is the commemoration of when the Jewish people were released from captivity in Egypt.

For Christian people throughout the world, Easter means the resurrection of Jesus from the dead. Jesus, being the Son of God, was falsely accused of several things including sedition and put to death on the cross. Even when He had the power to get off the cross, He realized that it was God's Will that He had to die to save us of our sins. Three days after being crucified on the cross, Jesus arose again, giving us the assurance that we too will one day rise in Christ.

Matthew 28:5-6 reads: "And the angel answered and said unto the women, Fear not ye: for I know that ye seek Jesus, which was crucified. He is not here: for he is risen, as he said. Come, see the place where the Lord lay."

Is your trust in Christ today?

April 13

On this day in history in 1861, during the War Between the States the Union troops who were held at Fort Sumter, South Carolina, surrendered to the Confederates. The Confederates had shelled the fort for more than 34 straight hours, but even so there were no Union fatalities.

The Confederates held the fort until February of 1865 when it was abandoned as Union General William T. Sherman left the nearby city of Savannah, on Georgia's coast. Sherman aimed to put pressure on Confederate General Robert E. Lee to force him to surrender.

Thirty-four hours of bombardments is a long time. Can you imagine how the people of Jericho felt after six days when the Children of Israel marched around their city in complete quietness? Then came the historical seventh day that Joshua 6:5 describes this way: "And it shall come to pass, that when they make a long blast with the ram's horn, and when ye hear the sound of the trumpet, all the people shall shout with a great shout; and the wall of the city shall fall down flat, and the people shall ascend up every man straight before him."

Joshua did not need any other help from others to win the battle, instead depending upon the Lord.

Do we depend upon the Lord to fight our battles?

April 14

On this day in history in 1865, President Abraham Lincoln was shot at Ford's Theater in Washington, D.C., as he and his wife, Mary Todd Lincoln, were in the audience watching the play, "My American Cousin." The president died the next morning. The War Between the States had just ended, and Confederate sympathizers could not or would not accept loss. When leaders are assassinated, at least there comes a time of reorganization.

Jesus' disciples were the same way. When Jesus was crucified, the disciples went into hiding. Some even scattered and went to other towns, only to return later. Even Peter, the strongest of the disciples, left and went fishing. Much like some of my own fishing trips, Peter caught nothing after fishing all night. But he did see the risen Jesus on the shore, giving him this command in John 21:17: "He saith unto him the third time, Simon, son of Jonas, lovest thou me? Peter was grieved because he said unto him the third time, Lovest thou me? And he said unto him, Lord, thou knowest all things; thou knowest that I love thee. Jesus said unto him, Feed my sheep."

Even in the vacuum of leadership, even when all seems lost, do we continue to feed the sheep of Jesus?

April 15

On this day in history in 1861, President Abraham Lincoln mobilized all federal troops. The move came just two days after Confederates fired upon South Carolina's Fort Sumter in Charleston's harbor. The Union troops stationed there surrendered. Ironically, four years later to the date, Lincoln died as a result of an assassin's bullet, having been shot the night before at Ford's Theater.

Judges 6, 7, and 8 tell of Gideon, a farmer who the Lord used to raise up an army.

Judges 7:1 reads: "Then Jerubbaal, who is Gideon, and all the people that were with him, rose up early, and pitched beside the well of Harod: so that the host of the Midianites were on the north side of them, by the hill of Moreh, in the valley."

As Gideon prepared for war, the Lord had another plan and directed it to him. The plan worked, Israel was saved, and afterward Gideon became the sixth Judge to rule Israel.

Are you following your plan for your life or God's plan?

April 16

On this day in history in 1968, the Pentagon announced that troops would be coming home from Vietnam. This did not work for me, though, because I went to Vietnam later that same year, in September. Many other troops still went after me and for several years to come. I suppose that the Pentagon just did not say *when* the troops would be coming home.

The folks at the Pentagon didn't heed the story about Gideon, who raised an army of thousands of men. Through a process of elimination, he sent all but three hundred home.

Judges 7:7 reads: "And the Lord said unto Gideon, By the three hundred men that lapped will I save you, and deliver the Midianites into thine hand: and let all the other people go every man unto his place."

What a blessing and relief it must be to know that the Lord will protect you.

Are you giving thanks to God for your blessings, and protection?

April 17

On this day in history in 1865, Federal troops arrested Mary Surratt at her boarding house in Washington D.C. She and six men were arrested for conspiracy to murder President Abraham Lincoln, with the group later tried before a military tribunal. All were later hanged.

Jesus was faced with a similar situation. This story can be found in John 8:1-11. A woman was charged for committing adultery, and the Law of Moses directed that she be stoned. Jesus was asked what to do.

Jesus speaks from John 8:7: "So when they continued asking him, he lifted up himself, and said unto them, He that is without sin among you, let him first cast a stone at her."

Jesus then writes on the ground – the Bible does not reveal what he had written – and all the accusers of the woman walked away.

Are you ready to cast a stone at someone? Jesus loved and forgave people. Will you at least try?

April 18

On this day in history in 1775, Paul Revere, William Dawes and Samuel Prescott rode through the towns of Massachusetts warning that the British regular troops were coming to. The phrase, "The British are coming! The British are coming!" that is attributed to Paul Revere is probably not true.

Henry Wadsworth Longfellow published a poem in 1861 in *Atlantic Monthly* entitled "The Midnight Ride of Paul Revere."

Throughout history Satan has tried to get us to believe lies or falsehoods. Satan is a great tempter. He will tell you things that are simply not true. Satan even tried to tempt Jesus.

Luke 4:1-3 reads: "And Jesus being full of the Holy Ghost returned from Jordan, and was led by the Spirit into the wilderness, Being, forty days tempted of the devil. And in those days, he did eat nothing: and when they were ended, he afterward hungered. And the devil said unto him, If, thou be the Son of God, command this stone that it be made bread."

Are you being watchful of the things that Satan tells us? Because we can also be tempted.

April 19

On this day in history in 1775, Lexington, Massachusetts, became the center of attention of the world in that the first shots of the American Revolution were fired there. Americans were tired of British rule and had wanted their independence from the monarchy. It would take several years, but America finally gained her independence.

Much has been said of freedom since that date in history. Perhaps Dr. Martin Luther King said it best in his "I Have a Dream" speech when he quoted from an old spiritual: "Free at last, free at last! Thank God Almighty, we are free at last!"

John 8:31-32 reads: "Then said Jesus to those Jews which believed on him, If, ye continue in my word, then are ye my disciples indeed; And ye shall know the truth, and the truth shall make you free."

Do you live a life of truth and freedom today?

April 20

On this day in history in 1998, The U.S. Air Force and Northrop Grumman unveiled its newest aircraft, the B-2 Bomber, sometimes called the Stealth Bomber. The B-2 could travel at speeds of Mach 0.80 at 40,000 feet or 530 miles per hour. The B-2 can hold 80 to 500 pounds of JDAM Global Positioning System (GPS) bombs or it can hold sixteen B83 nuclear bombs. That makes the B-2 a fast and large aircraft.

Another battle had taken place between a large man and much smaller teen. The teen was David, and the large man was Goliath, who stood at six cubits and a span, or what we know as a whopping 9-1/2 feet.

In 1 Samuel 17:49, we read more about this story: "And David put his hand in his bag, and took thence a stone, and slang it, and smote the Philistine in his forehead, that the stone sunk into his forehead; and he fell upon his face to the earth."

David trusted God for the victory. He did not need a B-2 bomber. I believe, however, that the rock traveled at the speed of a bomb and stuck the giant man called Goliath.

Is God fighting your battles today?

April 21

On this day in history in 1863, Congress established a mint in Denver, Colorado. The mint went into production as a small assay office. Because of gold and silver deposits found in the mountainous region around Denver, the mint soon began to grow. Money is one of those necessary curses that you can't live with or without.

In Matthew 22:15-22, Jesus is being questioned about money and taxes. In an effort to trick Jesus, the Pharisees ask Him about whom to give tribute. Jesus then asked for a piece of money and asked whose image was on the money. The Pharisees told him that it was Caesar's.

Jesus then says in Matthew 22:21: "They say unto him, Caesar's. Then saith he unto them, Render, therefore unto Caesar the things which art Caesar's; and unto God the things that are God's."

How do you handle your money? Do you give to Caesar his due? How about God and His due?

April 22

On this day in history in 1864, Congress passed legislation that allowed the inscription "In God We Trust" to be included on one- and two-cent coins. That same inscription would become our national motto in 1956, by a law passed by Congress and signed into effect by President Dwight D. Eisenhower. It remains our national motto today.

There are plenty of Bible verses about God and country in the Bible. Almost every book in the Old Testament alludes to God protecting his children, the Children of Israel.

Perhaps the most well-known Scripture about God and country is Psalms 33:12, which reads: "Blessed is the nation whose God is the Lord; and the people whom he hath chosen for his own inheritance."

As we think about this Scripture, let us also pray that God will be our God and bless America again.

April 23

This day in history is a difficult one from which to choose, and I'll try not to offend anyone.

On this day in history in 1900, the word hillbilly was first used in print in the *New York Journal*. If you don't know what a hillbilly is, then of course you ain't one. Then there are cousins of hillbillies who live in the flatter regions of the United States who are called rednecks. I can't explain that one, either; however, almost everyone has a trait or two of being a redneck or hillbilly, and some among us have enough traits to be overqualified.

The closest thing in the Bible that I could think of regarding this may be John the Baptist. Matthew 3:3-4 reads: "For this is he that was spoken of by the prophet Esaias, saying, The voice of one crying in the wilderness, Prepare ye the way of the Lord, make his paths straight. And the same John had his raiment of camel's hair, and a leathern girdle about his loins; and his meat was locusts and wild honey."

John the Baptist was also from the hill country of Judea. He was a bold man who spoke against Herod and his adultery with his sister—in-law Herodias. John the Baptist preached to multitudes and baptized many, including Jesus. All of this boldness ended up getting him beheaded because he spoke up against Herod and the way Herod loved dancers.

I will not ask if you are a hillbilly or redneck, but I will ask if you are being bold enough to proclaim Jesus or even to those higher than you in authority. Are you brave enough?

April 24

On this date in history in 1805, the U.S. Marines captured Derma, a Libyan suburb of Tripoli, in the first Barbary War (1801-05). The battle gave rise to the Marine Corps Hymn, written by Jacques Offenbach.

Music is a way of life. We use it and hear it almost everywhere we go, and even our car radios are almost always set to some type of music.

David wrote many songs, or psalms as they are also known, and among the most well-known is Psalms 100, with the first verse as this: "Make a joyful noise unto the Lord, all ye lands."

When we praise the Lord, we may not all be good or better at singing than another, but as long as we praise God, it is music to His ears. Whether we are in a battle or going out of a battle, let us remember to praise God with a song.

April 25

On this day in history in 1985, at the Eugene O'Neill Theatre in New York City, the play "Big River: The Adventures of Huckleberry Finn" opened on Broadway.

The musical, with words and music by Roger Miller, was adapted from a book by William Hauptman and based on Mark Twain's "The Adventures of Huckleberry Finn." With more than a thousand performances played out on stage, it was quite successful.

Huckleberry Finn was told at an early age that he must learn to read and write and go to church so Jesus could love him. While these things are important, it's not the truth about salvation.

In John 14:6, Jesus foretells His coming: "Jesus saith unto him, I am the way, the truth, and the life: no man cometh unto the Father, but by me."

As we think about this verse, let us put our faith in Jesus. He is our only hope for salvation. Do you trust Him?

April 26

On this day in history in 1865, John Wilkes Booth was shot and killed by Union troops in Northern Virginia. Booth had assassinated President Abraham Lincoln twelve days earlier at Ford's Theater in Washington, D.C. After being surrounded by Federal troops, Booth refused to give up because the War Between the States was not over. General Joseph E. Johnson, Confederate commander of the Army of Tennessee, had not yet surrendered to Union General William T. Sherman, although he soon would.

The passage of II Samuel 16:5-6 reads: "And when King David came to Bahurim, behold thence came out a man of the family of the House of Saul, whose name was Shimei, the son of Gera: he came forth and cursed as he came, and he cast stones at David, and at all the servants of King David; and all the people and all the mighty men were on his right hand and on his left."

Shimei and Booth had something in common: they both didn't like the leaders of their countries. Shimei threw rocks at his leader, while Booth shot his. Neither man could accept that everything does not always go the way it was planned.

Are you trusting in God for things to go His way in your life?

April 27

On this day in history in 1965, R.C. Duncan received a patent for the disposable diapers known as Pampers. The idea originated when Duncan was keeping his grandchildren, whom he loved but hated changing their diapers, especially the messy ones. His invention created an entirely new industry and has been well received by parents and grandparents alike.

Jesus mentions children several times in his ministry. One of these times is recorded in Mark 10:13-16. Verse 14 reads: "But when Jesus saw it, he was much displeased, and said unto them, Suffer the little children to come unto me, and forbid them not; for of such is the kingdom of God."

The disciples thought that Jesus had no time for children, but He corrected them with this verse. Jesus goes on to say that we must have the faith of a child to inherit God's Kingdom.

Do you love children? Will you inherit God's Kingdom?

April 28

On this day in history in 1914, Willis H. Carrier patented his design for an air conditioner. Can you imagine where would we be without that invention today, especially in South Georgia where summers are always hot and humid? Some inventions are really good, while others are not so good. The air conditioner was one of the best of all time.

In Matthew 13 Jesus gives us the parable of the sower. The sower's seed fell on the wayside, some in stony places, some in thorns, and some on good ground. The sower did not have a good harvest.

Matthew 13:5 reads: "Some fell upon stony places, where they had not much earth: and forthwith they sprung up, because they had no deepness of earth."

Seeds that fall into stony places is like sun shining on you without the benefit of air conditioning. You could wither in the heat and soon die.

Do you have an air conditioner for your soul or will it wither and die?

April 29

On this day in history in 1945, the U.S. Army's Seventh Division liberated the concentration camp at Dachau, Germany. An estimated 32,000 mostly Jewish prisoners were in the camp, including approximately some 3,000 waiting in boxcars on the train track. Most horribly, though, was that most of the prisoners in the boxcars were already dead from starvation and disease. A few days later, the cruel war in Europe would finally end.

Psalms 46:1-2 reads: "God is our refuge and strength, a very present help in trouble. Therefore, will not we fear, though the earth be removed, and though the mountains be carried into the midst of the sea."

Many lives were saved on this day of liberation in 1945. What do we have to fear when our trust is in God?

April 30

On this day in history in 1789, George Washington took the oath of office as the first president of the United States. He began his duties by giving thanks to the Almighty for the blessings the new country had received and the making of the Constitution of the United States of America.

In Acts 1:17, the Apostle Paul writes: "For therein is the righteousness of God revealed from faith to faith: as it is written, The just shall live by faith."

As the founders of our country had a faith in God, let us have that same faith for the betterment of our country. Are you living by faith?

May 1

On this day in history in 1931, the Empire State Building was dedicated and opened. At the time, it was the tallest building in the world at 102 stories. Whew! I would hate to climb those stairs. I'm sure that just standing at ground level and looking up at the building would make you dizzy. I know that looking down from the 102nd floor would. For a person who is scared of heights, it could be dangerous.

This reminds me of another tower. Genesis 11:4 reads: "And they said, go to, let us build us a city and a tower, whose top may reach unto heaven; and let us make us a name, lest we be scattered abroad upon the face of the whole earth."

When the Empire State Building was built, it was for commerce and trade. When the Tower of Babel was built, it was for man to reach into Heaven. One tower was for good, the other for the conceited. The Tower of Babel was for people who tried to trick God and become like Him. Boy, were they ever confused. God showed them, though, by confounding their tongues so they couldn't understand one another. According to Scripture, then, all the languages of the world came from Babel.

How is your language today? Are you trying to trick God? Are you trying to honor God? The choice is yours.

May 2

On this day in history in 1945, near the end of World War II, after twelve days of fierce house-to-house fighting, the Russian army captured Berlin. The Allies also announced the surrender of Nazi troops in Italy and part of Austria. Each day brought the war closer to an end. The Allies had to come from France and England as they headed to Berlin, and Russia had to come from the other direction. The Nazis were being pinned in with nowhere to go.

Judges 7:20 reads: "And the three companies blew the trumpets, and brake the pitchers, and held the lamps in their left hands, and the trumpets in their right hands to blow withal: and they cried, The sword of the Lord, and of Gideon."

This battle was opposite of the battles between Germany and Russia. This battle was quiet as well as successful. All the Army of Gideon had to do was break their pitchers so their light could shine, blow their trumpets so that a joyful noise could be heard, and shout about the Lord and Gideon.

One of the most fearful things in battle is noise. The opposing army did more damage to themselves than to Gideon's army.

In your battles today, are you caught up with the noise? What about calm in a time of fear? Are you trusting God?

May 3

On this day in history in 1965, the Sky Soldiers of the 173rd Airborne Brigade were deployed to South Vietnam as the first combat unit to arrive in South Vietnam. The 173rd consisted of 4th Battalion, 503rd Infantry; 3rd Battalion; 319th Airborne Artillery; Company E, 16th Armor; Troop E, 17th Cavalry; and the 355th Aviation Group. They were headquartered at Bien Hoa Air Base near Saigon. The 173rd also fought near the Cambodian border and in the Central Highlands of Vietnam. Twelve paratroopers of the 173rd won the Medal of Honor between 1965 and 1971.

The passage of 1 Chronicles 19:11-12 reads: "And the rest of the people he delivered unto the hand of Abishai his brother, and they set themselves in array against the children of Ammon. And he said, If the Syrians be too strong for me, then thou shalt help me: but if the children of Ammon be too strong for thee, then I will help thee."

In these verses, David's army is complete. They had their mighty men, then the soldiers. Like the 173rd Airborne, Infantry, Artillery, Aircraft, all were for one purpose, and that was to support one another, just as David's army was to support each other.

Are you supporting your brothers today? Those who are sick, lonely, in need of encouragement, or help? Then make yourself available to them to be an encourager.

May 4

On this day in history in 1864, the Union Army crossed the Rapidan River to confront Confederate General Robert E. Lee. In March of 1864, General Ulysses S. Grant was made commander-in-chief of Union forces. He went with General George Meade of the Army of the Potomac, and then sent General William T. Sherman to face Confederate General Joseph Johnston in Tennessee. After crossing the Rapidan River, the Union forces stalled because of the thickness of the wilderness. No fighting occurred this day, but Lee attacked the next day. The skirmish became the biggest campaign of the War Between the States, lasting into June at Petersburg, Virginia. There they faced off for the next nine months.

The passage of 1 Samuel 17:16 reads: "And the Philistine (Goliath) drew near morning and evening, and presented himself forty days."

Here the Philistine Army and the Army of Israel were at war with one another and at a standoff. In fact, hardly any fighting ever happened. The giant Goliath served only to intimidate the Army of the Israel. This went on for forty days, but then David came on the scene and thus the Philistine party was over.

Are you patiently waiting for something to happen in your life? Are you depending on God to be your helper in His own time?

May 5

On this day in history in 1945, six people from Oregon were killed by a hot-air balloon bomb. The high-altitude balloon bomb was one of tactics the Japanese utilized on the continental United States as they tried to win the war. The balloon had landed in the woods near Elsie Mitchell's home, and she and five children from her neighborhood were dragging it out of the woods when it exploded. The incident is believed to be the only time in World War II when America's civilians were killed.

Before the war was over, the Allies had dropped more than 160,000 tons of conventional bombs plus two atomic bombs over Japan. These actions cost the lives of approximately a half-million Japanese civilians. By honoring God, the Allies were blessed with victory.

Exodus 23:22 reads: "But if thou shalt indeed obey his voice, and do all that I speak; then I will be an enemy unto thine enemies, and an adversary unto thine adversaries."

Here Moses is giving laws to the newly-freed Children of Israel. Most of these promises are under the premise of "if you will, then I will." This verse teaches us to obey and do as commanded. The last part of the verse is that God will protect His children, and that He is an enemy to my enemy but with the condition His children must obey.

How is your "if you will, then I will" from God going? Are you following His will for your life? Is God defeating your enemies? Ask Him now to help you so that He will bless you.

May 6

On this day in history in 1941, Bob Hope gave his first USO show at March Field in California. USO stands for United States Organizations. Hope, who lived to be 100 years old, was one of the greatest of the great entertainers of the 20th century.

For more than sixty years, the "Bob Hope Show" entertained troops at home and overseas. He was even made an honorary veteran, although he never served in the military. Ask almost any serviceman or woman to tell you what Bob Hope means to them, and I'm sure the answer will always be positive. There is no other American entertainer I know whom I respect more than Bob Hope, as his show encouraged and uplifted servicemen and women. I remember parts of his show that were my favorites, including when Miss America would come along just to remind us what we were fighting for. And I believe that Bob Hope sacrificed more to entertain us than we did as servicemen and women to protect him.

Matthew 14:1-14 tells of another show, but not one as uplifting and humorous as Bob Hope's were. In fact, this one was plain murderous. Matthew 14:6 reads: "But when Herod's birthday was kept, the daughter of Herodias danced before them, and pleased Herod."

All the dancers in the Bob Hope show were good; however, I know of no one who lost their head over them.

What kind of shows do you watch? Is God pleased with your choice? What about your spouse?

May 7

On this day in history in 1941, Glenn Miller recorded "Chattanooga Choo-Choo," his most popular song that sold more than a million copies. It's still a favorite song for many today.

Like most struggling musicians, Miller's first band started in 1936, but it suffered from financial troubles. When he started performing again in 1938, though, it was a success, and mostly centered around a trombone and tenor saxophone. Miller set a different style of music called swing. With the magic of radio and television, Miller was to become a household name.

There are many musical instruments named in the Bible, as music was as much a way of life then as it is now. Probably one of the best musicians of the time was David, who played his harp to soothe King Saul. He also is credited with writing the Psalms. Many songs we have today are taken from Psalms.

Psalms 92:1 reads: "It is a good thing to give thanks unto the Lord, and to sing praises unto thy name, O most High."

The best way to give thanks to God is to lift up your voice of praise to Him. What better way than with a song? Each person has his or her own style of music. Neither is wrong; it's just a matter of preference, and its purpose is to praise God.

How are you praising God today? If you are not praising God today, how can you start?

May 8

On this day in history in 1914, Congress passed a joint resolution proclaiming the second Sunday in May as Mother's Day, an act that set aside one day a year just to honor mothers.

Exodus 20:12 reads: "Honor thy father and thy mother: that thy days may be long upon the land which the Lord thy God giveth thee."

This is the first commandment with a promise attached to it. When you see an older person, they probably have respect for their father and mother.

The chapter of Proverbs 31 is the most popular in the Bible about women. It tells of a godly woman's virtue, deeds, actions and love. You should take a few minutes to read that chapter to learn what a woman of God does.

Are you honoring your mother on Mother's Day?

May 9

On this day in history 1941, the Royal British Navy captured the German submarine U-110. The sub originally was sunk and then salvaged by the British and was found to contain several capital documents and plans. After it was salvaged, it was searched and looked over for better technology that might help Britain. The secret that the British had the submarine lasted for seven months until Prime Minister Winston Churchill told President Franklin D. Roosevelt about it in January of 1942.

Matthew 6:4 reads: "That thine alms may be in secret: and thy Father which seeth in secret himself shall reward thee openly."

No, I am not going to take up an offering at this time but only remind you that it is a perfect verse to urge people to give their tithes and offerings. God will reward you if it is done in secret.

Let's look at this verse a little differently. The British Navy sunk a submarine; they later recovered it. On the submarine were deciphering equipment and plans from Berlin, Germany. By keeping the salvage secret for seven months, the British were able to use the equipment to learn of other plans. If the Germans had known of the salvage of the submarine, they could have changed their codes, rendering the deciphering equipment worthless.

As secret as the operation was for the British, let us think for a moment how God blessed them. They were able to win the war with the help of the Allies and remain a free nation today.

Are you good at keeping secrets? Does God reward you for keeping those secrets? How are you being rewarded openly?

May 10

On this day in history in 1942 and 1943, the United States and Japan are both declared winners in the history books – at least for a little while.

In 1942, the U.S. forces in the Philippines began to surrender to the Japanese, a time when General MacArthur famously had to leave the islands but promised to return in relation to the Bataan Death March. At this point in World War II, it looked as if the Japanese were winning.

In 1943, U.S. troops invaded Attu in the Aleutian Islands to expel the Japanese troops, who had held two of those islands on the northwest coast of Alaska. The Battle of Attu was the major campaign of the Aleutian Islands. Kiska, another island, was also being held by the Japanese. Both islands were recaptured, Attu in June and Kiska in August. The reason for this battle is varied and speculative, but afterward the United States was winning and began a series of island-hopping to cut off Japanese supplies.

Luke 11:17 reads: "But he, knowing their thoughts, said unto them, Every, kingdom divided against itself is brought to desolation; and a house divided against a house falleth."

We have two stories about two battles for two reasons. Both forces were stretched thin, and neither had the superior force and nor control at this time. U.S. forces were finally getting enough weapons and supplies and would not be divided. After the Aleutians were recaptured, U.S. forces could then focus on other areas or islands. Because of advanced weaponry, the United States was able to unite and focus on a joint exercise and then won because it was able to join together and help each other.

Are you divided today in your house, your country, your religion, or your Christian life? There is hope to regroup and win the battle.

May 11

On this day in history in 1888, Irving Berlin was born. At the age of five, Berlin came to America from Imperial Russia. He published his first song in 1907, and in 1911 published "Alexander's Ragtime Band," a lively number that can get toes to tapping. Some of his other hits were "White Christmas," "God Bless America," Puttin' on the Ritz," Blue Skies," "Cheek to Cheek," "Happy Holidays," and "Easter Parade." Berlin was also a lyricist for "Annie Get Your Gun," "Yip-Yip Yaphank," "Miss Liberty," and others.

For a man who was an immigrant, he sure did embrace the American way of life, starring in several musicals and movies. He lived to be 101 years old.

Psalms 28:7 reads: "The Lord is my strength and my shield; my heart trusted in him, and I am helped: therefore, my heart greatly rejoiceth; and with my song will I praise Him."

Here David tells how his strength and joy come from singing. It seems that David was happiest when praising the Lord.

Irving Berlin probably was the same way, as most of his songs are of joy and happiness. There is also some humor in them, which helps prove the adage that we are happiest when we're doing something we love.

What makes you happy? Are you another David? Or are you Irving Berlin? Give God praise for your life and make the most of it.

May 12

On this day in history in 1900, Mildred Helen McAfee was born. She was an academic who attended the University of Chicago and Vassar College and went on to become the first director of the Women Accepted for Volunteer Emergency Service or WAVES. Moreover, she was the first woman to be commissioned in the U.S. Naval Reserves and was the first woman to receive the Navy Distinguished Service Medal.

The WAVES performed all sorts of duties but only onshore. At the end of World War II, 18 percent of clerical work was done by WAVES. The WAVES also allowed the men to be freed up from some jobs to go to fight the war.

Acts 16:14 reads: "And a certain woman named Lydia, a seller of purple, of the city of Thyatira, which worshiped God, heard us: whose heart the Lord had opened, that she attended unto the things which were spoken of Paul."

Lydia was a businesswoman in a man's world. She was converted by the Apostle Paul, and as a Christian she worked hard for the things of God and of her business, which allowed her the opportunity to be a leader of the community where she lived.

How trained are you today? Are you a useful servant? Will God recognize you for your dedication?

May 13

On this day in history in 1865, the Battle of Palmetto Ranch, the last land battle of the War Between the States, was fought in Texas on the outskirts of Brownsville. Union forces had left Brazos Island and headed to Brownsville where 350 Confederate troops had set up an outpost to wait for them. The Union had 800 men who almost became trapped in the bend of the Rio Grande River. Both Union and Confederate armies knew that General Robert E. Lee had already surrendered at Appomattox Courthouse. While the Confederates won the battle, they lost the war.

In the Battle of Palmetto Branch, Private John J. Williams of the 34th Indiana Infantry Regiment is thought to have been the last of the more than 600,000 soldiers who served in the war to die in the war.

Joshua 8:7 reads: "Then ye shall rise up from the ambush, and seize upon the city: for the Lord your God will deliver it into your hand."

Here Joshua tells of the second battle of Ai. Ai won the first battle against him because of sin in the camp of Israel. After cleansing the sin, Joshua is told by the Lord how to capture Ai, and the second time it was different because the Children of Israel won the battle and the war.

Do you listen to God and get Him to help with your battles?

May 14

On this day in history in 2018, the U.S. Embassy in Israel was moved from Tel-Aviv to Jerusalem. The plan had the approval of Congress for about 20 years, but it was President Donald J. Trump who ordered the embassy to finally be moved. Also, on this day in history 1948, Israel was given its independence from Great Britain and made a nation once again. Jerusalem had been the capital of Israel for centuries.

First in Genesis 14:18, "And Melchizedek king of Salem brought forth bread and wine: and he was the priest of the most, high God."

Jerusalem was Jebus, which brings in Jeru, the first part of the name Jerusalem, and this passage gives us Salem, the second part of Jeru-Salem; thus: Jerusalem.

After the Children of Israel left Egypt, Joshua didn't capture all the Jebusites. When David was anointed King of Israel, he led his army against the Jebusites. After capturing Jebu from the Jebusites, the city was renamed Jerusalem and is also known as the City of David.

Genesis 12:2-3 reads: "And I will make of thee a great nation, and I will bless thee, and make thy name great; and thou shalt be a blessing: And I will bless them that bless thee, and curse him that curseth thee: and in thee shall all families of the earth be blessed."

Are you being blessed today? Do you honor the Children of Israel?

May 15

On this day in history in 1948, Israel was attacked by Trans-Jordan Egypt, Syria, Iraq, and Lebanon only hours after Israel was declared an independent nation. This is called the Israel War of Independence. The surprise attack against the Nation of Israel was unorganized and not well thought out. The Israelites had only one command system and it worked fine. Israel also had three B-17 bombers purchased on the black market. Only one percent of Israelites were killed and just a few more for the Arabs. Thanks to World War II, Israel had a force that was trained to fight.

Egypt was the first country to sign a peace treaty with Israel. Jordan, Syria, and Lebanon were next. Iraq did not sign a peace treaty; instead, they withdrew and went home. The Israel War of Independence lasted about fourteen months, and while it would be Israel's first war, it would not be its last.

Joel 3:4 reads: "Yea, and what have ye, to do with me, O Tyre, and Sidon, and all the coasts of Palestine? Will ye render me a recompense? And if ye recompense me, swiftly and speedily will I return your recompense upon your own head."

The prophet Joel spoke about Israel being restored after the Battle of Armageddon. Israel is a nation but will not remain so forever, as the Last Battle will come and it will then be restored to its power and prestige.

Are you ready for Christ to return?

May 16

On this day in history in 1946, the Irving Berlin's musical "Annie Get Your Gun" opened at the Imperial Theater in New York City, the first of 1,147 performances. The most famous of songs from the production include "Doing What Comes Naturally," "The Girl That I Marry," "You Can't Get a Man with a Gun," "There's No Business Like Show Business," "My Defenses are Down," and "Anything You Can Do."

Another musical took place one night. I don't know what sort of Broadway reviews it would get, but a lot of people enjoyed the performance as outlined in Acts 16:25-26: "And at midnight Paul and Silas prayed, and sang praises unto God: and the prisoners heard them. And suddenly there was a great earthquake, so that the foundations of the prison were shaken: and immediately all the doors were opened, and every one's bands were loosed."

In the passage, the Apostle Paul and his friend Silas were missionaries for Christ and had gotten into trouble and then thrown into prison. While they were incarcerated, they put on a show of singing and praying so lively that it shook the foundations of the prison, allowing their chains to fall off and the doors to spring open.

The Philippian and his family were saved that night. After they were baptized, they then treated the wounds of the prisoners.

How would you react to such singing and praising God? Do you sing and praise God?

May 17

On this day in history in 1827, a young Andrew Johnson married a shy, timid girl named Eliza McCardle. Johnson would become the 17th president of the United States, but at the time of their wedding he was 18 and Eliza was 16. He was poor and had little or no education, while she was better off and had an education. She would become his teacher. Later he had a varied career in politics, while she remained at home and raised their five children. During the War Between the States, he served as military governor of Tennessee, and then Abraham Lincoln chose him to be his vice-president. Johnson became president after Lincoln was assassinated. Eliza Johnson moved to Washington, but because of her poor health, her oldest daughter, Martha, served as hostess of the White House.

Johnson survived impeachment for high crimes and misdemeanors by only one vote. He served out his remaining term before returning to Tennessee. In July 1875 he died, just after being elected senator, with his wife passing six months later.

Let me tell you a story of another couple. Their outcome was not as well as that of the Johnsons.

Acts 5:1-11 is the story. Verses 1-2 reads: "But a certain man named Ananias, with Sapphira his wife, sold a possession and kept back part of the price, his wife also being privy to it, and brought a certain part, and laid it at the apostles' feet."

So far everything is going okay for the couple, but now in this passage a problem arises. Ananias lies to the Holy Spirit about the money he is giving to the church. When he was confronted by Peter, he lies again and suddenly drops dead. Three hours later, Sapphira does the same thing and she also falls dead. The couple is both buried together, one not knowing the other had died. The moral of this story is to not lie to God or the Holy Spirit.

Exodus 20:3 reads, "Thou shalt have no other gods before me."

Is there another God in your life?

May 18

On this day in history in 1798, Benjamin Stoddert became the first Secretary of the Navy. He was tasked with rebuilding the Navy after the American Revolution ended. Stoddert served as a captain of a Pennsylvania regiment in the American Revolution. Outside of the military, he was a merchant in Georgetown, Maryland.

Stoddert fought private ships in the Quasi War with France. With limited ships and resources, he attacked the French ships in the Caribbean. He left the Navy with the legacy of an able administration, and he also built the Navy to defend our commerce on the high seas.

The Bible has no battleships listed that I can think of. One reason is because there were no Marines to go around thanking the Navy for the ride. Several ships are mentioned, yes, but no battleships, and one of those was carrying the disciples across a lake when a storm came up, as told in Matthew 14:23-24: "And when he had sent the multitudes away, he went up into a mountain apart to pray; and when the evening was come, he was there alone. But the ship was now in the midst of the sea, tossed with waves: for the wind was contrary."

Storms and rough weather were nothing uncommon for sailors. Jesus' disciples were scared and afraid, but the storm calmed down when Christ set foot on the ship. This was the time when Peter even tried to walk on water, but he took his eyes off Jesus and sank into the water.

Where are your eyes today? Does the presence of Jesus calm the storms in your life? If not, ask Jesus to be the captain of your ship.

May 19

On this day in history in 1864, the Battle of Spotsylvania Courthouse in Virginia came to an end, almost three weeks after Union General U.S. Grant crossed the Rapidan River in the wilderness. Instead of retreating, Grant moved further southward and the two armies met at Spotsylvania. General Robert E. Lee and his Confederates reached Spotsylvania first and dug in. When the Union army attacked, it could not uproot the Confederates. Grant retreated southward again.

At Spotsylvania the losses were Union 18,000 troops, with the Confederates losing 12,000 troops. From the time Grant crossed the Rapidan River until the end at Spotsylvania, the Union had lost 33,000 men.

Now here is a battle that was worse, if indeed things could get any worse.

Job 1:1 reads: "There was a man in the land of Uz, whose name was Job; and that man was perfect and upright, and one that feared God, and eschewed evil."

Job had ten children, seven thousand sheep, three thousand camels, five hundred yoke of oxen, five hundred she-asses, and a very great household, with the Bible explaining, "so that this name was the greatest of all the men of the east."

Job lost everything he had—everything!—when Satan destroyed him. Satan tried to get Job to turn against God, but he failed. Job never gave up on God, even when Job's own wife even turned against him. Through suffering and sorrow, along with self-righteous friends, Job never failed to worship God. God then restored him in the end because of his faithfulness. Job had ten more children and everything that he lost originally was repaid in double.

It pays to serve God. Are you being blessed today?

May 20

On this day in history in 1908, James Maitland Stewart was born, eventually becoming known simply as Jimmy Stewart. His parents owned a hardware store, but he was more interested in aviation. He had a noted military career as an Army Air Corps pilot and then later with the U.S. Air Force. He flew more than twenty missions in World War II, and then later served in the Vietnam War. In the Air Force Reserves, he rose to the rank of brigadier general. He is also the actor with the highest military ranking in history.

Stewart was nominated for five Academy Awards, winning one, and, among other awards, was feted with the Lifetime Achievement Award in 1985. Stewart once said, "I'd like people to remember me as someone who was good at his job and seemed to mean what he said."

Stewart and Moses were a lot alike. Neither man wanted the spotlight but both accepted it. Both men were military leaders and more likely than not always helping other people.

Exodus 4:10 reads: "And Moses said unto the Lord, O my Lord, I am not eloquent, neither heretofore, nor since thou hast spoken unto thy servant: but I am slow of speech, and of a slow tongue."

We are sometimes a lot like Moses in that we want someone else to speak for us. But then God says that he would rather that we speak ourselves. Does God want you today?

May 21

On this day in history in 1877, Henry Ossian Flipper graduated from the U.S. Military Academy at West Point. Flipper, a native of Thomasville, Georgia, was born a slave in 1856. During his four years at West Point, not the first white cadet spoke to him. After graduation he was assigned to the 10th U.S. Cavalry at Fort Sill, Oklahoma, an all African-American unit. Flipper died in Atlanta in 1940.

Have you ever heard of being treated like a leper? Leviticus 13:45-46 reads: "And the leper in whom the plague is, his clothes shall be rent, and his head bare, and he shall put a covering upon his upper lip, and shall cry, Unclean, unclean. All the days wherein the plague shall be in him he shall be defiled; he is unclean: he shall dwell alone; without the camp shall his habitation be."

Flipper must have known what a leper was in that he was treated like one. No one even said hello, good morning, goodnight or anything to him. Leprosy is a disease, but hatred is not.

How do you treat others today? What about different cultures or religions? Speaking to them in Christ's name is the least anyone can do for others.

May 22

On this day in history in 1939, Adolf Hitler and Benito Mussolini signed an agreement they called Pact of Steel, a joint effort to take control of the entire world and to help each other defend itself. Germany and Italy thus became the two largest and strongest Axis powers, which would lead to World War II.

In 1943 the Allies invaded Italy and began to conquer it, a move that proved more difficult than expected. Germany did, however, have to commit more troops to Italy, which led them away from France and the impending invasion there.

On June 4, 1944, six Allied divisions left Italy and headed for the invasion of France, an event that would become known as D-Day, and almost a year later German forces surrendered in Italy on May 2, 1945.

Joshua 23:13 reads: "Know for a certainty that the Lord your God will no more drive out any of these nations from before you; but they shall be snares and traps unto you, and scourges in your sides, and thorns in your eyes, until ye perish from off this good land which the Lord your God hath given you."

This is the last counsel of Joshua to Israel, as the passage speaks for itself.

Are you destroying your enemies who are ruining your life? If you let them stay, you are setting a snare for yourself.

May 23

On this day in history in 1923, Curley, a Crow Indian scout, was buried at the Little Big Horn National Cemetery in Montana. Curley was with Lieutenant Colonel George A. Custer and the 7th U.S. Cavalry. He was released from his duties along with four other scouts when they reported to Custer that a large group of Sioux Indians were just ahead of the cavalry. Custer did not believe them, and most of us know what happened then. Curley went to a ridge about a mile and a half away and through field glasses watched the massacre of Custer and his cavalry. When defeat was apparent, Curley felt his position was to warn General Alfred Terry and John Gibbon about the attack. Curley later moved to the Crow Indian Agency in Montana, where he died of pneumonia on May 21,1923.

The passage of 1 Samuel 26:4 reads: "David therefore sent out spies, and understood that Saul was come in very deed."

All military commands throughout history have used scouts or spies. In 1 Samuel 26, we read where David and King Saul used spies to find out about the other. In Verse 4, we discover that David knew just about every move Saul made. David even had several chances to kill King Saul but he would not.

Do you use spies today? Do you trust those spies? Do your spies tell you where your enemy is? How about television, the telephone and Facebook? Are they your enemies? How do you treat your enemies?

May 24

On this day in history in 1764, James Otis, a Boston lawyer, denounced taxation without representation and called for all other Colonists to do the same in opposition to the tax issues imposed upon them. Otis spoke often about these matters, and John Adams once said of him, "This is the first scene of the first act of opposition to British policies."

Otis served in several courts defending others because of British rule and laws. He was once beaten by a British official because of his actions and was left with severe brain damage. For the rest of his life, he suffered from mental illness, and then died in May of 1783 from injuries from a lightning strike.

The passage of 1 Kings 12:10 reads: "And the young men that were grown up with him spake unto him saying, Thus shalt thou speak unto this people that spake unto thee, saying, Thy father made our yoke heavy, but make thou it lighter unto us; thus shalt thou say unto them, My little finger shall be thicker than my father's loins."

King Rehoboam did not follow wisdom of Solomon, his father. Instead of helping his people, he was going to punish them more. There were no courts to defend against taxation. King Rehoboam then started doing evil against the Lord for the rest of his life.

Are you being a help or hinderance to your fellow man?

May 25

On this day in history in 1994, an absurd thing happened. Seventy-one years old George Swanson of Hempfield County, Pennsylvania, was buried. Sort of. Swanson, a veteran who had been a sergeant in World War II, died on March 31. After he was cremated, his ashes were buried in his 1984 Corvette, with his widow, Caroline, driving his ashes to the cemetery in her 1993 Corvette. Swanson's Corvette, at the time it was buried with his ashes, had only 27,000 miles on it. If that weren't absurd enough, the ladies of his church made a lap blanket for him and placed it in the car, and then someone cued up a cassette of Engelbert Humperdinck's "Release Me," ready to play on the Corvette's stereo system. The tag on Swanson's car read, "Hi, Pal," and was still attached to the car.

So much for the saying that you can't take it with you when you die, as Caroline Swanson later said, "You have a lot of people saying they want to take it with them. He took it with him." To each his own, I suppose.

Joshua 4:6 reads: "That this may be a sign among you, that when your children ask their fathers in time to come, saying, What mean ye by these stones?"

I don't know what type of monument, if any, is over George Swanson's grave. I also don't know what anyone would tell their children about this unusual grave.

If we could see the monument that Joshua was talking about, we would remember God's mercies, even today, hundreds of years after they were built. But if we saw the monument to George Swanson, it would remind us of his greed and foolishness.

What kind of a monument do you want?

May 26

On this day in history in 1864, President Abraham Lincoln signed an act to create the Montana Territory, which was part of the Louisiana Purchase and inhabited mostly by Indians. Montana had been inhabited for less than 15 years, and only then because gold was discovered there in the 1850s. Sidney Edgerton was Montana's first territorial governor but left office after six months of Indian warfare. Montana became the 41st state, some 25 years later.

Joshua 1:9 reads: "Have not I commanded thee? Be strong and of a good courage be not afraid, neither be thee dismayed: for the Lord thy God is with the withersoever thou goest."

I can only feel sorry for Edgerton. He was in a job he couldn't handle, whether it was because of the Indians, lawbreaking white men, extreme weather conditions or too few people, he wasn't suited for it. At least he had brains enough to leave before he went crazy, and that took courage and willpower.

Staying in a job that we are not suited for is a disaster waiting to happen, but be not dismayed, as other jobs are out there.

Do we trust God to find us that job?

May 27

On this day in history in 1941, the British Navy and British Air Force sank the *Bismarck*. More than two thousand Germans were killed in the attack.

In February of 1939, from Hamburg, Germany, the *Bismarck* was launched, an 823-foot long battleship with all the latest technology. Hitler hoped it would help Germany have better control of the seas.

James 4:14 reads: "Whereas ye know not what shall be on the morrow. For what is your life? It is even a vapor that appeareth for a little while and then vanisheth away."

The *Bismarck* had a short vapor, just over two years. Most of that time it was bottlenecked between France and Germany, and when it finally made it out to sea, it wreaked havoc on the ships around it. The plans that Hitler had for the *Bismarck* were never fulfilled, and that was for it to control everything. The British and their destroyers put an end to that, and its vapor was no more.

How is your life and vapor today? Is it widespread or just getting started? Only you can tell.

May 28

On this day in history in 1934, the Dionne quintuplets were born in Callander, Ontario, Canada, and named Annette, Cecile, Marie, Emilie and Yvonne. The quintuplets were the first to survive into childhood. They were born two months prematurely, with each of the five having her own incubator. Of the sisters, Annette and Cecile are still alive as of 2019. Emilie passed away in 1954 at the age of 20, Marie died in 1970 at 35 years old, and Yvonne died in 2001 at 67.

Genesis 25:24-26 reads: "And when her days to be delivered were fulfilled, behold there were twins in her womb. And the first come out red, all over like an, hairy garment: and they called his name Esau. And after that came his brother out and his hand took hold on Esau's heel; and his name was called Jacob: and Isaac was three score years old when she bore him."

Having twins wouldn't be as bad as having quintuplets, but twins would still be a handful. Having five girls would keep anyone busy.

God has a purpose for everything. Brothers Esau and Jacob were always fighting, which soon became more than sibling rivalry. Two nations would emerge from their battles. Esau married the daughters of Canaan; thus, those lands becoming the Arab nations as we know them today. Jacob married Laban's daughters, carrying on the Children of Israel's name. God showed He had a purpose for Jacob and Esau.

Does God have a purpose in your life? How are you showing it?

May 29

On this day in history in 1942, Hitler ordered all Jews to wear a yellow star on the left side of their coats. This order was suggested by Joseph Goebbels, the propaganda minister of the Nazi regime. Goebbels had made the extermination of the Jews a personal conquest, writing in his diary and often saying in public, "They are no longer human but beast."

Goebbels even wrote that extermination was barbaric but would not describe it any longer, adding. "There will not be very much left of the Jews."

Goebbels, his wife and children all died on May 1, 1945, in an act of murder-suicide.

Ezekiel 3:18 reads: "When I say unto the wicked, Thou, shalt surely die; and thou givest him not warning, Thou, shalt surely die, nor speakest to warn the wicked from his wicked way, to save his life; the same wicked man shall die in his iniquity; but his blood will I require at thine hand,"

In short, this is called do what I say or else. Someone forgot to tell Goebbels this or else he just didn't listen. If we don't tell others about the saving power of God's saving grace, there could be blood on our hands, as we could be held responsible for staying silent. But whether accepts that saving grace or not isn't your problem. I am not trying to be flippant about this, because we can't make anyone do anything. We can tell them about Jesus, yes, but this verse does not say that if they won't accept Christ, then their blood is on our hands. We tell, they hear, but the results are up to them.

Have you told someone about Christ? Whose blood is on your hands?

May 30

On this day in history, throughout the years has become traditionally known as Memorial Day. Across this country communities come together to honor the men and women who paid the ultimate price for our freedoms. They come from all different walks of life and diverse occupations to give their all for their country.

Thomas Paine wrote in *Common Sense*: "These are the times that try men's souls. The summer soldier and the sunshine Patriot will in this, crises, shrink, from the service of their country, but he that stands it now deserves the love and thanks of men and women."

Psalms 135:13 reads: "Thy name O Lord endureth forever; and thy memorial O Lord, throughout all generations."

The Lord's name will last forever and will be a memorial to Himself. The families of the men and women who paid the ultimate price for our freedoms need our prayer and support, lest we forget.

May 31

On this day in history in 1962, Adolf Eichmann was hanged. Eichmann was commander of Nazi operations that oversaw the murder of six million Jews during the holocaust of World War II.

Eichmann grew up in a middle-class family. He joined the Nazis in 1932 at the age of 26. He worked his way up the chain of command until he was one of the highest ranking and most powerful men of the Third Reich. He remained head of the B-4 unit of the Jewish "final solution" for the rest of the war.

After the war, he escaped the Allies and fled to Argentina, where he lived under the name of Ricardo Klement until he was captured by the Israeli Mossad on May 11, 1960. Eichmann was once quoted as saying, "I will leap into my grave laughing because of the feeling that I have five million human beings on my conscience is for me a source of extraordinary satisfaction."

Exodus 20:13; "Thou shalt not kill."

Hebrews 9:27; "And as it is appointed unto men once to die, but after this the judgment."

These two verses of Scripture tell us a lot about Eichmann. First, thou shalt not kill, but he did many, many, many, many, many, times over. Second is the judgment. I don't know what judgment Eichmann received after meeting the Lord after having killed so many.

God's acceptance of repentance is marvelous. We are saved by grace if we ask Him to forgive us. If Eichmann did not ask, he did not receive.

Heaven or Hell: Which will be your reward?

June 1

On this day in history in 1944, the British sent a coded message to the French Resistance telling them that the D-Day invasion was imminent. The Resistance was a contingent of undercover spies and citizens who worked tirelessly to set France free from the Germans, sometimes just to create a diversion and other times to take out a leader. It was a dangerous job, one the French did well. For the British to send such a message had to be encouraging for the French.

The Biblical story of Rahab in Joshua 2-6 is also an example of resistance. Rahab hid spies for the Children of Israel, even though she was from Jericho and not of Jewish descent. She had heard of God's children and was afraid but also believed in them.

Joshua 2:9 reads: "And she said unto the men, I know that the Lord hath given you the land, and that your terror is fallen upon us, and that all the inhabitants of the land faint because of you."

Rahab hid spies and then asked that her household be spared. She was granted that request. When the great walls of Jericho literally fell, she and her household were saved, and she went on to become the great-great-grandmother of David, King of Israel.

Is your resistance for or against God? Will God use you to help expand His kingdom?

June 2

On this day in history in 1835, P.T. Barnum launched his first traveling show, as everyone needs a good laugh every now and then. His main attraction was Joice Heth, an African-American who was supposedly George Washington's nurse. She was reported to be 161 years old. I doubt that I would have paid good money to see her, but I do wonder what she looked like.

P.T. Barnum joined with Hachaliah Bailey to form Barnum and Bailey Circus, and then in 1967 it was purchased by Ringling Bros. Circus. In May of 2017, the show closed, with Kenneth Feld of the Ringling family saying goodbye to what he called "the greatest show on Earth."

Proverbs 17:22 reads: "A merry heart doeth good like a medicine: but a broken spirit drieth the bones."

Laughter and a merry heart can go together. With a merry heart, you are not sick enough. With a merry heart and a broken spirit, the bones dry up. Being a happy or merry person makes you feel good and it also encourages those around you to be happy and merry. Being an old sour face helps no one.

Which are you? How do people react to you? Smile and laugh and it will make people wonder what you're up to.

June 3

On this day in history in 1959, the U.S. Air Force Academy in Denver, Colorado, held its first graduation ceremony. There are five service academies, with one for the Merchant Marines. The U.S. Marines don't have a service academy because it is a part of the Navy. The Marines are known to say to the Navy "thanks for the ride," as Navy ships and planes often transport Marines. These academies attract the best and brightest of American youth to be leaders in their particular branch of service and have many distinguished alumni.

The passage of 2 Timothy 2:15 reads: "Study to shew thyself approved unto God, a workman that needeth not to be ashamed, rightly dividing the word of truth."

To be a part of the Air Force Academy, you would surely have to study and use common sense, as it takes more than book smarts to fly an airplane.

Here Paul tells Timothy to study God's word to prove himself a leader.

Are you studying to be a leader today? Are you studying God's Word?

June 4

On this day in history, the Battle of Midway began and would last four days. Only one aircraft carrier, the *USS Yorktown*, was destroyed, but U.S. Forces sank four Japanese aircraft carriers. The Japanese Navy greatly outnumbered the U.S. Navy, plus the Japanese had not lost a battle since the war began.

Even though the battle was at sea, most of the fighting was done in the air. Both countries used Alaska's Aleutian Islands as a decoy. If the U.S. Pacific fleet was destroyed, then Japan would have a foothold on the Alaskan peninsula. If the U.S. fleet was successful, Japan would have no Navy.

When speaking of offensive behavior, let us look at Mark 9:42: "And whosoever shall offend one of these little ones that believe in me, it is better for him that a millstone, were hanged about his neck, and he were cast into the sea."

This verse warns us about being offensive against someone else. When we are offensive against God's children, we become doomed. When we are offensive against our enemies, we will be victorious.

Are you careful whom you offend? Trust God to let him lead you from offensive people.

June 5

On this day in history in 1944, during World War II, the first B-29 bombing raid hit the Japanese rail line in Bangkok, Thailand. The rail was a supply source for the Japanese.

The B-29 Superfortress was the largest of U.S. planes that was used in World War II. The B-29 had a 5,592-mile delivery range at a speed of 356 miles per hour. It was a four-engine jet with a 141-foot wingspan. It was used in World War II and in Korea and is best known as being the type of bomber that dropped the atomic bomb on Japan. The name of the aircraft that dropped the bomb was *Enola Gay*.

The passage of 1 Samuel 25:10 reads: "And Nabal answered David's servants, and said who is David. And who is the son of Jesse? There be many servants now a days that break away every man from his master."

Samuel the prophet had died. David was still running from King Saul and did not have time to gather supplies. He then sent his men to ask Nabal for supplies but Nabal refused and insulted David and his men. Nabal's wife, Abigale, after learning of her husband's rudeness, gathered supplies for David. After Nabal died, Abigale became David's wife.

How well protected is your supply chain? Are you going with no supplies? What about what you have? Are you using it for God's purpose?

June 6

On this day in history in 1944, the D-Day invasion of France began. More than 400,000 soldiers from England, America, and Canada as one unit repelled the Germans from France. Bombs and aircraft of all types pounded the German defenses for weeks, then at dawn on June 6, the day arrived.

Several people I know were personally involved in D-Day. Here's one story. England had been at war since 1939, and a shortage of men left some of the war duties to be filled with women. On a British destroyer in the English Channel, Maria Ross fired the first shot to start the invasion. She had met her husband-to-be, Wade Ross, in England and then moved to America, to here in Georgia, after the war to marry him. I knew Maria as a friend and taught her in Sunday School during the last years of her life. No one would believe by looking at her that she was a gunner on a destroyer. She was a most gracious lady whom I loved dearly.

I also had an uncle who was involved in D-Day. He later served at the Battle of the Bulge. My father was slow to get to Europe. He crossed over two weeks after D-Day and served in clean-up operations.

Women have always played a part in every war. Consider the story of Jael in Judges 4-5. Jabin, the king of Canaan, declared war against Israel, which was led by the prophetess Deborah and another man named Barak.

Judges 4:23 reads: "So God subdued on that day Jabin the King of Canaan before the Children of Israel."

The Children of Israel were winning the battle. Jabin ran for his life, but Jael let him rest in her tent. While he was asleep, Jael put a tent spike to his head and hammered it in, killing him. God and His chosen people won the battle.

How are you fighting your battles today? Are you awake and alert or asleep?

June 7

On this day in history in 1917, the British 2nd Army dealt a crushing defeat to the Germans at Messines Ridge. The battle brought a halt to German advancement that was slow and to the point. British forces for the past 18 months had dug tunnels and then set off nearly a ton of explosives that could be heard as far away as London. The German losses were ten thousand killed and seven thousand taken as prisoners of war. The Germans were forced to retreat and lost ground on the western front.

Judges 3:31 reads: "And after him was Shamgar the son of Anath, which slew the Philistines, six hundred men with an ox goad: and he also delivered Israel."

Hidden explosives and an ox goad were unusual methods of warfare, but both worked. Shamgar surely had the Lord with him, as did the British. With this many killed in action and both battles being won, it was an answer to prayer. Both armies of the British and Israel were victorious.

What weapons do you use to fight your battles?

June 8

On this day in history in 1944, U.S. General Omar Bradley and his troops from Omaha Beach linked up with British troops from Gold Beach at Colleville-sur–Mer. Russian premier Joseph Stalin sent a message to British Prime Minister Winston Churchill that the success at Normandy was a joy to us all. Stalin had promised to step up offensive attacks on the eastern front. Hitler could not move his troops to the west to oppose the Allies from coming from Normandy. General Dwight D. Eisenhower, commander of Allied forces, knew the importance of not being divided.

Matthew 12:25 reads: "And Jesus knew their thoughts and said unto them, every kingdom divided against itself is brought to desolation; and every city or house divided against itself shall not stand."

When Eisenhower ordered the British and Americans to unite, he knew that they could work together. They also provided a stronger force against the Germans.

In our lives we must be able to unite in order to have more perfect lives. You can't argue with your neighbor and have a community of peace.

How is your neighbor? How can you help to unite your community? How can you help to unite your church? How can you unite your own Christian testimony?

June 9

On this day in history in 1943, Congress passed legislation that allowed for payroll taxes to be withheld from the paychecks of Americans. For the good, it's easier to pay your taxes a little at a time. For the bad, you don't really know how much in taxes are being paid. For the good, everyone pays and it provides a steady source of income for the government. For the bad, if you write a check at the end of the year, you'll know how much taxes you really pay. This legislation stopped that.

Try this method. At the end of the year when you are preparing to pay your taxes, add up taxes from W-2s, 1099s, and any other forms for the amount of taxes you pay. Now that you have this all added up, then write a check for this amount. Now put the check in a savings account for your future.

The passage of 1 Kings 12:4 reads: "Thy father made our yoke grievous: now therefore, make thou the grievous service of the father, and his heavy yoke which he put upon us, lighter and we will serve thee."

The people were asking for relief of some of their taxes. Rehoboam, the King of Israel, told them that he would think about it. After consultations pro and con, Rehoboam took the latter's advice. His reply is found in 1 Kings 12:10-19. Verse 19 reads: "So Israel rebelled against the house of David until this day."

I know that you probably dislike paying taxes as much as I do, but it is a necessary evil. When leaders will not listen to you complain or try to change things, it makes it worse.

Ask God to guide you in this matter. He can and is willing to help.

June 10

On this day in history in 1965, two men earned the Medal of Honor at the battle of Dong Xoai in South Vietnam. First Lieutenant Charles O. Williams took command of his Special Forces camp when his commander was wounded. He took a 3.5-inch rocket launcher and asked for help in knocking out a machine gun position. CM3 Marvin G. Shields, a Navy Seabee, stepped forward to help Williams. They attacked the machine gun position and destroyed it. Returning to the camp, Shields was mortally wounded. President Lyndon Johnson presented Williams with the Medal of Honor on June 23, 1966, and then presented the Medal of Honor to the widow of Shields on September 13, 1966.

When the Children of Israel were dividing the land that God gave them, it came time for Caleb to get his land.

Joshua 14:10-12 tells us the story. Verse 12 reads: "Now therefore give me this mountain, whereof the Lord spake in that day for thou heardest in that day how the Anakims were there, and that the cities were great and fenced: if so be the Lord will be with me then I shall be able to drive them out, as the Lord said."

Caleb, Williams and Shields all acted the way a person should. They gave of themselves that others would be safe.

Do you act toward others in a way that makes them safe?

June 11

On this day in history in 1979, the actor John Wayne died. He was 72 years old and had battled cancer for ten years. Born Marion Morrison in 1907 in Iowa, his family moved to Glendale, California, where he finished high school. He attended the University of Southern California for two years on a football scholarship. Marion's first role was in the "The Big Trail." He then changed his name to John Wayne when the directors thought that the name Marion was not strong enough. He later starred in movies such as "Stagecoach," "Fort Apache," "She Wore a Yellow Ribbon," "Rio Grande," "The Quiet Man," and "The Man Who Shot Liberty Valance." He also produced movies such as "The Alamo" and "The Green Berets."

Offscreen John Wayne was a political conservative who earned his nickname of Duke after that of his favorite dog.

John 3:1-4 tells us of a story about a tough and rugged man who could have been another John Wayne, one who even lived in a wilderness for a while.

Matthew 3:4 reads: "And the same John had his raiment of Camel's hair, and a leather girdle about his loins; and his meat was locus and wild honey."

His name was John the Baptist, and if you could wear clothes like the ones he wore, you would have to be a strong man.

June 12

On this day in history in 1987, President Ronald Reagan spoke to Mikhail Gorbachev regarding the Berlin Wall, urging, "Mr. Gorbachev, tear down this wall!"

Gorbachev was the secretary general of the Communist Party of the Soviet Union. After World War II, Berlin fell into the hands of the Allies. The British and American forces gave up their half of the city, but the Russians did not.

During the 1960s, the Russians built a wall to separate East and West Berlin. When Reagan told Gorbachev to tear down the wall, the Russian economy was at an all-time low and the burden of keeping the people under bondage was expensive. The wall came down on November 9, 1989.

The Berlin Wall was not the first wall to fall. Consider Jericho. The Children of Israel marched around the city for seven days. Not a sound was made and the silence had to be deafening. In battle there are two major problems. One is silence, and the other is noise.

Joshua 6:10 reads: "So the people shouted when the Priest blew the trumpet: and it came to pass, when the people heard the sound of the trumpet and the people shouted with a great shout, that the wall fell down flat, so that the people went up into the city, every man straight before him, and they took the city."

This time the noise destroyed a wall and the Children of Israel were victorious.

How is your shouting today? Do you praise God when the walls in your life have fallen?

June 13

On this day in history, the lighter side of moments of history have occurred.

First, in 1415, Henry the Navigator sought to explore Africa after sailing from Portugal. I'm sure he had his reasons, but why does that make history?

Second, in 1789, Elizabeth "Eliza" Schuyler, maybe better known as Mrs. Alexander Hamilton, served George Washington some ice cream but no mention is made of its flavor.

Third, in 1825, Walter Hunt invented the safety pin, selling the patent for $400 after he found out the hard way that it could hurt.

Fourth, in 1888, Congress created the Department of Labor. Somehow Congress and Labor do not seem to go together.

Fifth, in 1912, Captain Albert Berry parachuted out of an airplane, with both airplane and man landing safely.

The Bible also has its moments of laughter or joyfulness.

First, in Genesis 21:2, a 99-year-old woman was visited by an angel and told that by the same time the next year she would have a child.

Second, in Nehemiah 8:12, the prophet Ezra read the book of law to the Children of Israel. The people understood the law and celebrated having it.

Third, in Psalms 137:3, the captives were required to sing a song; in fact, they were required to sing a song of Zion. They were happy to do it.

Fourth, Ecclesiastes 3:4 reads, "A time to weep, and a time to laugh; a time to mourn and a time to dance."

Yes, today in history is a day to laugh and is a sign of joy. Are you a joyful person?

June 14

On this day in history in different years, two things happened regarding the U.S. flag. In 1777 the Continental Congress in Philadelphia adopted the Stars and Strips as the national flag. The flag was to have thirteen stripes alternating between red and white, and then its corner was to have a thirteen white stars against a blue field.

The second thing to happen was that in 1954, President Dwight Eisenhower signed an order adding the phrase "under God" to the Pledge of Allegiance. The pledge had been written in 1892 by Francis Bellamy. In 1923, the pledge was changed to add "the flag of the United States of America." When Eisenhower asked Congress to change it in 1954 to add "under God," Bellamy's daughter objected but was overruled.

On May 20, 1916, President Woodrow Wilson officially proclaimed June 14 of every year as Flag Day.

Isaiah 59:19 reads: "So shall they fear the name of the Lord from the west, and his glory from the rising of the sun. When the enemy shall come in like a flood, the Spirit of the Lord shall lift up a standard against him."

The U.S. flag is the standard flag of our country, but there are other standard flags such as the Christian flag, state or local flags, civic clubs, and the like.

What kind of standard do you represent? Is the standard of God at least a part of yours?

June 15

On this day in history in 1864, the U.S. Government purchased the Curtis-Lee Mansion in Arlington at public auction for $26,800. The property had been confiscated for unpaid taxes of $92.07. The owner of the property was Mary Curtis Lee, the wife of Confederate General Robert E. Lee. After she died, her son sued in 1882 for the return of the property. By a 5-4 decision of the Supreme Court, Lee won his case, but by then more than six thousand Union soldiers were buried there. Lee then sold the estate to the U.S. Government for $150,000. It is now known as Arlington National Cemetery. On May 13,1864, Private William Chrisman became the first soldier to be buried there.

Arlington would be a nice place to be buried, but for me it is too crowded. I want a place of quiet solitude. Of course, I'll be dead and won't know or care either way, but it's not the burial place that counts.

Hebrews 9:27 reads "And as it is appointed unto men once to die, but after this the judgment."

It matters not where we are buried. What matters is this: are you ready to die and face the judgment of Christ?

June 16

On this day in history in 1896, a tsunami hit Japan after an earthquake struck 120 miles away from its coastline, bringing about huge water displacement. Most people living inland didn't know about the tsunami until the next morning.

That particular region of Japan is vulnerable to tsunamis, with several reported in 869, 1611, and 1933. About a third of earthquakes causes tsunami, with some having walls of water as high as 115 feet.

Exodus 14:27 reads: "And Moses stretched forth his hand over the sea, and the sea returned to his strength when the morning appeared; and the Egyptians fled against it; and the Lord overthrew the Egyptians in the mist of the sea."

The children were leaving Egypt and bondage, as they thought Pharaoh had been defeated. He had not, and then followed through with plans to bring them back to bondage. The Children of Israel were between Pharaoh's army and the deep blue sea when the Lord told Moses to lift his hand over the sea, causing it to separate. The people then crossed the sea over dry land without fear of drowning. When they reached the other side, Moses again lifted his hand and the water returned to normal. The problem for the Egyptians is that the water began falling on their own heads, and when they tried to run to escape, every one of them drowned

Are you trying to escape from God's presence? Don't, because you can't. He is always near.

June 17

On this day in history in 1885, the Statue of Liberty arrived in New York Harbor after having been shipped from France in 350 pieces and 200 containers. A year later it was dedicated by President Grover Cleveland as a symbol of freedom and democracy. The statue cost the French an estimated $250,000, or about $5.5 million today. The statue was erected on Bedloe's Island, whose name was later changed to Liberty Island. Nearby Ellis Island soon became the main center for immigration in 1892. Sixty years later, the statue was designated a national monument by President Calvin Coolidge.

Statues are not a good thing in the Bible, as most are associated with other gods and idols. There is one that I can think of, although there may be more that I have not thought of, and it's found in Numbers 21:8: "And the Lord said to Moses, make thee a fiery serpent and set it upon a pole: and it shall come to pass that everyone that is bitten, when he looked upon it, shall live."

The statue the Lord approved of had a different purpose. By faith a person who looked upon the statue would be healed. Today the symbol of a doctor or medical practice is a serpent on a pole or a sword.

Do you need to see a doctor? God blesses them also, or at least some of them. Better yet, ask God to make you well. He may just be the doctor you need.

ne 18

On this day in history in 1983, Sally Ride became the first American woman in space. Russian Cosmonaut Valentina V. Tereshkova was the first woman ever to go into outer space. And American Shannon Lucid set a space record of 188 days living in space.

During Ride's space journey, she tested a shuttle robot arm she helped to design. These female astronauts had to be smart and work hard. Training was difficult, sometimes terrible. More than six thousand women applied for the job.

Let's look at hardworking women in the Bible. While there are several, Lydia is mentioned in Acts 16. She is classified as the first convert to Christianity in Europe.

Acts 16:14-15 reads: "And a certain woman named Lydia, a seller of purple of the city of Thyatira, which worshipped God, heard us: whose heart the Lord opened, that she attended unto the things were spoken of Paul. And when she was baptized and her household, she besought us saying, if ye have judged me to be faithful to the Lord, come into my house and abide there. And she constrained us."

Lydia was a businesswoman. She had to be strong and smart to compete in business. She worked hard and was even able to keep guests in her house. She also believed in God.

Are you being a Lydia? Do you trust God? Is Jesus your savior? Do you study God's word?

June 19

On this day in history in 1910, the first Father's Day was celebrated in Spokane, Washington. Now Father's Day is celebrated in 46 countries, although most are on different days to fit different customs. The United States celebrates Father's Day on the third Sunday in June.

I like the idea of June 19 myself. That date is my father's birthday. Let me tell you a little about him. He was born in 1920, just in time to be old enough for World War II, where he served in England and France. After he died at age 92, I found out that he had earned two Bronze Stars, but he rarely talked about his war experiences. If anyone pressed him for details, he just became quiet.

My father had four children, three boys and one daughter. I overheard him telling a friend about his children, with the conversation going like this: I have four children of whom I'm proud. My oldest son is the assistant plant manager of a vegetable oil processing plant. My second son works for the United States Postal Service as a rural letter carrier. My third son works for the City of Macon as a building inspector and blueprints examiner. Then there's my daughter who's going to school and has been all her life, with grades 1 through 12 in the county school system, followed by six years of college, and then 30 years of teaching. When she retired, she began substitute teaching. I don't know if she will ever get out of school.

Proverbs 20:7 reads: "The just man walketh in his integrity: his children are blessed after him."

My dad walked in God's integrity, and I hope that my children will be able to say the same of me.

Are you walking in the integrity of God?

June 20

On this day in history in 1943, Operation Bellicose began for Britain. This was a new type of bombing raid that was called shuttle bombing. British airplanes left England and bombed a steel factory in Germany, but instead of returning home they flew to airbases in Algeria for refueling, and then to Italy and the naval base in La Spezia in Liguria. This shuttle strategy enabled Britain to make two attacks on one trip. The steel factory in Germany made V-2 rockets but was completely shut down because of the bombing.

The Army of Israel was at war with the Philistines. Goliath was a mighty warrior for the Philistines, standing more than nine feet tall. He was the aggressor against Israel. The Bible tells us that the youthful David opposed Goliath. Going out to meet Goliath, David picked up five stones, one for Goliath and the others for his four brothers.

The passage of 1 Samuel 17:45 reads: "Then said David to the Philistine, thou comest to me with a sword and a spear, and with a shield: but I Come to thee in the name of the Lord of host, the God of the armies of Israel, whom thou hath defied."

David told Goliath his plan of action, and then with one stone killed his aggressor and set the Philistine army in disarray. That's a classic example of killing two birds with one stone.

Who fights your battles? Do you have more than one battle to fight? Ask God for help.

June 21

On this day in history in 1913, Georgia Broadwick became the first woman to jump from an airplane. She joined the circus skydiving circuit when she was 15, and became the first person to use a pullcord to open a parachute. She was also the first to land in water, be an instructor, and teach the Army how to parachute. Broadwick was only five feet tall and weighed a mere 85 pounds. She retired in 1923 with 1,100 jumps. She died in 1979.

Miriam was the sister of Moses and Aaron. She was a trendsetter as a prophetess of Israel and a leader in the Exodus. She was probably the young lady who watched over Moses when he was placed among the reeds in the Nile River before Pharaoh's daughter rescued him. She contracted leprosy after rebelling against Moses' leadership. But Moses quickly interceded for her and she was healed. The next time she was mentioned is at the time of her death and burial at Kadesh in the wilderness.

Exodus 15:20-21 reads: "And Marion the Prophetess the sister of Aaron, took a timbrel in her hand; and all the women went out after her with timbrels and with dances. And Miriam answered them, sing ye to the Lord for he hath triumphed gloriously; the horse and his rider hath he thrown into the sea."

Miriam, the prophetess served the Lord with music and song.

What better way to proclaim the power of God?

June 22

On this day in history in 1944, the Servicemen's Readjustment Act of 1944, also known as the G.I. Bill, was created. The bill created a hospital system for veterans returning from service, low-cost housing loans, stipends for college and technical schools, unemployment benefits, and farm and business loans. Servicewomen were also covered by the bill.

The bill was controversial but passed because of the "bonus war" of the 1920s and 1930s. World War I Veterans were promised money for readjustments after the war, but it didn't take effect until 1945. What good is readjustment money 25 years later?

The passage of 2 Kings 9:15 reads "But King Joram was returned to be healed of his wounds which the Syrians had given them, (When he fought with Hazael, King of Syria). And Jehu said, if it be in your minds then let none go forth nor escape out of the city, to go to tell it in Jezreel."

King Joram needed a Veterans Administration hospital when he returned home, as he suffered battle wounds. He may have needed a college loan to find another line of work. Of course, he would have been unable to work so he could have gotten an unemployment check. None of this happened for King Joram, but this was the plan for U.S. veterans returning home from war. The plan is still in effect today.

Will you ask God for help with your wounds?

June 23

On this date in history in 1865, Confederate General Stand Waite, who was also a Cherokee Indian chief, surrendered with the last of the big armies of the Confederacy at Fort Towson in the Oklahoma Territory. The war had long been over in the east. After Waite surrendered, only a few small armies remained.

Until the very end, Waite would not hear of surrender. His hit-and-run tactics caused much trouble among the Union troops. He attacked small towns, supply chains, food depots, anything that he could use for his own gain. When the war was over, he returned to his home in Honey Creek in the Oklahoma Territory.

David sang a song after a war with the Philistines. In this battle David became ill and was almost killed. His men wanted him to stay behind for that reason. After being successful in battle and the enemy defeated, David wrote a song.

The passage of 2 Samuel 22:2-4 reads: "And he said the Lord is my rock and my fortress and my deliverer; The God of my rock in him will I trust: he is my shield, and the horn of my salvation my high tower, and my refuge, my savior; thou savest me from violence. I will call on the Lord, who is worthy to be praised: so shall I be saved from mine enemies."

To the victor comes the praise. I'm sure that the general who opposed Waite could have sung this song, as could his army.

Are you living a victorious life? Can you sing this song with David?

June 24

On this day in history in 1989, the United States invaded Panama in a successful attempt to overthrow Manual Noriega, its dictator. Noriega had been indicted by a grand jury in Miami on charges of money laundering and drug trafficking. Tensions were high between Panama and the United States since the indictment, and twenty thousand troops were sent to Panama and affected the overthrow. Noriega surrendered in January of 1990, was found guilty of all charges, and then sentenced to 40 years in prison. He was extradited to Panama, where he died in May 2017.

The late Peter Marshall, chaplain of the U.S. Senate, is quoted as saying, "May we think of freedom, not as the right to do as we please, but as the opportunity to do what is right."

Psalms 119:44-46 reads: "So shall I keep the law continually for ever and ever. And I will walk at Liberty, for I seek thy precepts. I will speak of thy testimonies also before Kings and will not be ashamed."

The difference between David and Noriega was that one wanted to keep the law, while the other one did not. David is thought of as a man whom God loved, while Noriega did not follow God nor keep His commandments.

We have the same choices in what we do today. Which journey will you take?

June 25

On this day in history in 1868, President Andrew Johnson signed legislation that created the 8-hour workday for federal employees, a law that has not been changed since. Throughout history, states and companies have adopted these sets of laws that provided for a better workforce since long hours and a need for rest will affect your daily lives. Since then, in most instances, employees have felt better and worked harder for their employers.

Genesis 2:2 reads: "And on the seventh day God ended His work which He had made; and he rested on the seventh day from all his work which he had made."

This verse tells us that even God rested on the seventh day. We don't know how many hours He worked on the first six days, but we know that He rested on the seventh.

God set an example for us to follow. Do you get enough rest? Do you follow God's example?

June 26

On this day in history in 1813, John Tyler married Letitia Christian in a month traditionally known for weddings and graduations. The Tylers would have eight children. In 1839 Letitia suffered a stroke that left her paralyzed and unable to fulfill her role in life, and then in 1841 she suffered another stroke and died.

In 1844 Tyler married a New York socialite named Julia Gardiner, making him the first of his occupation to get married. Julia was thirty years younger than her husband, and together they had seven children. Tyler had now fathered 15 children, the most of any man in his position. He was the tenth president of the United States.

Weddings are always popular events, but let's see what the Bible says about marriages. Mary, the mother of Jesus, loved to attend weddings. In fact, the first miracle Jesus performed was at a wedding in Cana.

John 2:6-8 reads: "And there was set six waterpots of stone, after the manner of the purifying of the Jews, containing two or three firkins apiece. Jesus saith unto them, fill the waterpots with water. And they filled them up to the brim. And he saith unto them, draw out now, and bear it unto the governor of the feast. And they bare it."

The wine was good, Mary was happy, and Jesus would now begin his ministry.

Are you doing good today? Do you make your family proud? Ask God to help.

June 27

On this day in history in 1932, Father Francis P. Duffy died. He was a Catholic chaplain of the 69th Infantry Regiment. The old 69th was made up mostly of Irish-Americans and other immigrants from New York City. Father Duffy was to become the most decorated cleric in the history of the army.

Ezekiel 22:30 reads: "And I sought for a man among them, that they should make up a hedge and stand in the gap, before me and the land that I should not destroy it: but I found none."

Ezekiel and the rest of Israel were held captive in Babylon. Ezekiel was a prophet who prophesied that Israel was to build a hedge. God could not find one, so they were now in captivity.

Father Duffy of the fighting 69th was the type of man God was looking for. He stood in the gap and helped rescue men from the battlefield and also offered comfort in times of hard fighting.

Are you standing in the gap for your land and America? Are you standing in the gap of your land for the sake of God and His word? God still needs this kind of men.

June 28

On this day in history two very important things happened five years apart that are both related.

The first is that in 1914, a Serbian national assassinated Austrian Archduke Franz Ferdinand and his wife, Sophia, an event that started World War I. The second occurred in 1919 when the Treaty of Versailles was signed in Paris, an act that formally ended World War I.

Romans 14:19 reads "Let us therefore follow after the things which make for peace and things where with one may edify another."

Paul writes that we are to seek peace, but sometimes we are not able to afford that peace.

We should always ask God to lead us in our search for peace. Are you seeking peace today?

June 29

On this day in history in 1767, the British parliament approved the Townsend Revenue Act, which was a tax on glass, lead, paper, and tea that was sent to America from England. This was probably the straw that broke the camel's back as far as taxation without representation is concerned. It was the next to last straw over high taxes. Even if a bill is termed as revenue, income or tariffs, it is still just another tax. That was in 1767 and in 2018, and the only difference between then and now is that at least we are represented now, such as it is.

Luke 2:1 reads: "And it came to pass in those days, that there went out a decree from Caesar Augustus that all the world should be taxed."

Here is another tax that no one loved, especially Joseph. Joseph had to leave his home and take with him his wife, Mary, who was with child, and travel to Bethlehem to pay taxes. There was no postal service back then to send in a payment. The journey was going to be hard for an expectant Mary, for their trip was on a donkey and the land was hilly. Everything turned out fine, though, as Mary had her baby and Joseph paid his taxes and made friends with shepherds and an innkeeper. Everyone in Bethlehem loved Mary's baby, a little boy whose name was Jesus.

We all undergo hardships from time to time. Just remember to do what is right and things will turn out okay. If you take Jesus on your journey, He will be the best friend you can have. Would you meet Him now?

June 30

On this day in history, two things are brought to mind. Some of us have reaped the results of the first event in 1950, but very few of us have succeeded in attaining the second since it occurred in 1953.

In 1950, President Harry S. Truman ordered ground troops into Korea. Personally, I know plenty of Korean war veterans.

Then in 1953, the first Chevrolet Corvette rolled off the assembly line in Flint, Michigan. While many of us have wanted one, few actually paid the high price tag to actually own one.

Matthew 6:33 reads: "But seek ye first the kingdom of God, and his righteousness, and all these things shall be added unto you."

We did not seek that trip to South Korea, nor did we want to go. But go, we did, and we carried out our duties the way we should have.

Many of us want a Corvette, and many of us have sought one, but very few people I know has ever reached the prize of owning one.

When we seek after the things of the world, we forget about God. When we seek God, the things of the world do not matter.

Are you seeking after God or the world?

July 1

On this day in history in 1980, President Jimmy Carter signed legislation that provided two acres of land near the Lincoln Memorial for the Vietnam Veterans Memorial. The memorial honors the men and women who served in the unpopular Vietnam War. It has the names of the 58,195 names, in chronological order, of those who died or are listed as missing in action in Vietnam. There is also a three-quarter size replica of the wall that travels across the country for people to see. Both walls are sometimes referred to as "The Wall That Heals."

Exodus 3:15 reads: "And God said moreover unto Moses, thus shalt thou say unto the Children of Israel, The Lord God of our fathers, the God of Abraham, the God of Isaac, and the God of Jacob hath sent me unto you: this is my name for ever, and this is my memorial unto all generations."

As a memorial to the Children of Israel, God told them who He was. The God of Abraham, Isaac, and Jacob is what God refers to as forever when His name is mentioned.

The Wall that Heals in Washington is a powerful memorial and has brought healing to many men and women. But God's memorial is more powerful than any other, for He is a living memorial.

The God of Abraham, Isaac, and Jacob can be your God also. Will you let him rule in your life?

July 2

On this day in history in 1881, President James A. Garfield was shot after having been in office for only four months. He lived just 80 days after being shot.

Charles Guiteau, a lawyer and seeker of political office, was charged in the shooting. The reason he gave was that Garfield wouldn't give him a job. Guiteau was deemed sane by a jury, and then found guilty and was hanged on June 30, 1882.

Chester A. Arthur was then named the 20th president. Arthur had been Garfield's vice-president.

As a strange afternote, Garfield's spine is kept as a historical artifact by the National Museum of Health in Washington, D.C.

Someone is always trying to kill leaders. Ehud, the second judge of Israel, killed Eglon, the King of Moab. Judges 3:21 reads: "And Ehud put forth his left hand, and took the dagger from his right thigh and thrust it into his belly."

Ehud was able to escape by leaving the king's palace and shutting the doors behind him to the king's chambers. Ehud just acted naturally once he was past the doors. One way of getting rid of your enemies is to kill the leaders, and God had inspired Ehud to kill Eglon.

Does God inspire you to do things? Are you sure it's God? Check with Scripture to see if it's God's will.

July 3

On this day in history in 1940, the British launched Operation Catapult. The French had already fallen to the Germans and the only thing that stopped England from being next was the English Channel. Operation Catapult was intended for the British to capture the French ships. The ships in the ports of England would be no problem or at least offer very little resistance. But the French ships at the Oran, Algeria, port were different. The British surrounded the harbor and demanded surrender. They were given four options of joining the British naval forces to fight the Germans, turning the ships over to the British, disarming them, or scuttling them and making them useless.

The French rejected all of these options, so another option was offered, and that was to go to the French West Indies, disarm the ships, and then turn them over to the U.S. Navy The French wouldn't accept that option, either, so the British opened fire. Some 1,250 French sailors were killed, the battleship *Dunkerque* was damaged, and the *Bretagne* and the *Providence* were destroyed. The next day the British prime minister told the House of Commons that he would leave his actions to be judged by history.

The passage 1 Samuel 18:3 reads: "Then Jonathan and David made a covenant, because he loved him as his own soul."

Jonathan was the son of King Saul, and David was the son of Jesse the Bethlehemite. David was a warrior, while Jonathan was not. They both loved and respected each other in spite of their differences. David would soon be the next King of Israel.

Saul wanted to kill David but never could. David had several chances to kill King Saul but would not, saying that he would not kill God's anointed. To put it mildly, King Saul hated David. Jonathan loved David, and as long as Jonathan was alive David would be his friend.

Who are your friends? Who are your enemies? How do you treat them?

July 4

On this day in history in1776, the American colonies declared their independence from England. What can I say about it that the majority of Americans don't already know? So, let's look at other happenings for the 4th of July.

In 1826, former presidents John Adams and Thomas Jefferson die. Adams's last words were, "That ol' Jefferson still lives." But in fact, Jefferson had died about three hours earlier. Neither knew of the other's demise.

In 1863, during the War Between the States, Vicksburg fell into Union hands, a move that cut the Confederacy in half in a sort of divide and conquer move.

In 1917, U.S. troops marched to the tomb of Marquis de Lafayette in France. Lafayette was a Revolutionary War hero for the United States in its fight for independence.

In 1997, the spaceship *Pathfinder* landed on Mars.
God has blessed America from its beginning. Our leaders were mostly Godfearing men. Those who were not at least respected the institute of Christianity.

The passage 2 Chronicles 7:14 reads; "If my people which are called by my name, shall humble themselves, and pray, and seek my face, and turn from their wicked ways; then will I hear from heaven, and will forgive their sins, and will heal their land."

This is a great promise for our land for today and tomorrow. When we call upon God, He hears us, and we should ask Him to help us remain as one nation under His guidance.

July 5

On this day in history in 1950, Private Kenneth Shadrick, a 19-year-old infantryman, became the first American reported killed in South Korea. Shadrick had just fired a bazooka at a Soviet-made tank when he looked up to see if he hit his target. That's when he was hit by machinegun fire.

The total number of Americans killed in Korea varies from 36,516 to 54,246. The 54,000-plus number counts for any serviceman in the world who died for any reason. For example, if a serviceman was killed in a car accident, he would be included in that number. The smaller number is probably more accurate.

Exodus 20:13 reads: "Thou shalt not kill."

This is a good rule to live by, but being in a war makes things a little different. In war, it's kill or be killed.

Judges 20:46 reads: "So that all which fell that day of Benjamin were twenty and five thousand men that drew the sword; all these were men of valor."

The Tribe of Benjamin was in a civil war against the other tribes of Israel. The Tribe of Judea was the first to fight. For the first two days, things were not going well, but on the third day things were different and Benjamin was defeated.

Are your enemies being defeated? Are you doing this in God's will?

July 6

On this day in history in 1976, the United States Naval Academy admitted women for the first time. There were 81 midshipmen admitted to the class, with Elizabeth Anne Rowe as the first woman to graduate in 1980. Four years later, Kristine Holderied became the first female to graduate at the top of her class.

In 1845, the school, known then as the Naval School, was organized. In 1850, its name was changed to the U.S. Naval Academy. The curriculum was changed to four years and all cadets were to spend summers serving on ships, a rule that remains the same today as then.

Acts 9:36 reads: "Now there was at Joppa a certain disciple named Tabitha, which by interpretation is called Dorcas: this woman was full of good works and almsdeeds which she did."

Tabitha was a well-respected lady of the community. She was a seamstress and had a lot of good deeds to her credit. At her death, her friends sent for Peter to come where she was. Peter asked everyone to leave the room, and then told Tabitha to rise. After hearing Peter's voice, she sat up, and then stood up, and Peter, lending her a hand, presented her to her friends. What a miracle that was.

Do you have the faith of Tabitha and her friends? Do you live expecting a miracle?

July 7

On this day in history in 1981, President Ronald Reagan nominated Sandra Day O'Conner for a seat on the Supreme Court. She was the first woman to be nominated for this job. On September 21, the U.S. Senate unanimously approved her appointment, and four days later she was sworn in by Chief Justice Warren Burger as the first female Supreme Court justice.

Born Sandra Day, she earned a law degree from Stanford Law School. After graduation she married classmate John Jay O'Conner III. She then served in the public sector as a deputy county attorney, and next worked in West Germany for three years as a private attorney while her husband served a tour in the military. Three children later, she returned to Arizona and served as an assistant state's attorney. She served on the Supreme Court until her retirement in 2005.

Esther 2:17 reads: "And the King loved Esther above all women, and she obtained grace and favor in his sight over all the Virgins; so that he set the Royal Crown upon her head and made her queen instead of Vashti."

Sandra Day O'Conner and Esther were similar because they both influenced laws and worked for the betterment of the people they served. O'Conner ruled on the constitutionality of laws and set forth a standard that people had to abide by.

Esther was about the same. As queen she had an influence on actions taken by others that affected her people. Her uncle told her that she had come to the kingdom for such a time as this. Such could also be said of Sandra Day O'Conner.

Are you here for such a time as this? What does that mean for you?

July 8

On this day in history in 1776, a bell made of copper and tin rang out from the tower of the Pennsylvania statehouse. The bell is now known as the Liberty Bell, and the statehouse is now known as Independence Hall.

On July 4,1776 the Declaration of Independence was signed but not read to the public. It was sent to be printed, and when it was completed it was read on July 8, 1776. The Liberty Bell rang out to summon the people together for its first public reading.

In 1976 the Liberty Bell was moved to a new pavilion about a hundred yards away from Independence Hall. Now about a million visitors tour and see the Liberty Bell each year.

Exodus 34:28 reads: "And he was there with the Lord forty days and forty nights; he did neither eat bread, nor drink water. And he wrote upon the tablets the words of the covenant, the ten commandments."

This is a verse about how we received the Ten Commandments. God passed them to Moses, and then Moses printed them on two stone tablets so that he could read them to the people of Israel.

Have you read the Declaration of Independence? Have you read the Ten Commandments? Both are worth reading.

July 9

On this day in history in 1947, General Dwight D. Eisenhower appointed Francis Blanchfield to be a lieutenant colonel in the U.S. Army. She was the first female to attain permanent rank in the military. Blanchfield had been a member of the Army Nurse Corps since 1917 and secured the rank when the Army-Navy Nurse Act became law in 1947. Blanchfield received the Florence Nightingale Award from the International Red Cross. Today, the hospital at Fort Campbell, Kentucky, is named in her honor.

When King Saul and Jonathan, his son, died in battle, Jonathan had a son named Mephibosheth left at home. When word of Jonathan's death arrived, his nurse fled with Mephibosheth. In her haste she fell, and the boy became lame in both legs. The nurse was able to get him to safety at the home of Ammiel in Lo-debar.

The passage of 2 Samuel 9:1 reads; "And David said, Is there yet any that is left of the house of Saul, that I may shew his kindness for Jonathan's sake."

Mephibosheth's nurse took care of him after the accident. King David wanted to honor his friend Jonathan and searched for Mephibosheth and brought him to the palace of the king. Mephibosheth stayed there for the rest of his life. Anything he wanted, he was afforded. He even sat at the king's table.

How do you treat your enemies and friends?

July 10

On this date in in history in 1998, the U.S. military delivered the remains of First Lieutenant Michael Blassie to his family in St. Louis, Missouri. Blassie was an Air Force pilot whose body was placed in Arlington National Cemetery in the Tomb of the Unknown Soldier for the Vietnam War. His remains were confirmed by DNA testing, which means there will be no unknown soldier from the Vietnam War. I'm glad. Everyone needs closure for their lost loved ones.

Galatians 1:22-24 reads: "And was unknown by face unto the churches of Judea, which were in Christ: But they had heard only, that he which persecuted us in times past now preacheth the faith which once he destroyed. And they glorified God in me."

The Apostle Paul was an unknown person. Simply put, no one knew him. They had heard of him, and they knew all about him, but they didn't know what he looked like.

Blassie was the same way. People knew him, they had heard of him, but after being lost in Vietnam they had no way of identifying him. The Apostle Paul said in the last verse that God was "glorified" in him. Blassie's family was glorified because their son, brother, cousin, and friend had been found.

Are you lost? Could you be a blessing and glorify God in yourself if you accepted Christ? Why not give it a try?

July 11

On this day in history in 1918, Enrico Caruso recorded "Over There," a song penned by George M. Cohen. Every war needs a song, and from the mid-1910s through the 1950s, musicals were tremendously popular and the most watched movies and plays of any other genre. The likes of Cohen, Rogers and Hammerstein, George Gershwin and others had a bonanza writing songs and plays that seemed to draw the nation together. Songs like "Over There" reminded the people of the war going on and to pray for the troops.

Psalms 107:1-2 reads: "O give thanks unto the Lord for he is good: for his mercy endureth forever. Let the redeemed of the Lord say so, whom he hath redeemed from the hand of the enemy;"

David reminds us that the Lord is good to us and that we need to give thanks to Him. Most of David's psalms give praise to God, as he was a man after God's own heart. We can be also like David when we give God praise and repent of our sins. Like the song "Over There," we are reminded of what's happening in other lands.

David tells us what is happening in our lives. When we give God praise, our lives will just flow better.

July 12

On this day in history in 1862, President Abraham Lincoln signed a law creating the U.S. Army Medal of Honor for non-commissioned officers and privates who distinguish themselves by their gallantry in action. The previous year, in December of 1861, the Navy Medal of Honor was created.

In 1863 the Medal of Honor became a permanent military decoration available to all servicemen in all branches of service. It is conferred upon going above and beyond the call of duty. Since the War Between the States, more than 3,400 men and one woman have received the award.

The passages of 2 Timothy 4:7-8 reads: "I have fought a good fight, I have finished my course, I have kept the faith: Henceforth there is laid up for me a crown of righteousness, which the Lord, the righteous judge, shall give me at that day: and not me only, but unto all them also that love his appearing."

Paul tells us about his crown of righteousness. We can have the same kind of crown that Paul has if we seek after God and do His will.

Do you want that crown? Do you follow God? Why not start today?

July 13

On this day in history in 1863, opponents of the Civil War draft began, followed by three days of rioting in New York City. During the riots, more than a thousand casualties occurred.

President Abraham Lincoln had signed the legislation for the draft and young men protested the law. The war was about as popular then as the Vietnam War was in the 1960s, which means no one cared for it. But the draft was the only way to equip an army in an unpopular war such as the War Between the States, the Korean War, or the Vietnam Conflict. Ironically, some of the thousand men probably could have survived the war more than the rioting.

A protest is defined as to make objection to or speak strongly against. Using this definition, we are all guilty of protest almost every day.

Jeremiah 11:7 reads: "For I earnestly protested unto your fathers in the day that I brought them out of Egypt, even to this day, rising early and protesting saying Obey my voice."

When the Children of Israel left Egypt, God made a covenant with them. Most covenants are simple: if you will, I will. God had promised to protect Israel and make them a strong nation. The Children of Israel had promised to worship God, and only God. Now the Children of Israel had broken that covenant.

Do you protest God? Have you broken your covenant with God?

July 14

On this day in history in 1798, Congress passed the Sedition Act, which made it a federal crime to write, publish, or utter false or malicious statements about the government. Nowadays, we see it every day, as it has become common practice to defy the government. The Sedition Act was repealed in 1920.

Romans 13:9 reads: "For this thou shalt not commit adultery, Thou, shalt not kill, thou shalt not steal, Thou, shalt not bear false witness, Thou, shalt not covet; and if there be any other commandment, it is briefly comprehended in this saying, namely, thou shalt love thy neighbor as thyself."

The Apostle Paul, speaking to the Romans, tells most of the Ten Commandments before wrapping it up with the commandment that Jesus gave during his ministry: Thou shalt love thy neighbor as thyself.

Following this commandment generally covers all the rest. Who is your neighbor? Everyone. Whom should you love? Everyone. What if I just don't like them? Just stay away from them.

Love and like are two different things. For example, I love fishing. I really do. But if I eat fish, it could kill me because I am allergic to them. So, then, I love them but I don't like them and just stay away. Just the same, you can stay away from people and not hate them.

Do you love your neighbor as you love yourself?

July 15

On this day in history in 1806, Lieutenant Zebulon Pike headed out on a mission to explore the American Southwest. He was to find the headwaters to the Arkansas and Red rivers and then he was to investigate Spanish settlements in New Mexico. Pike reached Colorado and spotted what is now Pike's Peak, the highest mountain in the Front Mountains of the Rockies. In New Mexico, the Spanish charged Pike with illegal entry into Spanish territory, a complete 180-degree spin on today's immigration issues. Pike was taken to the border of the Louisiana Purchase in Texas and released.

In an attempt by Aaron Burr to capture part of the Southwest Territory for his own country, Pike was implicated but later exonerated of any crime. He later served as a brigadier general in the War of 1812. He was killed at York, Canada, in April of 1813.

Joshua 2:1 reads: "And Joshua the sun of Nun sent out of Shittim two men to spy secretly, saying, Go view the land even Jericho. And they went and came into an harlot's house, whose' name was Rahab and lodged there."

In Biblical times spies were used much like today. The most noted spies were the ones who spied out the land and did not trust God. Where could spies stay? They were enemies of Jericho. They went into the harlot's house and were later able to escape.

How do you observe the enemy today? What do you do about them?

July 16

On this day in history in 1945, the first atom bomb was tested. The Manhattan Project had come to an end at almost 5:30 in the morning on this date. The tower holding the bomb was vaporized. Planning on this test began in 1939, with noted scientists from around the world working on the project.

Italian Physicist Enrico Fermi met with Navy officials first. Then Albert Einstein wrote a letter to President Franklin D. Roosevelt saying such an explosion was possible. Germany was the first choice of the Allies of where to drop the bomb but by then the Nazis had already surrendered, so Japan was next. On August 6 and 9, the atomic bomb was dropped on Hiroshima and Nagasaki Japan respectively. The war was over.

Joshua 6:5 reads: "And it shall come to pass, that when they make a long blast with the ram's horn and when ye hear the sound of the trumpet, all the people shall shout with a great shout; and the wall shall fall down flat, and the people shall ascend up every man straight before him."

Joshua didn't need the atomic bomb to win his battle. The Lord had told Joshua what was going to happen.

When God fights your battle, you win. Are you depending on God today?

July 17

On this day in history in 1898, the Spanish-American war ended. At the end of the war, all Spanish territories in Central America and the Pacific were finally out of Spain's hands. Only Cuba was still fighting Spain for its independence. The *USS Maine* was an American battleship anchored in Havana Harbor during that time, and while America wanted independence for Cuba, the United States remained neutral until the *Maine* was bombed and sunk. The sinking of the *Maine* is still unexplained, but afterward America entered into that war.

Commander George Dewey of the U.S. Navy had captured the Philippines on May 1. General William Shafter led U.S. ground troops including Teddy Roosevelt and his Rough Riders in an effort to force the Spanish Navy out to sea. At sea the land batteries, the artillery, opened fire on them and every ship was damaged or destroyed. The Spanish Navy surrendered in 1898. From that time, America has become a world power.

Joshua 5:6 reads: "For the Children of Israel walked forty years in the wilderness, until all the people that were men of war, which came out of Egypt, were consumed, because they obeyed not the voice of the Lord: unto whom the Lord sware that he would not shew them the land, which the sware unto their fathers that he would give us, a land that floweth with milk and honey,"

The Children of Israel had been in a war much like Spain and America. They had been promised a land flowing with milk and honey, but they did not possess it as the Lord had commanded. The Spanish, too, had a promised land, but they could not keep it because they were unprepared for such conflict. Israel would win their next battle, and the Spanish would lose theirs.

Are you prepared for your next battle?

July 18

On this day in history in 1940, Franklin Delano Roosevelt was nominated for his third term for president of the United States. He would later become a four-term president, a feat no other president ever achieved. Because of rising pressure in Europe before World War II, Roosevelt said it was his duty to continue serving as president, and in 1944 he was elected to his fourth term. He died in office on April 12, 1945, and was succeeded by Vice-President Harry S. Truman.

In 1947, the 22nd amendment to the Constitution passed that placed two-term limits on the presidency, with it ratified in 1951.

The passage of 2 Thessalonians 2:13 reads: "But we are bound to give thanks always to God for you, brethren beloved of the Lord, because God hath from the beginning chosen you to salvation through sanctification of the spirit and belief of the truth."

We are to give thanks for our leaders, and although we may not always agree with them, we must respect their office. The president has a term limit, but members of Congress don't. Maybe we should rethink that idea. Another way to impose term limits is to simply to not vote for the person in office. We as Americans have a choice to vote for whom we wish. If you want term limits, then don't vote for that candidate anymore.

God has chosen us. Have we chosen God?

July 19

On this day in history in 1943, the United States bombed a railroad yard in Rome, Italy, in an effort to break the will of the Italian people. It worked. President Roosevelt and British Prime Minister Winston Churchill had told the Italians to reject Mussolini and live for Italy. With the railroads destroyed, the Italians went into a panic. Mussolini had convinced them that the Allies would not attack the Holy City, but he was wrong. The Italians lost their confidence in their leader.

Then Hitler and Mussolini met in northern Italy in an effort to revive the Italians. Mussolini kept fighting because he feared Hitler. Despite low morale, Mussolini would not tell Hitler the truth. Italy had been defeated. Hitler no longer trusted Mussolini, and after their meeting he ordered Field Marshall Erwin Rommel to take over occupied Greece in case Mussolini surrendered.

Psalms 73:28 reads: "But it is good for me to draw near to God; I have put my trust in the Lord God, that I may declare thy works."

Mussolini had lost not only the trust of his country, but also trust in himself. He could have had that trust restored if he had turned to God. Even King David in all his greatness trusted God. Mussolini could not proclaim the works of God. David trusted God and no one else.

Do you trust in yourself? Do you trust in God's guidance?

July 20

On this day in history in 1969, Neil Armstrong, an American astronaut, became the first person to walk on the moon, saying these immortal words, "That's one small step for man, one giant leap for mankind."

The American effort to put a man on the moon started on May 25, 1961, when President John F. Kennedy spoke to a joint session of Congress, calling for more space exploration. In 1966, National Aeronautics and Space Administration (NASA) launched an unmanned Apollo mission to test the structure of spacecraft. In October of 1968, Apollo 7 became the first manned mission. In December of 1968, Apollo 8 took three men to the dark side of the moon. At 9:30 in the morning of July 16, 1969, Apollo 11 lifted off from Kennedy Space Center with Neil Armstrong, Edwin "Buzz" Aldrin Jr. and Michael Collins on board. Apollo 11 went into moon's orbit on July 19, and the next day the landing craft named *Eagle* made its descent. At 10:56 p.m., Armstrong set foot on the moon, with Buzz Aldrin joining him at 11:11 p.m. The two planted the American flag and left a plaque. They even talked to President Richard Nixon from the moon. At 12:56 a.m. on July 22, Apollo 11 headed for home, arriving at 12:51p.m. on July 24.

Genesis 1:16 reads: "And God made two great lights; the greater light to rule the day and the lesser light to rule the night: he made the stars also."

As exciting as it was to hear of this happening, I'm sure it was more so thrilling to be a participant. Oh, what a story they will have to tell their grandchildren.

What else will they be able to tell about God's existence?

July 21

On this day in history in 1930, Congress created the Veterans Administration. Is it a good thing? A bad thing? Take your pick. The VA is in charge of helping veterans from all the branches of the service, helping them to make decisions about school, home loans, college or trade schools, illnesses and anything else they may need. The VA is on the frontline to help returning veterans from all over the world, and it has a hospital system for veterans, so with the high cost of medical care, it is certainly a good thing for veterans. The only drawback is that the overriding cost of healthcare makes it difficult for the VA to see all veterans and give them adequate care.

Revelation 13:3 reads: "And I saw one of his heads as it were wounded to death; and his deadly wound was healed: and all the world wondered after the beast."

In this chapter of Revelation, the Beast is coming out of the sea and is a big, imposing monster. It has ten heads with one that was wounded and then healed. Somehow the Beast lived through it and many wondered how that could have happened.

Have you ever seen a person healed? Were you amazed? Was a doctor used? Have you seen anyone healed by faith? Ask God to heal you and your friends.

July 22

On this day in history in 1942, the systematic deportation of Jews began in Warsaw Poland. The Jews had already been imprisoned in a ghetto lined with barbed wire. Later, a brick wall was placed around it as well. Heinrich Himmler, commander of the Nazi SS unit, ordered the ghetto cleaned and depopulated.

The concentration camps of Treblinka I and II had been established not far from Warsaw, and in the next seven weeks more than 250,000 Jews had been sent to these camps and gassed to death. Before the war was over in 1945, some 700,000 Polish Jews—with some estimates as high as 900,000—had been put to death by gas. It is hard to comprehend the suffering the Jews went through before their deaths. The pure hatefulness was enough for anyone to fear. I cannot imagine what God has done and will do to those responsible for such atrocities.

Esther 3:13 reads: "And the letters were sent by posts into all the Kings providences, to destroy, to kill, and to cause to perish, all Jews, both young and old, little children and women, in one day even upon the Thirteenth day of the twelfth month, which is the month Adar, and to take the spoil of them for a prey."

In Esther, we read about a man called Haman, who was a top assistant to King Ahasuerus. His goal in life was to eliminate Jews. He even devised a way to do it and ordered it carried out. After hearing of Haman's plans, Esther went to see the king. He listened to her, and then took action of his own. He had Haman hanged, and the Jews were allowed to defend themselves. Esther's uncle, Mordecai, became the king's main commander. Before he was hanged, Haman did not kill any Jews, but he was punished anyway.

What will the Germans get for killing so many Jewish people? Do you trust God? What will be your reward?

July 23

On this day in history in 1793, Roger Sherman died. Sherman was a patriot from Connecticut who was one of five people appointed to write the Declaration of Independence and the only American to sign all four of the great state papers of the United States, including the Continental Association, the Declaration of Independence, the Articles of Confederation, and the Constitution. It is said that Thomas Jefferson once remarked of Sherman that he never said a foolish thing in his life.

The passage of 1 Kings 3:19 reads: "Give therefore thy servant an understanding heart to judge thy people, that I may discern between good and bad: for who is able to judge this thy so great of people."

Solomon, the third king of Israel, asked God for wisdom. He could have asked for riches or the power to rule the entire world, yet he merely asked for wisdom.

Roger Sherman was a man of great wisdom, using it for his country.

What are you using for your country? What are you using for God? Wisdom is what all of us need. Have you asked God for wisdom? What has He given you?

July 24

On this day in history in 1943, British bombers raided Hamburg, Germany, by night while the Americans bombed it by day. The Americans called it Operation Blitz, and the British called it Operation Gomorrah. The British dropped 2,300 tons of incendiary bombs on Hamburg in just a few hours. Of the 791 planes that flew that night, the British lost only 12 aircraft. The 8th U.S. Air Force started two days of daylight bombing runs, with two of these over Hamburg. The British flew 17,000 bomber sorties carrying 9,000 tons of explosives. This was the beginning of the end for Germany.

Genesis 19:24 reads: "Then the Lord rained upon Sodom and Gomorrah brimstone and fire from the Lord out of heaven."

Just as the British destroyed Hamburg with fire, the Lord destroyed Sodom and Gomorrah with fire and brimstone sent from Heaven.

What type of life are you living? Hamburg was almost destroyed, but what about the city you live in? Will God destroy it as He did Sodom and Gomorrah? What if the life of your town depended on your life?

July 25

On this day in history in 1978, Louise Joy Brown was born in Oldham, England, as the world's first so-called test-tube baby. The process is actually known as in-vitro fertilization (IVF) and is now quite common. At least five couples I know personally were successful with IVF, but I also know of several cases when it didn't work.

Jeremiah 29:11 reads: "For I know the plans I have for you, declares the Lord, plans to prosper you and not to harm you, plans to give you a hope and a future."

God knows what is in store for each of us, just as He knew what He was doing with Louise Joy Brown. With God's promises, we will be blessed and have a future through Him if we accept Him as our Savior.

July 26

On this day in history in 1775, the Continental Congress created the United States Post Office, and its name was later changed to the United States Postal Service. Benjamin Franklin became our first postmaster general in 1753 in Philadelphia. The British fired Franklin in 1774 because of his political activities, but then Congress rehired him until 1776, when he became ambassador to France. Because of Franklin, routes were established to carry the mail from Florida to Maine.

Today there are more than forty thousand post offices in the United States. The USPS delivers mail to every address in the United States, Puerto Rico, Guam, American Virgin Islands and American Samoa. The USPS receives no tax dollars except for Visually Impaired Material that Congress requires to be delivered. In remote locations, the USPS still uses mules to deliver the mail. If the price of gasoline rises by just one penny, it will cost the USPS $8 million a year.

The passage of 2 Kings 19:10 reads: "Thus shalt ye speak to Hezekiah, King of Judea, saying, Let not thy God in whom thou trustest deceive thee, saying, Jerusalem shall not be delivered into the hands of Assyria."

This verse is a play on words. Sennacherib is telling Hezekiah that he will conquer Jerusalem in spite of what God said. Hezekiah prays to God and gets assurance that Jerusalem will not belong to Assyria. Without a battle, the Assyrian army is destroyed by angels.

Messengers are as important now as in Hezekiah's time. The USPS helps us out and delivers our messages to where they are going. The fastest way to get a message to God is to pray.

July 27

On this day in history in 1943, Russian leader Joseph Stalin issued order number 227 that became known as the Not One Step Backward order. The order proclaimed that "panic-makers and cowards" must be liquidated on the spot. No retreat or withdrawal without the consent of higher headquarters was allowed. They would be traitors if these orders were not followed.

Germany had been having success against the Russians but had suffered a setback when they attacked Stalingrad. They lost a lot of land in this defeat. Their next site was Leningrad, but that attack was also repelled as Russian troops were finally beginning to fight back. Being shot on the spot would be an encouragement to anyone.

The passage of 1 Samuel 25:37-38 reads: "But it came to pass in the morning, when the wine had gone out of Nabal, and his wife had told him these things, that his heart died within him, and he became as a stone. And it came to pass about ten days after, that the Lord smote Nabal and he died."

Nabal was a greedy man and a coward. He did not stand up against David in an honest way or help David out with what he needed. When his wife told him about her meeting with David, the coward in Nabal came out. God then struck him, and he fell down and died.

Are you a coward? I can understand fear but not being a coward. Ask God to help you face your problems and glorify Him.

July 28

On this day in history in 2018, I was thinking about my life. Most of my childhood I was brought up in a small shotgun house with no indoor plumbing. Today, after living in that shotgun house, then military barracks, then tents on training missions, then a hooch in Vietnam, and later a singlewide trailer, then brick houses, and finally a doublewide mobile home, I still have a place to look forward to coming home.

John 14:1-3 is a very well-known passage of Scripture: "Let not your heart be troubled ye believe in God, believe also in me. In my Father's house are many mansions; if it were not so I would have told you. I go to prepare a place for you, And if I go and prepared place for you. I will come again and receive you unto myself that where I am there ye may be also."

No matter in what type of housing we live in, we can always be assured that a mansion is waiting for those of us who are children of God.

Are you ready for your mansion? Do you trust God?

July 29

On this day in history in 1924, my mother, Maxine Beall, was born. She was later to become a basketball star in school, a schoolteacher, and a Sunday School teacher. She loved to travel. My daddy watched her play basketball while she was in high school. They later dated, and then after World War II, they married and had four children.

In our phases of life, we sometimes reach the stage of thinking that we know it all. John Wooden, a former basketball coach for the University of California at Los Angeles, put it this way, "It's what you learn after you know it all that counts." I have a friend who says he knows everything in every book in the Universe but those are his words.

The passage of 2 Timothy 2:15: reads: "Study to shew thyself approved unto God, a workman that needeth not to be ashamed, rightly dividing the word of truth."

As we go through our lives and pass the know-it-all stage, let us study and learn what God would have us to do.

What are you doing? How can you improve?

July 30

During the long hot summer months of 1787, the Constitutional Convention met in Philadelphia. These men were given the responsibility of forming a new government for our young nation.

The preamble of the Constitution reads: "We the people of the United States, in order to form a more perfect union, established justice, insure domestic tranquility, provide for the common defense, promote the General welfare and secure the blessings of Liberty, to ourselves and our prosperity, do ordain and established this Constitution of the United States of America."

Just as tranquility means peace in our Constitution, Jesus gives us the peace that we need to not be afraid.

John 14:27 reads: "Peace I leave you, my peace I give unto you; not as the world giveth, give I unto you, Let, not your heart be troubled, neither let it be afraid."

The writers of the Constitution were the type of people who could not afford to be afraid, for a great responsibility was on their shoulders.

God can give you peace if you ask it of Him.

July 31

On this day in history in 1928, MGM's Leo the Lion roared for the first time. Its roar was at the beginning of the first MGM movie with sound, and that movie was "White Shadow on the South Sea." It was based on a book by Fredrick O`Brien and his life in the South Pacific. Leo has been portrayed by seven lions, but only one, that first one, was named Leo. Howard Dietz of MGM pictures patterned the lion after the mascot of Columbia University, his alma mater. The music that accompanies Leo is "Roar, Lion, Roar," Columbia's theme song.

Daniel 6:16 reads: "Then the King commanded, and they brought Daniel, and cast him into the den of lions. Now the King spake and said unto Daniel, Thy God whom thou serveth continually, he will deliver thee."

We have all heard the story of Daniel and the lion's den when the Lord shut the mouth of Leo and the rest of the lions. Daniel slept well that night, much better than the king who had cast him into the den.

Are you facing Leo and a den of lions today? Are you prepared for it? Ask God to give you the courage that you need.

August 1

On this day in history in 1779, Francis Scott Key was born. He was educated in Annapolis, Maryland, and later became a lawyer who was appointed as a U.S. District Attorney. He was a religious man who opposed the War of 1812. When the British captured Washington D.C. in 1814, Dr. William Beans was also captured. Key was asked to negotiate his release from prison. The British agreed to release Beans, with Key and another officer overseeing the exchange the next day. But as it were, the bombardment of Fort McHenry took place that night. As dawn arose the next morning Key could see the American flag still flying and quickly wrote a poem entitled "Defense of Fort McHenry." Later it was set to music and became a popular song called "The Star-Spangled Banner." It became our national anthem in 1933.

Psalms 5:3 reads: "My voice shalt thou hear in the morning, O Lord, in the morning will I direct my prayer unto thee and will look up."

King David looked up to God in the morning. He wanted to see the beauty of sunrise as he prayed.

Key also looked up to see what was going on when he saw the U.S. flag still flying.

Even in war, and especially that night, I'm sure Key praised God. He would also say a prayer in the form of a song, one that would inspire millions.

Is your heart renewed today? Have you looked up to see God's beautiful creation? Why not start now?

August 2

On this day in history in 1923, President Warren G. Harding, the nation's 29th president, died of a stroke in California. He had been to Alaska to get away from Washington D.C., because of impending scandals. Harding was elected by a landslide but was not a very effective leader. The scandals involved corruption and fraud in the Interior, Justice and Veterans departments, plus there were rumors of extramarital affairs. Vice-President Calvin Coolidge was sworn into office by his father the next day in Vermont.

In Matthew 7:15-20, Jesus tells us about good and evil fruit, with Verse 17 reading: "Even as every good tree bringeth forth good fruit; but a corrupt tree bringeth forth evil fruit."

How do you tell the difference? If it is good, it came from a good tree. If a person is good, then their actions will be good. If a person is bad, then their actions will be bad. We are sometimes confused about what's good and what's bad. You may have several situations that are good or bad.

God's word will tell us what's what. Do you read God's word?

August 3

On this day in history in 1797, Lord Jeffrey Amherst died. Amherst was the British general famous for leading the British against the French during the Seven Years War. Another fact in his rise in history is how he treated the American Indians before the War of Independence. Amherst was the first person to use biological weapons. He suggested that Colonel Henry Bouquet use smallpox-infested blankets to put down an Indian uprising in the Ohio Valley. Bouquet did this with great success, and about 75 percent of the Indians died from exposure to the virus. Amherst returned to England in 1763 and declined to come to America again.

Ecclesiastes 6:2 reads: "A man to whom God hath given riches, wealth, and honor, so that he wanteth nothing for his soul of all that he desireth, yet God giveth him not power to eat thereof, but a stranger eateth it: this is vanity and it is an evil disease."

Amherst may have suggested a disease to kill the Indians but he also had a disease called vanity. Like smallpox, vanity has no cure except through God.

Regardless of what your life may be, vanity can be cured only by God. Do you have that disease?

August 4

On this day in history in 1944, Anne Frank, a young Jewish girl, was captured by the Nazis. She was found hiding with the rest of her family in a secret apartment in Amsterdam. The Franks had left Germany in 1933 when the Nazis overran the Netherlands between 1942-1944. The young Anne stayed in hiding and kept a diary of everything going on around her. It was published after she died in a German concentration camp and widely read as a glimpse of life during the time of the Holocaust.

This reminds me of another story about a Jewish girl named Esther. She was a beautiful young lady who King Ahasuerus liked, but he didn't know she was Jewish. After a plot to destroy the Jews, Esther had to reveal herself in order to save her people. Her husband took action to protect Esther and her fellow Jews.

Esther 7:3 reads: "Then Esther, the Queen, answered and said, If I have found favor in thy sight, O King, and if it pleases the King, let my life be given me at my petition, and my people at my request."

Esther has a written record of her request for her life and the life of other Jews. Both Anne Frank and Esther rose to an occasion to help their people.

Are you helping your people today? Will the things in your life account for something next week, next year, in the next decade or even a century from now?

August 5

On this day in history in 1914, Germany started the first battle of World War I. The assault of Germany against Liege, Belgium began with three armies or 34 Divisions of troops. That meant more than 1.5 million troops just from Germany were in the battle. Liege fell into German hands on August 15, 1914, after Germany had to bring in extra guns. The on August 18, Germany began its advance through Belgium and marched toward France.

Joshua 10:28 reads: "And that day Joshua took Makkedah, and smite it with the edge of the sword, and the king thereof he utterly destroyed, them and all the souls that were therein; he let none remain: and he did to the King of Makkedah, as he did unto the king of Jericho."

The 10th chapter of Joshua tells of the Children of Israel and how the Lord led them in conquering the land that He had promised them. The Germans conquered Belgium and France in World War I, but they were not led of God, and in the end the forces that opposed them stood fast and defeated them. Joshua followed the Lord in battle. He withstood his enemies and honored God with his actions.

What are your actions telling you about God's will? Are you serving God the way Joshua did?

August 6

On this day in history in 1945, at 8:16 a.m., Japanese time, the B-26 bomber named *Enola Gay* dropped the first atomic bomb over Hiroshima, Japan. Approximately 80,000 people were killed and 35,000 injured that day and another 60,000 would die before the end of the year. President Franklin D. Roosevelt made the decision to drop the atomic bomb after estimates that more than a million lives could be lost if the United States launched an invasion of Japan.

Revelation 16:16 reads: "And he gathered them together unto a place in the Hebrew tongue, Armageddon."

The dropping of the atomic bomb is likened unto the battle to end all time. Chapter 16 of Revelation tells us of the wrath of God and how it will be poured out on the earth in the last days. The bomb that was dropped over Hiroshima will be small in comparison to what will happen in the last days of this earth.

Are you ready for that battle? What about the outcome of that battle?

August 7

On this day in history in 1942, the first offensive operation in the Pacific began when the First U.S. Marine Division landed on five of the Solomon Islands to begin the attack. U.S. military forces had been reeling because of the loss of men and supplies when Japan attacked Pearl Harbor on December 7, 1941. The attack on the Solomon Islands caught the Japanese off guard and allowed the Marines to take a major airfield on Guadalcanal. The Japanese regrouped and fierce hand-to-hand fighting occurred. In February 1943 the Japanese secretly retreated and abandoned the islands. The Japanese lost 25,000 men, while the U.S. lost 1,600. Both sides each lost 24 ships.

Isaiah 1:15 reads: "And when ye spread forth your hands, I will hide mine eyes from you: yea, when we make many prayers, I will not hear: your hands are full of blood."

God is telling the Children of Israel that when they open and spread their hands, it does not affect Him. The hands of the Children of Israel are full of blood and are contaminated, dirty, stinky, and even look bad. Until the children confess their sins, their hands are of no use to them.

After the Japanese abandoned Guadalcanal, I'm sure thankfulness and joy were in the camp. Their hands could now be cleaned.

Your hands must be clean to give God praise. Are your hands free of sin today? Ask God to cleanse them for you.

August 8

On this day in history in 1974, President Richard M. Nixon announced that he would retire effective at noon on August 9. Shortly before the midday hour, the president and his wife, Patricia, boarded Marine One, leaving Washington to return to their home in San Clemente, California.

Nixon said in his resignation statement, "By taking this action, I hope that I will have hastened the start of the process of healing which is so desperately needed in America."

Nixon became the first president to resign from office. That same day at noon, Vice-President Gerald R. Ford was sworn in as the 38th president. He later pardoned Nixon of any crimes he may have committed.

The second chapter of 2 Kings tells of Elijah and Elisha. These two men are hard to keep separate in my mind, and my wife told me to remember that J comes before S that is in their names.

The passage of 2 Kings 2:11 reads: "And it came to pass, as they still went on, and talked, that, behold, there appeared a chariot of fire and horses of fire, and parted them both asunder; and Elijah went up by a whirlwind into heaven."

Nixon went up into sky with the helicopter's whirlwind and returned to California as a disgraced president just because greed had taken over his life.

What kind of life do you live?

August 9

On this day in history in 2010, Steven Slater, a JetBlue flight attendant, quit his job in a most unusual way. Since I'm always on the lookout for something on the jovial side of life, this story fit the bill. After Slater's JetBlue flight landed in New York, he got into a heated discussion with a passenger over her luggage. Slater lost his temper, grabbed the plane's public address system and cursed out the passenger. Then he deployed the aircraft emergency chute, grabbed two beers, jumped out of the plane and slid down the chute. Realizing he forgot his own luggage, he clamored up the chute, retrieved his bags, and then slid back down again.

Later Slater was arrested and pleaded guilty to two counts of attempted criminal mischief. He was ordered to go to substance abuse counseling and pay JetBlue $10,000 to replace the chute. His fifteen minutes of fame had then come to an expensive end.

The passage of 1 Samuel 17:49 reads: "And David put his hand in his bag and took thence a stone, and slang it, and smote the Philistine in his forehead, that the stone sunk into his forehead; and he fell upon his face to the earth."

Another man had his fifteen minutes of fame and is recorded in the first book of Samuel. That man was Goliath. He came out to harass the army of Israel for many days. When a small teenager challenged the giant, his ridicule became worse. David gave Goliath's fifteen minutes of fame, let's just say, a rocky finish.

Are you living your fifteen minutes of fame? Do you trust God to help make wise decisions?

August 10

On this day in history in 1821, Missouri became the 24th state of the United States of America, with its name taken from a Native American tribe. Missouri was controversial from the start. It was part of the Louisiana Purchase and was admitted to the Union as a slave state. It was also the first state that was geographically completely west of the Mississippi River.

In 1861, all slave states seceded from the Union except Missouri. Most of the Confederate forces from Missouri were not much more than ruthless outlaws anyway, and they continued to terrorize Missouri even after the war.

These outlaws could be compared to the Gibeonites found in Joshua 9. The Gibeonites were afraid of the Children of Israel and did not want to be their next victims, so they made a league with Israel under false pretenses, but then God punished Israel for not doing what He told them to do.

Joshua 9:6 reads: "And they went to Joshua unto the camp at Gilgal, and said unto him and to the men of Israel, we be come from a far country: now, therefore, make ye a league with us."

Joshua did not check them out to see if they were truthful. I realize that you have to trust other people, but you should check them out first.

Do you follow God's instructions?

August 11

On this day in history in 1984, President Ronald Reagan made a joke about bombing Russia. While testing the microphone in preparation for a speech, Reagan said, "My fellow Americans, I am pleased to tell that today I have signed legislation that would outlaw Russia forever. We begin bombing in five minutes."

Of course, most of the people knowingly laughed at the joke, but a few Democrats almost had a cow. It seems that Reagan was always making a joke about something.

Another incident took place in a cave. King Saul was trying to kill David, but he was tired out and went into a cave to sleep that night.

First Samuel 24:3 reads: "And he came to the sheep cotes, by the way, where was a cave; and Saul went in to cover his feet: and David and his men remained in the sides of the cave."

While King Saul slept, David would not allow his men to hurt him. After all, Saul was still king. David called Saul the next morning and bowed himself before him, saying, "I could have killed you." King Saul lifted his eyes and told David that he was more righteous than himself.

Are you doing what is right today? Do you honor God?

August 12

On this day in history in 1961, construction of the Berlin Wall began. Berlin had been divided into the east and west since World War II when the Russian army captured half of the city. The other half was claimed by the Americans and British.

After the end of World War II, during the 1950s and 60s, Berliners from the east moved freely to the west. That went on until East Berlin built a barbed-wire fence to keep out West Berlin. Later a concrete wall took its place.

Over the years, more than 80 people were killed trying to cross the wall from East Berlin to freedom in West Berlin. The Russians even installed minefields to keep people in. Soon the Berlin Wall became a symbol of the Cold War. Even when western governments protested the wall, the Russians paid no attention.

There was another wall that was built around a city, and that city was Jerusalem. The wall was for protection of its people, not to keep them fenced in. It was built by men who were afraid of their enemies.

Nehemiah 4:17 reads: "They which builded on the wall, and they that bare burdens, with those that laded, everyone with one of his hands wrought in the work, and with the other handheld a weapon."

This kind of wall is what we need, not one made of hate but of concern for our safety.

What kind of wall do you have today?

August 13

On this day in history in 1781, Patriot forces led by Colonel William Harding and Brigadier General Francis Marion, also was known as the Swamp Fox, led British Major Thomas Fraser and his 450 men into an ambush at Parker's Ferry, South Carolina.

Also on this day three thousand soldiers sailed on a French fleet to aid the Patriots. The French had left St. Dominque in the Caribbean for the Chesapeake Bay where British General Charles Cornwallis had set up his headquarters. While the French defeated the British at sea, General George Washington attacked Cornwallis's position, thus trapping him and effectively ending the war.

The passage of 2 Chronicles 13:13 reads: "But Jeroboam caused an ambushment to come about behind them; so, they were before Judah, and the ambushment was behind them."

Jeroboam was King over Israel, and Abijah reigned over Judah. They both began a war between the two nations. Judah was caught in the ambush; however, the priest blew the trumpet and the soldiers gave a shout and broke the ambush. Israel was defeated that day, and half of its army was killed. Judah won because they relied on the Lord.

Are you victorious in your life today? Do you trust the Lord?

August 14

On this day in history in 1945, Japanese Emperor Hirohito announced that Japan had surrendered to the Allies and accepted the terms of the Potsdam Conference. The actual surrender date was on August 10, but the Soviets and Japanese were still fighting in Manchuria, and the United States was still fighting in the Pacific against the Japanese. A Japanese submarine sank two American ships east of Okinawa. When news of the surrender came, more than a thousand Japanese troops stormed the Imperial Palace to find war documents and destroy them but were repulsed by forces loyal to Emperor Hirohito.

John 18:10 reads: "Then Simon Peter having a sword drew it, and smote the high priest's servant, and cut off his right ear. The servant's name was Malchus."

Not everyone is ready to surrender. Even Peter, a disciple of Jesus, was not ready for Jesus to be carried away by soldiers.

Jesus didn't put up a fight, so Peter did. He was loyal to Jesus as long as he carried a sword in his hand. Today that weapon would probably be a pistol. It's easier to defend ourselves with a weapon rather than to surrender peacefully.

Have you surrendered your life to Christ? What are you hiding behind?

August 15

On this day in history in 1939, the movie "The Wizard of Oz" premiered in Hollywood, California. Judy Garland, its lead actress, became famous because of the movie, as did the song "Somewhere Over the Rainbow." Most of us know the beautiful and cheery song, even decades after it was first released.

Genesis 9:13-15 reads: "I do set my bow in the clouds, and it shall be a token of a covenant between me and the earth. And it shall come to pass, when I bring a cloud over the earth, that the bow shall be seen in the cloud: and I will remember my covenant, which is between me and you and every living creature of all flesh; and the water shall no more become a flood to destroy all flesh."

The rainbow in the clouds appeared right after Noah and his family left the ark as a promise from God to humans that He will never again destroy the earth with water. The title alone of "Somewhere Over the Rainbow" reminds us of God's promise.

What songs are you singing today? Do they uplift God? Do they bring praise to God?

August 16

On this day in history in 1812, U.S. General William Hull surrendered at Fort Detroit, Michigan, without a fight. Hull was a veteran of the American Revolution. He had lost hope of defending the fort against the British and Indians. His daughter and grandchildren were at the fort, too. The army was taken to Canada as prisoners while militiamen were allowed to return home. In 1813 William Henry Harrison, who would one day become president of the U.S., recaptured Fort Detroit.

In 1814, Hull was court-martialed for cowardness and neglect and sentenced to die. But President James Madison revoked the sentence because of Hull's service in the Revolutionary War.

Isaiah 42:4 reads: "He shall not fail nor be discouraged, until he has set judgment in the earth: and the isles shall wait for his law."

Isaiah 42 reminds us that God will always be faithful and will encourage us. When we trust In God, we can live our lives with joy. God will not fail us, and we will not be discouraged.

If Hull had read this verse for his morning devotion, he may not have been discouraged; instead, he was afraid for himself and his family.

Are you feeling discouraged? Do you have faith that God will not fail you?

August 17

On this day in history in 1943, U.S. General George S. Patton and the U.S. 7th Army beat British Field Marshall Bernard L. Montgomery and his 8th Army to Messina, Sicily. This unofficial race brought an end to the conquest of Sicily.

Patton believed in the use of tank warfare as the future of war. He was a tough commander and had a love-hate relationship with his troops. He met his end in December of 1945 in a hospital in Germany from injuries sustained in an automobile accident.

Hebrews 12:1 reads: "Wherefore seeing we also are compassed about with so great a cloud of witnesses, let us lay aside every weight, and the sin which doth so easily beset us, and let run with patience the race that is set before us."

The "unofficial race" was won by Patton, as he had laid away all weights to help win the war. Both the British and Americans wanted the war to end, but the Germans were the weights that had to be laid aside. After the Allies captured Messina, it was now a race to Italy, then France, and then Germany. The prize of the race for the Allies was ridding the world of Hitler.

Are you running a race today? What is your goal? Can you see the finish line?

August 18

On this day in history in 1872, Aaron Montgomery Ward mailed out his first mail order catalogue. It was a one-page paper with a hundred items and their prices listed. Ward was born in New Jersey and schooled in Michigan before moving to and working in Chicago.

In 1872 he began the company known as Montgomery Ward. It was a mail order house, but later Ward opened retail stores as well. George R. Thorne, Ward's brother-in-law, bought a half-interest in the business for $500. In 1888, Montgomery Ward saw sales of $1 million a year. When Ward died in 1913, the company's annual sales had risen to $40 million.

Deuteronomy 29:5 reads: "And I have led you forty years in the wilderness: Your clothes are not waxen old upon you, and thy shoe is not waxen old upon thy foot."

God's protection upon his children reached to their physical and spiritual needs. Spiritual needs occur when God will protect his people as long as they worship Him, while physical needs reached to their shoes and clothes. In other words, they just didn't wear out.

How is your life? Does God take care of your spiritual and physical needs?

August 19

On this day in history in 1856, Gail Borden received a patent for the process of producing condensed milk. Instant food had just hit the market, and condensed milk was a welcome item. It has many uses from cooking and baking to pastry-making, and it keeps for a long period of time. In most cases, cooks can just add water and have a sustainable milk product. No longer was there a need for homes to have cows at hand for fresh milk, and no matter where you are in the world, you can have milk, even if it is in a can. Milk is and always has been a precious and important commodity globally.

Exodus 3:8 reads: "And I am come down to deliver them out of the hand of the Egyptian and to bring them up out of the land unto a good land and a large, unto a land flowing with milk and honey; unto the place of the Canaanites; and the Hittites, and the Amorites, and the Perizzites, and the Hivites, and the Jebusites."

We know the story of how God spoke to Moses from a burning bush. God told Moses to pull off his shoes, and then from the burning bush He gave Moses instructions on how to handle Pharaoh. But before Moses got to Pharaoh, he first had to win over his own people.

When we look at the land that God gave the Children of Israel, we can tell that God has blessed the Israelites. To live in a land flowing with milk and honey is to live in a good place.

Gail Borden helped the world to be able to be a better place because of his experiment.

How are you helping the world?

August 20

On this day in history in 1804, Sargent Charles Floyd died. Floyd had volunteered to join Lewis and Clark on their journey of exploration to the Pacific Ocean. He was the only member of the party to die on the trip.

Lewis and Clark had left St. Louis, Missouri, three months earlier. Floyd, a native of Kentucky, had suffered for days with symptoms pointing to cholic. After Lewis and Clark returned home and told others about Floyd, it was thought that he had appendicitis. At the time, no doctor alive could help him get over the illness as there was no cure or operation that could help. Floyd was buried in Sioux City, Iowa, on a bluff overlooking the Missouri River. That spot is now known as Floyd's Bluff.

Deuteronomy 34:4-6 reads: "And the Lord said unto him, this is the land that I sware unto Abraham, unto Isaac, and unto Jacob, saying, I will give it unto thy seed: I have cause thee to see it with thine eyes, but thou shalt not go over thither. So, Moses the servant of the Lord died there in the land of Moab, according to the, word of the Lord. And he buried him in a valley in the land of Moab, over against Beth-peor: but no man knoweth of his sepulcher unto this day."

Moses was able to see the Promised Land and he enjoyed looking at it. When he died, God buried him but no one knows where that place is located and likely his grave will never be found.

Most of us know where we will be buried, while Moses did not. What happens after death is what is important. Floyd didn't see his earthly destination of the Pacific Ocean, but Moses saw his in the Promised Land.

Will you see yours? What about your eternal life? Will you see it?

August 21

On this date in history in 1883, Frank James went on trial in Gallatin, Missouri, for robbery and murder. The trial was moved from the courthouse to the local opera house to accommodate the overflow crowd who wanted to see one of the sensational James brothers in person. Frank James had turned himself in to authorities in October 1882, after his brother Jesse James was shot dead in a conspiracy to collect reward money. Frank feared the same would happen to him.

Jesse and Frank James and their gang had robbed and killed many people for more than two decades. Ironically, they always gave the money to some needy soul. The public called them heroes who took money from banks, railroads, and the rich, and with it in turn helped the poor.

The Missourians were unwilling to convict Frank James, but the State of Alabama and the State of Missouri tried to convict him again, but it was of no use. In late 1833, Frank James became a free man. He died in 1915 at his family home at age 72.

Exodus 20:13 reads: "Thou shalt not kill."

Exodus 20:15: reads "Thou shalt not steal."

Hebrews 9:27 reads: "And it is appointed once to die, but after this the judgment."

I'm not sure if Frank James was guilty of everything for which he was accused, but I do know that like every other man, he would one day die. What type of judgment he received depended on God.

We all know of cases where people get away with crimes. One day we will stand before God. What will you say?

August 22

On this day in history in 1775, King George III of England proclaimed that the American colonies were in open rebellion. Really? Why, thank you very much. We're glad you noticed. We had given the king so many hints with the Quartering Act, Stamp Act and Tea Tax. America also had no representatives in government or Parliament. The country also had no chance of freedom or survival other than to resist the king.

Joshua 24:14 reads: "Now therefore fear the Lord and serve him in sincerity and in truth: and put away the gods which your fathers served on the other side of the flood, and in Egypt, and serve ye the Lord."

Many in the American colonies felt that they existed only for England and no other reason, plus the Church of England was pushed down the throats of the Colonists as the only religion. The Colonists wanted a better way of life, and that's why they came to America in the first place. But England had other ideas and still wanted the Colonists to answer to the throne, but that's not what they wanted. Instead, they wanted to be like Joshua and choose whom they wanted to serve.

As we know now, that open state of rebellion soon became an open state of war, one for independence, freedom of religion, and choices as to how they were to live their lives then and how we live our lives today.

What choices have we made? Are you in a state of rebellion against God?

August 23

On this day in history in 1913, two groups of people united to form Veterans of Foreign Wars (VFW). It is the largest group of organized veterans in this country.

In 1899, a group of Spanish-American War veterans and another from the Philippines Insurrection of 1899-1902 formed the VFW. The organization is comprised of men and women in active duty or honorably discharged veterans who have served in a combat zone. Their motto is "Honor the dead by helping the living."

The VFW and its auxiliaries work to help veterans by developing friendships, donating blood, funding college scholarships, teaching patriotism, and respecting the flag. It also extends the institutions of American freedoms and protects and defends the Constitution of the United States of America from all enemies foreign and domestic.

Psalms 40:1-2 reads: "God is our refuge and strength, a very present help in trouble, Therefore, we will not fear, though the earth be removed and though the mountains be carried into the mist of the sea."

These verses tell us how God is our strength and our helper. We can always trust God. Sometimes we may need help from our fellow man as well. For combat veterans, that help may come from the VFW. For ourselves and our neighbors and friends, that help can come from God.

Agust 24

On this date in history in 1942, in World War II, U.S. forces delivered another crushing blow to the Japanese. The Japanese aircraft carrier *Ryuho* was sunk in the East Solomon Islands. The main part of the success of the mission was the volunteer coast watchers who had spotted a large Japanese force headed toward Guadalcanal. The coast watchers then alerted three U.S. carriers of Japanese movement, which allowed the U.S. to intercept the Japanese. The American ship, the *USS Enterprise*, was damaged but would return to duty before the end of the war.

As a footnote, future President John F. Kennedy and his crew were rescued because of the coast watchers when their ship sank in 1943 near the Solomon Islands.

Acts 23:27 reads: "This man was taken of the Jews, and should have been killed of them: then came I with an Army and rescued him, having understood that he was a Roman."

The coast watchers helped the U.S. Forces when things got bad.

Are you helping someone today?

August 25

On this day in history in 1830, a famous race occurred that was sponsored by B&O Railroad. The locomotive Tom Thumb—often called an iron horse—entered into a race with a horse-drawn car led by a live gray horse. At the starting signal the horse-drawn car got off to a clear lead but the iron horse caught up with and passed it. About the time the Tom Thumb was ahead, its blower belt came off the pulley and caused the engine to lose its steam. By then, it was too late to overtake the live horse. The living, breathing gray horse won.

The passage of 2 Timothy 4:17 reads: "I have fought a good fight, I have finished my course, I have kept the faith. Henceforth, there is laid up for me a crown of righteousness, which the Lord, the righteous judge shall give me at that day and not to me only, but unto all them also that love his appearing."

How are you running your race today?

August 26

On this day in history in 1920, the 19th Amendment to the U.S. Constitution was passed. The amendment gave women the right to vote. Well, not exactly. It actually prohibited state and federal governments from denying the right to vote to citizens of the United States based on their gender. That could cover almost any race or gender of all people. Since the women's suffrage movement was front and center at that time, it mostly applied to women. On August 26 of each year, this date has been called Women's Suffrage Day. That started in 1973 and is proclaimed each year by the president.

John 4:14 reads: "But whosoever drinketh of the water that I shall give him shall never thirst; but the water that I shall give him shall be in him a well of water springing up into eternal life."

Jesus proved that He respected all people. Here He is talking to the Jews, the most despised race of people of the time. Jesus had met a Samarian woman at the well. The Samarians were the most hated among the Jews. Jesus offered her a drink of living water and told her all about herself and the things she had done in life.

How would you feel if Jesus came to you and started telling you about the things that you have done? Even the things that very, very, very, very, very, few people know about? That's when Jesus told the woman about the living water.

Do you know about this living water? Have you sipped of that water?

August 27

On this date in history in 1872, Congress passed a law making the Latin phrase "E Pluribus Unum" our nation's motto. The phrase means "Out of many, one," and is included on the Great Seal of the United States. And yes, it sounds like Greek to me. In 1873, a law passed by Congress declared the phrase appear on all U.S. money. It also explains what America is about. Many people, nationalities, colors and religions have united together for one cause, and that is for the United States of America.

Psalms 133:1 reads: "Behold how good and how pleasant it is for brethren to dwell together in unity."

This does not mean that we all have to think alike nor agree with one another. But it does mean that we should be agreeable and united in our differences. As the Psalmist David wrote, "It is pleasant for brethren to live together in unity."

We do not think as our neighbor does. Do we respect their opinions? Do we trust God to lead us in our thinking? Why not give it a try?

August 28

On this day in history in 1776, General George Washington had moved his men to safety across the East River to Manhattan in New York. The move was made necessary by the fact that the British were chasing the Colonials and greatly outnumbered them. Washington had lost the Battle of Long Island in New York, and he was trapped and defeated. After finding two boats, he ferried his men across the river to fight again. The next day, a heavy fog kept the British ships off the river and the army in their quarters.

Mark 4:39 reads: "And he arose and rebuked the wind, and said unto the sea, Peace be still. And the winds ceased and there was a great calm."

Jesus and his disciples were in a boat when a storm arose and almost sank the boat. Jesus, who had been sleeping, was awakened and questioned about the storm. Jesus raised his hand to the water and said, "Peace, be still." The storm rolled away.

The fog on the East River allowed Washington and his troops to escape. A storm in Jesus' time made the disciples afraid.

A storm is in our lives right now. Will we be afraid, or will we say, "Peace be still?" Sleeping through a storm can be relaxing, but not sleeping through a storm can be scary.

What are you doing? Are you afraid of the storm? Why not be able to sleep through the storm? God has the solution if you ask for His guidance.

August 29

On this day in history in 2005, Hurricane Katrina hit New Orleans and caused much damage and loss of life, with those numbers about 1,800. It also affected the rest of Louisiana and Mississippi. In 2017, on this date, Hurricane Harvey caused so much damage in Texas that it made parts of it look as if it were an island chain when before it had been landlocked. The impact of both hurricanes will be felt for a long time.

Isaiah 43:2 reads: "When thou, passes through the waters, I will be with thee and through the rivers, they shall not overflow thee; when thou walkest through the fire, thou shalt not be burned; neither shall the flame kindle upon thee."

This verse reminds us that God will be with us through the storms in our lives. As we know, a storm does not always mean a weather storm. It could be almost anything, including the loss of a loved one, an illness or disease, financial difficulties, or almost anything.

How do you handle your storms? Are they weather-related or emotions-related? In either case, ask God to lead you through your storms.

August 30

On this day in history in 1967, Thurgood Marshall became the first African-American to be confirmed as a justice on the Supreme Court of the United States. Marshall's parents had taught him about the Constitution, and additionally one of his teachers once made him read the it as punishment for misbehavior.

Marshall graduated from Lincoln University in 1930. He then applied to the University of Maryland School of Law but was refused entry because of segregation. He instead attended Howard University Law School, an historically African-American school in Washington, D.C. Upon graduation, Marshall then sued the University of Maryland School of Law because of their discriminatory admission policies.

Marshall later became the chief counsel for the National Association for the Advancement of Colored People (NAACP). He was only 32 years old. He also argued 32 cases before the Supreme Court, winning 29 of them. For 24 years, he served on the Supreme Court before retiring because of ill health.

Acts 8:31 reads: "And he said, How, can I, except some man should guide me? And he desired Phillip that he would come up and sit with him."

Another leader of African descent who had an important position in life is not named. He is only known as the Ethiopian eunuch. He was the treasurer for Queen Candace of Ethiopia. He was returning to Ethiopia from Jerusalem where he had gone to worship when Phillip joined him. The leader asked Phillip to help him understand God's word, so Phillip preached to him the words of Christ. The Ethiopian believed the word and was baptized.

Marshall helped many people in his life.

How many have you helped? Is God calling you to teach others?

August 31

On this day in history in 1916, during World War I, a U.S. Citizen named Harry Butters was killed fighting for the British in the Battle of Somme in France. Butters was mostly raised in England where he attended Beaumont College in Old Windsor. When the war broke out in 1914, Butters rallied to the cause and joined the British Army. He received a commission in the Royal Artillery, 24th division, 107th Brigade in April of 1915.

After arriving in France, Butters met Winston Churchill, who was serving as a battalion commander on the western front. When asked about his commission and being an American, Butters said "I just lied to them."

At the battle of Somme, his battery took a direct hit and all were killed, including Butters. He is buried at his request in the Commonwealth Graves Commission Cemetery just south of Albert, France. His headstone reads "An American Citizen."

John 15:13 reads: "Greater love hath no man than this, that a man lay down his life for his friend."

Butters was a friend to the British. He lived there, went to school there, served in their Army, and even died for them, giving his life for his friends. He died for what he believed.

Are you willing to do the same?

September 1

On this day in history in 1836, the first known white women settled west of the Rockies. Narcissa and Marcus Whitman and Eliza and Henry Spalding were missionary couples who had left New York for the West. Narcissa wrote of the journey, "We are determined to convert the benighted one living in darkness of heathenism to Christianity."

Eliza and Henry Spalding (no relation to Henry or Spalding counties in Georgia) left and went to Idaho, while the Whitmans went to Washington State where they started a mission for the Cayuse Indians. Their mission went well for eleven years until a smallpox epidemic broke out. With no immunity of the disease, the Indians blamed the Whitmans' God for the disease, and then attacked and killed the missionaries. Narcissa Whitman was the first white woman to live and then die west of the Rockies.

Acts 18:26 reads: "And he began to speak boldly in the synagogue: whom when Aquila and Priscilla had heard, they took him unto them, and expounded unto him the way of God more perfectly."

In the Book of Acts is written the story of another missionary couple named Aquilla and Priscilla. Aquila taught in the synagogue every Sabbath. When Paul was persecuted in Corinth, Aquila and Priscilla went to be with him, and there they separated with Paul going one way and Aquila and Priscilla another. Aquila and Priscilla were able and willing to take a young preacher under their wing to train, educate, and instruct him about God.

Are you willing to help a younger preacher? Are you the teacher that a young person needs? Why not start now?

September 2

On this day in history in 1944, George Herbert Walker Bush, an aviator with the U.S. Navy, was serving as a torpedo bomber pilot in the Pacific. Bush would later become the 41st president of the United States.

During a bombing mission on this date, Bush's aircraft was hit by Japanese antiaircraft gunfire. He was forced to jump out of the plane, and then treaded water for four hours before being rescued. Bush's bravery earned him the Distinguished Flying Cross.

(This would have been the one time that I would want to jump out of a plane, but with a parachute, of course.)

The event was Bush's second time cheating death in a crash. Later in 1944, he was reassigned to Norfolk Naval Base to teach young men to fly. He was discharged in 1944 after the Japanese surrendered.

Numbers 13:32-33 reads: "And they brought up an evil report of the land which they had searched unto the Children of Israel, saying, The land through which we have gone to search it, is a land that eateth up the inhabitants thereof, and all the people that we saw in it are men of great statue. And there we saw the giants, the sons of Anak, which came of the giants: and we were in our own sights as grasshoppers and so we were in their sights."

Joshua and Caleb were young men who were leaders and two of the twelve spies who searched the land of Canaan. They showed as much bravery as Bush. The two men brought back favorable reports while the other ten spies were scared and gave bad reports. Joshua and Caleb acted on faith as to what God told them to do.

Do you have the faith to stand up against spies? It takes courage to take a stand. Are you taking a stand?

September 3

On this day in history in 1954, the last episode of "The Lone Ranger" was broadcast on the radio, but the television series would last until 1957. The story is about a Texas Ranger who survived an ambush and was nursed back to health by Tonto, his Indian friend. In order to keep his identity a secret, the Lone Ranger wore a mask and as such was often thought of as an outlaw.

As long as the show ran, no one was killed, not even the so-called bad guys. The Lone Ranger always settled his case and then rode off to another mission. There seemed to be a lot of cases to be solved in the wild, wild west, as the last show number was 2,956.

The passage of 1 Timothy 1:2 reads: "Unto Timothy, my own son in the faith: Grace, mercy, and peace from God our Father and Jesus Christ our Lord."

Let me tell you of two other men who walked around preaching and helping others. They weren't quite as exciting as the Lone Ranger but exciting, nonetheless. They are the Apostle Paul and his young friend Timothy. Paul was the leader who made three missionary journeys before being put to death in Rome. Timothy was a young man upon whom Paul depended for help and support. He was a young preacher, just learning how to preach. Paul even thought of Timothy as a son. The two men preached and helped one another and even suffered trials together. When Paul was in prison, he sent for Timothy to help him.

Do you have a son in Christ? Do you have a young person to be an example to? Look around and find one with whom to start. The time will not be a waste.

September 4

On this day in history in 1945, Japanese forces on Wake Island surrendered two days after the Japanese officially surrendered onboard the *USS Missouri*.

The U.S. had control of Wake Island until December 7, 1941. On that date Japanese captured or attacked several of the Pacific islands. While invading Wake Island, the Japanese lost 820 men to the U.S. loss of 120. The U.S. decided not to recapture the island but to stare them out. Japanese Rear Admiral Shigematsu Sakaibara ordered the 96 American prisoners of war to be executed on trumped-up charges of using a radio. Japanese forces lost 1,300 men from starvation and another 600 from the occasional Allies air raids. American forces finally landed on Wake Island. When the war was over, Sakaibara was tried for war crimes and executed in 1947.

Joshua 10:26 reads: "And afterward Joshua smote them, and slew them, and then hanged them on five trees: and they were hanging upon the trees until the evening."

Joshua called this the Battle at Gibeon. Adoni-zedek, the king of Jerusalem, as well as four other kings and their armies were getting ready to fight Gibeon. Gibeon sent word to Joshua that he needed help, and Joshua caught the five kings while they were hiding in a cave.

The five kings went against God's will. When you go against God's will and His people, you pay for it. The Japanese leaders could have surrendered at any time, but instead chose to starve. The five kings decided to stay in a cave until they were captured because pride got in their way.

Does pride get into your way?

September 5

On this day in history in 1882, in New York City, some ten thousand men marched in the nation's first Labor Day Parade. The parade brought attention to the fact that some men worked fourteen hours a day with no time off. There were also issue of child and slave labor. The workers made little money, and their workplaces were dirty. The labor movements of the time did not want to overthrow the government. They just wanted a piece of the American pie.

Today, Labor Day is considered the unofficial end of summer unless you live in Georgia where it seems to stay summer until October. Labor Day is also mostly considered a back-to-school time and the last day of a three-day weekend.

Luke 10:7 reads: "And in the same house remain, eating and drinking such things as they give: for the laborer is worthy of his hire. Go not from house to house."

Jesus sent out seventy disciples. He told them that the harvest was ready and plentiful. Jesus then gave instruction on how and where to stay and for them to not be moving around.

Are you a good laborer today? Will Heaven be your goal and reward for the work you are doing?

September 6

On this day in history in 1620, the *Mayflower* set sail for America, arriving on November 9, 1620. Rough seas made for a treacherous trip. The *Mayflower* had a crew of 30 men and 120 passengers of mostly Puritans seeking a better and safer place to live and worship. Upon arriving in America everyone signed the Mayflower Compact, which was written to establish legal order and to quell increasing strife within the ranks. The *Mayflower* wintered in America and returned to England in April of 1621.

The Apostle Paul had been arrested and tried for preaching the Gospel. To avoid punishment, he asked to be sent to Rome because he was a Roman citizen. It was almost winter as he made his way to Rome. Sailing in the winter is dangerous, so most ships find a safe harbor, an inland canal, or a river to anchor for the winter in order to get out of the weather. The ship Paul was on wouldn't stop because of small harbors were difficult to maneuver and the need by the owner to hurry up to Rome.

Paul then gave this warning in Acts 27:10: "And said unto them, Sirs, I perceive that this voyage will be with hurt and much damage, not only for the lading and ship, but also of our lives."

After the ship set sail, a storm arose. Paul then told the people on the ship that no lives would be lost, but only the ship would be damaged.

Are you sailing through life today? Do you have any cares? Will God protect your ship?

September 7

On this day in history in 1776, during the Revolutionary War an American submersible named *Turtle*—named as such in that it resembled a turtle—attempted to attach a time bomb to the *Eagle*, the flagship of British Admiral Richard Howe. The *Turtle* was the first submarine ship ever used in war.

David Bushnell started making underwater mines while attending Yale University and found that a submarine was the best way to deliver the mines. That's how he developed the *Turtle*. Several other attempts were made to attach mines to other ships but without success.

Bushnell was given a commission with the Army Corps of Engineers by General George Washington. Bushnell then tried to develop a floating mine, but that didn't work either. After the Revolutionary War ended, Bushnell was over the U.S. Army Corps of Engineers at West Point.

The Apostle Paul writes to Timothy in Verse 2:15 and tells him what direction in life to take: "Study to shew thyself approved unto God, a workman that needeth not to be ashamed, rightly dividing the word of truth."

It is a good thing to learn to study. Having knowledge and intelligence helps you in life but having an intelligent life in Christ is even better. We, just as Timothy, need to study God's word, as life is much easier with God.

What are you studying today?

September 8

On this day in history in 1974, President Gerald Ford issued a pardon to disgraced former President Richard Nixon. Nixon was charged with illegal activities during the Watergate investigation. He bowed to public pressure to resign the presidency and became the first ever to do so. The pardon was full, free and absolute for any crimes Nixon may have committed while in office.

Twenty-seven years later, the John F. Kennedy Library presented its Profile in Courage award to Gerald Ford for his pardon of Nixon. In pardoning Nixon, Ford had put his country above his own political future and at the same time brought needed closure to the Watergate affair. Ford lost the next election in 1976 to Jimmy Carter. Ford died on December 26, 2006, at the age of 93.

When we talk about a man with courage, let's look at Job. God gave Satan permission to tempt Job and did it to such a degree that it would have been all over for the majority of us. But not Job. He suffered great losses but never lost faith in God. Even Job's friends and his wife could not convince Job that he did something wrong because he had done no wrong. After Job's trials, God rewarded him for his faithfulness.

Job 42:12 reads: "So the Lord blessed the later end of Job, more than his beginning: for he had fourteen thousand sheep, and six thousand camels, and a thousand yoke of oxen, and a thousand she asses."

Job's courage to stand with God and stay faithful was rewarding in the end. All that Job lost, God replaced two-fold. That is called faithfulness. Job had ten children, and then he had ten more. Children cannot be replaced.

How is your courage and, faithfulness?

September 9

On this day in history in 1836, Abraham Lincoln earned his license to practice law in Illinois. What a pleasure to get a law license, especially if someone were like Lincoln and had so many failures in life.

Life is bumpy at best and sometimes the smooth things in life are bumpy. Let us look at some of the bumps in Lincoln's life. He was defeated in a seat for the state legislature, he failed in business, his sweetheart died, he was defeated for speaker for the Illinois statehouse, he suffered depression, and he was defeated for a seat in the U.S. Senate. But being elected to the office of president of the United States was one of his successes, and what a success it was.

Philippians 2:14 reads: "I press toward the mark for the prize of the high calling of God in Christ Jesus."

We all have successes and failures in life, and how we handle our failures will, in effect, measure our successes. Just as Abraham Lincoln never gave up after so many failures, neither did the Apostle Paul. Paul said to press forward and never retreat. God had a special calling for him. Lincoln could have said the same thing. Lincoln was to be a president while Paul was to be a preacher and evangelist and both were successful.

How about you? What is your calling? Will you be a success?

September 10

On this day in history in 1955, the television show "Gunsmoke" began its twenty-year run. James Arness was the star of the show and played Marshal Matt Dillon for the entire run. The character of Miss Kitty ran a saloon while the character of Doc Adams patched up people's gunshot wounds. As those in my generation grew up with "Gunsmoke," we saw how the wild west was won and watched as towns became cities and territories became states. Even after a good fight, we always knew that the bad guy would get caught.

The passage of 2 Chronicles 22:9 reads: "And he sought Ahaziah: and they caught him (for he was hid in Samaria), and brought him to Jehu: and when they had slain him, they buried him: Because said they, he is the son of Jehoshaphat, who sought the Lord with all his heart. So, the house of Ahaziah had no power to keep still the Kingdom."

God turned His wrath on Ahaziah and his evildoing. The king of the other armies captured Ahaziah and he was killed. When you are in rebellion against God, you always lose, as God, like Marshal Dillon, always gets his man.

Is God after you? Are you running from Him?

September 11

On this day in history in 1965, the U.S. Army's First Cavalry Division (airmobile) arrived in South Vietnam, a move that brought the U.S. troop strength up to 125,000 men. The First Cavalry was the Army's first full division in Vietnam and introduced a new concept to fighting using helicopters to move troops around the battlefield. The First Cavalry was the only division in Vietnam to fight in all four corps, and as a result the awards for the division and its men were plentiful. They included presidential unit citations, 25 Medals of Honor, 120 Distinguished Awards, 2,766 Silver Stars, 2,697 Distinguished Flying Crosses, and 8,408 Bronze Stars for Valor. I was a part of the First Cavalry and I enjoyed it immensely.

The Children of Israel were raising an Army to fight the Midianites, a heathen people who gave their sons and daughters to the Children of Israel to marry. This was not in keeping with God's commandments. God had sent a plague on the Children of Israel who married the Midianites. Finally a priest put an end to those marriages and the plagues stopped. Now the Children of Israel were gathering an army to fight and kill the enemy, as outlined in Numbers 31:6: "And Moses sent them to the war, a thousand of every tribe, them and Phinehas, the son of Eleazar the priest, to the war with the holy instruments, and the trumpets to blow in his hand."

Moses was doing what God wanted him to do, and that was kill and capture the enemy. That is what the First Cavalry did in Vietnam. As part of an Army, both Moses and the First Cavalry were good at their jobs.

Do you do your job? If not, then follow the advice of a drill sergeant and step it up, soldier.

September 12

On a day in history in 1969—not this exact date but at some point close to it—I was serving with the First Cavalry Division in Vietnam. I had received word that a friend and fellow classmate named Larry was coming to Vietnam so I tried to find out where he would be stationed, to no avail. I just waited and checked with incoming personnel to see if he could be found, and then one day I was fortunate when I asked about him. I was told that someone with his last name had gone to the post exchange, the PX, as it's known, so I hurried over to see if I could find him. Goodness gracious, but there he was.

"Hello, Larry," I said to him. "Welcome to Vietnam."

Larry turned around and gave me a short hug and a vigorous handshake. After a few minutes of catching up, we had to say our goodbyes and go our separate ways.

The next time I saw Larry was our high school class reunion in 1976. He told me that he didn't want to be welcomed to Vietnam. Later, in 2018, I was giving a speech and saw my friend in the audience.

"Hello, Larry," I smiled at him. "Welcome home."

Everyone laughed when I told the story, and Larry told me that he was glad to be home.

Proverbs 18:24 reads: "A man that hath friends must shew himself friendly: and there is a friend that sticketh closer than a brother."

We all have friends in this life. Some are better than others. Proverbs tells us that a real friend is better than a brother.

I hope that you have a friend. Will you work to make at least one friend? God will be your friend and never fail you.

September 13

On this day in history in 1862, during the War Between the States, Union soldiers of the 27th Indiana regiment found a copy of Confederate General Robert E. Lee's special order 191. The order was found in an abandoned Confederate campsite and wrapped around three cigars. The papers were addressed to General D.H. Hill and passed up the chain of command until it reached Union General George McClellan. McClellan gloated over the plans, boasting, "Here is a paper with which if I cannot whip Bobby Lee, I will be willing to go home."

McClellan's boasting turned to caution. He waited 18 hours before he started to execute his plan to attack Lee, which gave Lee enough time to realize what McClellan was up to. Lee was able to close a few gaps in his plan, and then the Confederates would go on to victory at Antietam culminating in the bloodiest day of fighting in U.S. history with more than 22,000 dead, wounded or missing.

Proverbs 8:13 reads: "The fear of the Lord is to hate evil: pride, and arrogancy, and the evil way, and the forward mouth do I hate."

McClellan should have learned this verse in Sunday school. What was reported to him was meant for the good of the Union, but he instead turned it into a downfall.

Have you fallen lately? God will help you to stand strong.

September 14

On this day in history in 1847, U.S. forces, including Marines under the leadership of U.S. Army General Winfield Scott, invaded Mexico in the Mexican-American War. Scott and his forces landed at Vera Cruz and captured the city the next day. Less than six months later, American forces captured Mexico City and hoisted the American flag over the halls of Montezuma. The Marine Corps hymn was borne of that battle. Mexico City was the first foreign capital city under which the American flag had been flown. In February 1848, a treaty was signed that set the border between the United States and Mexico as the Rio Grande and westward to the Pacific Ocean.

Malachi 1:5 reads: "And your eyes shall see and ye shall say, The Lord will be magnified from the border of Israel."

Israel is being magnified by the Lord because of its borders. America, too, is magnified by the Lord because of its borders. When we honor God, our borders will be expanded and our influences will be greater. Just as with the war with Mexico, we won and our borders were expanded.

Are your borders being expanded? With every battle we win, God will expand our borders.

September 15

On this day in history in 1916, in the Battle of Somme the British used tanks as weaponry for the first time in history. The tanks were too slow, though, as they were plagued with mechanical problems and moving over uncertain terrain. General Douglas Haig saw their potential, though, and ordered hundreds more. The Battle of Somme was a disaster for the British, but it did free up troops that the Germans had assigned to fight in the ten-month long Battle of Verdun, the longest and costliest battle of the war for Britain and Germany.

Here's an example of another long battle. Jacob was the son of Abraham's son, Isaac. When Jacob married, he gained a father-in-law, Laban, who was real trouble.

Genesis 29:25 reads: "And it came to pass that in the morning, behold it was Leah: and he said to Laban, what is this thou hast done unto me? Did not I serve with thee for Rachel? Wherefore then has thou beguiled me?"

Jacob had wanted to marry Rachel; instead, he married Leah after working for Laban seven years. Next, Jacob worked another seven years for Rachel. This time he got the right girl along with her two handmaids, and then came a barrage of cattle and goats. After several changes in wages, Jacob had enough. He left, taking his cattle and goats with him. God had really blessed Jacob. When Jacob left, Laban came after him. Jacob had received a blessing from his father. He was also blessed of God.

Do you faithfully serve God? Are you a good servant both to God and your life?

September 16

On this day in history in 1776, the Battle of Harlem Heights in the American Revolution restored the confidence of Americans. The day before, the British had captured New York City. General George Washington encouraged his troops to dig in and hold the line. Captain Thomas Knowlton was then sent with his rangers to engage the British. Washington then attacked the British right flank, which enabled the British to retreat a short distance. The Battle of Harlem Heights renewed a belief in Washington and his army. Knowlton was killed in the fighting.

Hebrew 10:35 reads: "Cast not away therefore your confidence, which hath great recompence of reward."

The colonial army had lost its confidence, and the young nation seeking its independence had also lost its confidence. When your confidence is lost, you're fighting a lost cause. Confidence makes your life brighter.

How is your confidence today? Are you fighting a lost cause? Ask Jesus to restore your life and confidence.

September 17

On this day in history in 1972, the television show M*A*S*H, a comedy-drama taking place in the Korean War, premiered on CBS. M*A*S*H showed us many facets of war, including its horrors, the drama of the situation, the humor that everyone had to have to keep going, and the human sacrifices of war. In Korea, few soldiers bothered with things such as adhering to the dress code, making their beds, and following military protocol and discipline because they figured they couldn't be sent anyplace worse than Korea. M*A*S*H also depicted career soldiers alongside draftees who did not want to be there in the first place. It was a truly funny and good show, even if it was on the liberal side.

Ecclesiastes 3:4 reads: "A time to weep, and a time to laugh; a time to mourn, and a time to dance."

In this verse, King Solomon is listing the seasons of life. For every season of life, there is also a reason for it. When we weep, it will soon be over, for then we can laugh. When we laugh, we just feel better.

What is your life about today? A time to mourn or laugh? We can do both as situations and seasons of our lives change. Try laughing a little more each day.

September 18

On this day in history in 1947, the U.S. Air Force was established as a separate military branch of the armed forces. President Harry Truman signed the bill onboard the *Sacred Cow*, a C-54 transport used for presidential flights that later became known as Air Force One. U.S. officials had been exploring air power since 1903 when the Wright Brothers made their first flight at Kitty Hawk in North Carolina. When World War I began, the Army Air Force had only five planes. In World War II, that number grew to 80,000 planes. Today the Air Force has only 5,700 active aircraft.

Isaiah 40:31 reads: "But they that wait upon the Lord shall renew their strength; they shall mount up with wings as eagles; they shall run, and not be weary; and they shall walk and not faint."

The U.S. Air Force is much like the eagle. Eagles can soar high above the earth to get above the storm. They can dive to catch their prey at high speeds and hit their target with pinpoint accuracy. The eagle and the Air Force control the skies, making battles easier.

Do you soar like eagles today?

September 19

On this day in history in 1796, George Washington's farewell address was published in newspapers as an open letter to the American public. By declining a third term as president, Washington let the world know that the United States would be governed by the people. Washington's main theme in the address was about religion and morality, and he reminded the people that the among the pillars of private morality, religion was, in his word, "indispensable."

Exodus 20:2-3 reads: "I am the Lord thy God, which have brought thee out of the land of Egypt, out of the house of bondage. Thou shalt have no other gods before me."

This is what Washington meant when he said indispensable. We have all been in bondage in one way or another. When we put God first in our lives, then the ropes of bondage will be broken.

Are you free of bondage today?

September 20

On this day in history in 1863, the Battle of Chickamauga ended. As wounded Union soldiers were brought to nearby Chattanooga, Tennessee, they were surprised to find a female doctor tending their wounds. Her name was Mary Edwards Walker. No. She is not related to our Walker clan.

A graduate of Syracuse Medical College, she became one of America's first female doctors. She dressed in gold-striped trousers and a green surgeon's sash, topped with a straw hat adorned with an ostrich feather. A woman in trousers instead of a dress would have shocked anyone in that day and age.

In 1865, Walker was awarded the Medal of Honor for her service, but it was rescinded in 1916 as undeserved. It was reinstated in 1997. She remains the only female to be awarded the Medal of Honor.

Walker was truly a good Samaritan. Just like the Good Samaritan in the Book of Luke, she gave comfort and care to others.

Luke 10:34 reads: "And went to him and bound up his wounds, pouring in oil and wine, and set him on his own beast, and brought him to an inn and took care of him."

What a blessing it is to have someone to bind your wounds. Walker was so good at medicine and healing that she received a medal for her efforts.

What will we receive for our service? Will we be given a medal? Ask God to guide you so that you may receive a crown of glory for your service.

September 21

On this day in history in 1942, the U.S. B-29 Superfortress took its maiden flight from Seattle, Washington. The B-29 was Boeing's answer to a plane that could fly higher, faster and longer than any other. It had four engines to help push it along and carried a payload almost as heavy as it was. It flew at heights of thirty to forty thousand feet.

The B-29 made its first run on June 5, 1944, against Bangkok in preparation for the Allies liberation of Burma (now Myanmar). The most famous B-29, though, was the *Enola Gay* and *Bock's Car*. On August 6 and 9, 1945, respectively, they took off from the Marianas Island with a 10,000-pound bomb and headed for Japan. We know how that story ends.

Since the beginning of time mankind has sought ways to kill each other faster and so we continue to improve our weaponry. Why not seek peace instead? I do believe that a good defense makes a good offense, and as long as two countries are talking, there is always hope for peace.

John 14:27 reads: "Peace I leave with you, my peace I give unto you: not as the world giveth, give I unto you. Let not your heart be troubled, neither let it be afraid."

We can all have the peace that Jesus gives. It's different from world peace. With the peace of God, we will have comfort. With God's peace we will not be afraid. Trust in God for His peace. All our troubles will not be over, but we will have calm assurance from Him while going through them.

September 22

On this day in history in 1914, one German U-boat sank three British cruisers in just over an hour. The Germans had begun a great naval buildup before World War I even started, and their submarines were far superior to those of other nations. This battle alerted other nations of the effectiveness of submarine warfare. The U.S. was neutral at that time of the war but dropped that neutrality because of the presence of German U-boats. The entry of the U.S. into the war brought men, materials, and ships into the war and also turned the tide of war against the Germans based on our sheer manpower.

Exodus 13:16 reads: "And I will make thy seed as the dust of the earth: so that if a man can number, the dust of the earth: then shall thy seed also be numbered."

When God promised this to Abraham, the young man didn't have children, although he would have only one son later in life. The seed of Abraham would grow into a great nation that's still a great nation today. Just as the Germans were defeated by our manpower, all nations who stand against Israel will be defeated also.

Are you building up your power? Will God help or hurt that power? What is God doing for you?

September 23

On this day in history in 1968, a skinny 19-year-old left his hometown in South Georgia and went to Atlanta International Airport, now Hartsfield-Jackson International Airport. He was headed to Seattle, Washington, to Fort Lewis and from there to Vietnam. That young man was me.

Traveling to Atlanta was enough to scare anyone to death. At the airport, I shook my daddy's hand, hugged my mama, and kissed my girlfriend goodbye. As I turned to walk down that long corridor to the boarding gate, I realized I was frightened, anxious, terrified, nervous, and scared. My thoughts were running wild, and I kept asking myself questions that I couldn't answer. Only time would tell as to which way my life would go. During those moments, I then realized how so many soldiers felt going down those long corridors to airplanes that would take them to parts unknown, among them my brother before me, my father in World War II, and others in military uniform, all headed to the same place that I was. I kept repeating to myself that only time would tell.

Joshua 1:9 reads: "Have not I commanded thee? Be strong and of a good courage; be not afraid, neither be thou dismayed: for the Lord thy God is with thee whithersoever thou goest."

I was raised in a Christian home and had heard this Scripture often. At least the part that states, "Be not afraid." As I think about this verse, it reminds me of how afraid I really was.

Is the Lord giving you courage? Are you afraid or even scared? Put your trust in God.

September 24

On this day in history in 1906, President Theodore Roosevelt proclaimed Devil's Tower in northeastern Wyoming as the nation's first national monument. As a veteran who has had many chances to see beautiful places at home and around the world, I realize that we have many right here in the United States. But I have yet to see Devil's Tower. There are many places I would like to see again and others I had seen where I felt I had wasted my time. Overall, though, Mother Nature is something else.

Genesis 1:1 reads: "In the beginning God created the heaven and the earth."

Genesis 1:31 reads: "And God saw everything he had made and behold, it was very good, and the evening and the morning were the sixth day."

Each day as we look around, we can see changes in the scenery. As the seasons change, we can see something different each day.

Let us remember that the God of the universe made all things for us to enjoy. Are you enjoying God's creations?

September 25

On this day in history in 1789, Congress sent twelve amendments to the states for ratification. Ten were accepted and two were refused. The ten that passed are known as the Bill of Rights. Since that time, additional amendments have been added to the Constitution, while several others have been proposed and rejected. This, as we know, is how the laws are made in America. If we keep faithful to the Bill of Rights, we will live a good life.

Galatians 5:14 reads: "For all the law is fulfilled in one word, even in this; Thou shalt love thy neighbor as thyself."

The Apostle Paul, in his letter to the Galatians, tells them about love, and love is the complete law in one word. If we love, we need nothing else.

Do you love your neighbor?

September 26

On this day in history in 1892, John Phillip Sousa played "The Liberty Bell March" for the first time. Sousa was and is still known for other marches and compositions including "Semper Fidelis – The Marine Corps March" from 1888; "Glory to the Yankee Navy" from 1909; "U.S. Field Artillery – The Army Goes Marching Along" from 1917; the "Black Horse Troop – Troop A"; "107th Cavalry – Ohio National Guard" from 1924; and the "Salvation Army March" from 1930. His most popular work, however, is "Stars and Stripes Forever."

In this time in our history, we must continue to press on and teach others about our flag and the respect it deserves.

Exodus 17:11 reads: "And it came to pass, when Moses held up his hands, that Israel prevailed; And when he let down his, hands, Amalek prevailed."

Israel and the army of Amalek were at war. If Moses lifted his hands, Israel would win. If Moses rested his arms or let them fall, Amalek would start winning. Moses' hands were a national banner for Israel, just as our flag is our national banner.

When we tell others about Moses, let us also tell them about our flag and its status as a national banner. When we raise our national banner, we win. When the national banner is not lifted, we all lose.

Are you raising a banner today?

September 27

On this day in history in 1968, I became very, very, very, confused. People who know me said that I have always been confused, but nevertheless, here is a riddle that led to my confusion.

Today is my birthday. I was born in 1948, so as of 2018, I was seventy years old, yet I have had only 69 birthdays. Think about that for a moment.

When I left Fort Lewis, Washington, for Vietnam, I left on September 26 late in the afternoon. Our flight landed in Alaska for refueling before we journeyed on to Japan. We landed in Japan and were allowed off the plane. I asked a military policeman the time of day, and he said a little after 12:30 a.m. (for you lifers, that's 0030). I then asked him what the date was. He looked at me strangely before answering that it was September 28.

What happened to September 27? Going east to west, you cross the International Date Line and jump ahead by one day. To give you an example, if it's 4:00 a.m. on the 10th, you jump to 4:00 a.m. on the 11th. All you have done is cross an imaginary line in the Pacific that's known as the International Date Line. I was going to Vietnam from east to west, so I jumped from the 26th to supposedly the 27th. I crossed the International Date Line at midnight and went straight to the 28th, so I did not have a 20th birthday. Now, I ask again: How old am I?

This riddle is true. It is not made up nor is it a joke and only explains why I'm always confused over the number of birthdays I've had.

Genesis 21:6 reads: "And Sarah said, God hath made me to laugh, so that all that hear will laugh with me."

I know how Sarah felt.

Try laughing at your own confusion. You'll feel better. God guarantees it.

September 28

In this season in history of every year, football is just beginning from high school and college to the pros. Football is a fall season sport, but I would like to focus on one player.

Pat Tillman was a student at Arizona State University who was a burley 200-pound linebacker who helped lead his team to the Rose Bowl in 1997. After college, he played football for the Arizona Cardinals, and in 2000, he set a team record for tackles of 224 in a single season.

After the terrorist attacks of September 11, 2001, or as we refer to it now as 9/11, Tillman started to think about his future. He served out his contract with the Cardinals but didn't renew it the next year. Instead, he chose to join the army with his brother, where they both became Rangers. On April 22, 2004, Tillman was killed by friendly fire while he was on patrol Afghanistan. He was just 27 years old. Afterward, one of his coaches remarked, "The spirit of Pat Tillman is the heart of this country."

Matthew 19:29 reads: "And everyone that hath forsaken houses, or brethren, or sisters, or father, or mother, or wife, or children, or lands, for my name's sake shall receive an hundredfold, and shall have everlasting life."

Tillman gave up fame and fortune for his country. What have you given up?

September 29

On this day in history in 1980, American General Francis Marion, also known as the Swamp Fox, surprised British forces at Black Mingo Creek, South Carolina. British forces were having an easy time against the Colonists. Morale was low, troops were leaving, and the outlook was grim. Marion gathered a few citizens to counterattack the British, and after only 15 minutes of fighting, the British scattered. The skirmish turned out to be one of the turning points in the War for Independence.

Psalms 139:23 reads: "Search me, O God, and know my heart: try me and know my thoughts."

Just like the Psalmist David, I'm sure that there was plenty of soul-searching by the Colonists. There seemed to be more "what if" questions than answers. After the battle, though, the Colonists would live to fight another day.

What are you searching your soul for today? Ask God, and He will lead you.

September 30

Benjamin Franklin once remarked, "After crosses and losses, men grow humbler and wiser."

Let's think back over this statement and consider some of our crosses and losses. The result of this quotation is certainly true. The more crosses we bear, we do indeed grow wiser.

Matthew 7:24 reads: "Therefore whosoever heareth these saying of mine and doeth them, I will like him unto a wise man, which built his house upon a rock."

As we act upon the Word of God, we become wiser. When we have crosses to bear in our lives, we become wiser. When we have losses in our lives, we become wiser. So, then, it seems as if we should all be very wise. We will even be able to build our house upon a rock.

Are you getting humbler and wiser? Are your crosses and losses getting bigger or smaller?

October 1

On this day in history in 1890, Congress created Yosemite National Park. The natural wonders of Yosemite include giant sequoia trees and Half Dome, the imposing granite landmark that dominates the park. President Benjamin Harrison signed the bill that protected 1,500 square miles of Yosemite for campers, hikers and nature lovers. American Indians were the main residents of Yosemite Valley until 1849 until the coming of the California gold rush.

In 1864, President Abraham Lincoln was convinced to save Yosemite Valley and Mariposa Grove by putting it in the California Trust, a move that saved Yosemite Valley and several groves of sequoia. In 1889, environmentalists John Muir and Robert V. Johnson lobbied Congress for Yosemite's national park status.

Yosemite has more than three million visitors a year. Its beauty and wilderness are almost beyond compare.

John 1:23 reads: "He said, I am the voice of one crying in the wilderness, make straight the way of the Lord, as said the prophet Esaias."

John the Baptist could have felt right at home in Yosemite Valley with its stunning wilderness. John's crying was telling others about Jesus. In Yosemite, you can almost hear God speak by just sitting still and listening to nature around you. John wanted everyone to be ready to meet Jesus. Nature's crying out at Yosemite wants the same thing.

Do you hear God's call on your life today? Have you heeded that call?

October 2

On this day in history in 1919, President Woodrow Wilson suffered a massive stroke. Wilson had poured all his strength into getting the Treaty of Versailles signed to end World War I and to have the League of Nations adopted. When the treaty went before the Senate Foreign Relations Committee chaired by Wilson's longtime rival Henry Cabot Lodge, that made the fight even harder. Wilson himself went before the committee to argue for its approval. When that failed, he left on a tour of America to take his message to the American people. In Colorado he became ill and returned to Washington. He suffered the stroke and was partially paralyzed for the rest of his life. Wilson's friends in the Senate voted against the treaty to save it from amendments that Lodge had put in. Then the treaty failed to get the two-third votes needed in the Senate to pass.

Wilson was awarded the Nobel Peace Prize in 1919. He served the rest of his term and then spent the rest of his life in retirement until his death in 1924.

The passage of 2 Kings 20:1 reads: "In those days was Hezekiah sick unto death. And the Prophet Isaiah the son of Amos came to him and said unto him, Thus, saith the Lord, set thine house in order; for thou shalt die and not live."

Wilson and Hezekiah had a lot in common. They were both leaders and had great responsibilities. Both had become sick and recovered somewhat. I'm sure a lot of prayers went up for both of them.

How is your health today? Has anyone told you to set your house in order? It would not be a bad idea. We do not know when our time will be up.

October 3

On this day in history in 1968, at Camp Evans in South Vietnam, a CH-47 helicopter and a C-7 Caribou airplane collided and killed 24 American servicemen. At that time in my life, it was the worst tragedy I have ever witnessed. I had been in Vietnam only six days and was in line at the repelling tower for training to repel from a helicopter. Most of the people around me were like I was: a newcomer to Vietnam.

Almost immediately after the crash, we knew that there were no survivors. At the moment of impact of the crash, I saw the two aircraft spiral to the ground. I got a really sick feeling in my stomach. We gazed at what was happening and were told to get back in line. While tragedies still happen, training goes on. Every single time I think of those 24 servicemen, I say a prayer for their families.

The passage of 2 Samuel 12:20 reads: "Then David arose from the earth, and washed, and anointed himself and changed his apparel, and came into the house of the Lord, and worshipped: then he came to his own house; and when he required, they set bread before him and he did eat."

David lost a son to a sickness, and he did not want to rejoice in that fact. Instead, he arose and gave God praise, going to the temple first. After he refreshed himself, he went home to eat and visit his wife and comfort her.

I don't know how David felt, as I have never lost a son or daughter. I do pray that I will still be able to give God praise and worship Him if it ever happens. As I learned in Vietnam on that day those men lost their lives, life goes on.

Do you give God praise like David?

October 4

On this day in history in 1861, President Abraham Lincoln observed a balloon demonstration near Washington, D.C.

Control of the airways has always been a necessity, as a view from above lets you see more land, just as a ride in an airplane lets you see much below. Confederates and Union armies both used balloons to gather military information. Even before the War Between the States, experiments with balloons had already started.

Thaddeus S.C. Lowe was a balloon inventor from Ohio. In April 1861, he took a flight that floated to Unionville, South Carolina, where he was arrested for being a spy but released a short time later. Lowe became head of the Union Army Balloon Corps in 1861. Some of the Union generals approved of the idea, while others did not. Lowe resigned in 1863 and the Balloon Corps was disbanded in August of that year. Lowe died in California in 1913 at the age of 80.

Proverbs 30:19 reads: "The way of the eagle in the air; the way of the serpent upon a rock, the way of a ship in the mist of the sea; and the way of a man with a maid."

Solomon tells us here that he just can't understand what it's like to be an eagle to soar and see your prey from so high in the air. This is what was so difficult to comprehend in 1861. Today so many of us have flown in an airplane that we couldn't possibly understand that concept. Flying high like an eagle, we can see things around us.

Do we observe things around us from ground level? Do you see your brethren? How you can help them?

October 5

On.this day in history in L892, Emmett Dalton, of the Dalton Gang, was the lone survivor of five bandits, that attempted their final crime spree in Coffeeville, Kansas. After serving 15 years of a life sentence, he was pardoned.

Later Dalton said, "The biggest fool on earth is the one who thinks he can beat the law, that crime can be made to pay. It never paid and it never will and was the one big lesson of the Coffeeville raid."

The passage of 2 Corinthians 1L:26 reads: "In journeyings often, in perils of water, in perils of robbers, in perils by my own countrymen, in perils by the heather, in perils in the city, in perils in the wilderness, in perils in the sea, in perils among false brethren."

The Apostle Paul is talking about the perils of being a preacher, teacher and missionary. He describes some of the dangers he faced. Yet Paul was once a persecutor of Christians. Both of these men changed their lives and started living differently for the good. Emmett Dalton said that crime doesn't pay, and Paul said to repent and be saved. Has your life been changed?

October 6

On this day in history in 1955, the glass ceiling of the Army Nurse Corps was broken when Edward T. Lyon became its first male member some 54 years after the all-female unit was formed. Male nurses had the same education and training as female nurses and were usually orderlies who were put into another field of training or service. Male nurses quickly established their worth in field hospitals, rescue teams, airborne units, and field units across the world. Today male nurses make up about a third of the Army Nurse Corps.

Luke 10:33-34 reads: "But a Good Samaritan as he journeyed came to where he was: and when he saw him, he had compassion on him. And he went to him and bound up his wounds, pouring in oil and wine, and set him on his own beast, and brought him to an Inn, and took care of him."

We don't know if the Good Samaritan was a nurse, but we do know that he gave first aid and bound up the man's wounds and cared for him. The men of the Army Nurse Corps do the same thing as the women in caring for and healing soldiers.

Would you fit in helping others? Have you given first aid to the fallen? Why not help someone today?

October 7

On this day in history in 2001, Operation Enduring Freedom began as a global war on terror launched by President George W. Bush. It affected countries worldwide that harbored and trained terrorists. The first target was Afghanistan, with Al-Qaeda and the Taliban in its crosshairs. It also effected the Philippines, Trans-Sahara, Somalia, the Republic of Georgia, and Kyrgyzstan. The main goal was to stop terrorists from working and being trained.

Psalms 91:5 reads: "Thou shalt not be afraid for the terror by night; nor for the arrow that flieth by day."

The Psalmist David tells us to not be afraid of terror. That sounds easy, but he is right. We have fought to rid the world of terror. As long as people reject God and His word, we will have terrorism. To stop terrorism, we must pray and follow God's call in our own lives. We should always be able and willing to tell others about Christ.

Have you told anyone about Christ? Now would be a good time to start.

October 8

On this day in history in 1918, U.S. Army Corporal Alvin C. York, reportedly killed 20 men and captured 132 others in the Argonne Forest near the Meuse River in France. York was later awarded the Medal of Honor for his actions and also promoted to sergeant.

York was born in a small cabin on the Tennessee-Kentucky border, one of eleven children. The family lived off farming and hunting. After experiencing a religious experience and conversion, he became a Christian around 1915.

When York was drafted, he protested as a conscientious objector but was denied. He joined the 82nd Infantry Division and went to France in May 1918.

As York and others from his battalion were trying to take a valley, they came under machinegun fire. A superior officer was killed, leaving York in charge. He kept firing at the Germans. In order to find York, the Germans had to lift their heads above the trench. York said of that day, "Every time I saw a head, I just touched it off." He kept yelling for the rest to surrender and finally they did.

Jonah 4:1-2 reads: "But it displeased Jonah exceedingly, and he was very angry. And he prayed unto the Lord, and said, I pray thee O Lord, was this not my saying, when I was yet in my country? Therefore, I fled before unto Tarshish: for I know that thou art a gracious God and merciful, slow to anger, and of great kindness and repentest thee of evil."

Just like Jonah, we do things that we don't like or want to do but do them anyway for the good of others. Jonah didn't want to go to Nineveh, and Alvin York didn't want to go to war. Both went anyway and did their jobs well. Having the courage to do what is right is an example of being a good soldier or Christian.

Are you doing what is right?

October 9

On this day in history in 1766, James Forten was born the grandson of a slave but the son of free blacks. He was at Independence Hall when the Declaration of Independence was read. At the age of fourteen, he went to sea to fight the British. In 1781, the ship that he was on was captured and he became a prisoner of war. During that time, he made friends with the ship captain's son. The captain of the ship even offered to take Forten to England, but his reply was this, "I have been taken prisoner for the liberties of my country and never will prove a traitor to her interest." Forten remained a prisoner for seven months before being exchanged. After the war ended, Forten worked for a Philadelphia sailmaker and eventually bought the business. He became rich, then encouraged other black men to help defend Philadelphia in the War of 1812. He later organized an antislavery society, supported *The Abolitionist* newspaper, helped runaway slaves and extended a helping hand to all people.

Another man who had great personality was Joseph, the son of Jacob, and he was a spoiled brat. His brothers despised him and got a chance to sell him as a slave. Potiphar bought him and eventually made him his head of household. Potiphar became angry with Joseph when Potiphar's wife accused Joseph of molesting her. Potiphar had him put in prison where he soon became the main trustee. He even interpreted dreams of other prisoners. When Pharaoh had a dream he didn't understand, he was told about Joseph. Pharaoh called Joseph and was told by him that only God could interpret dreams. After God revealed the dream to Joseph, it was then told to Pharaoh. Pharaoh promoted him on the spot to second in the kingdom. Imagine being a prisoner one day, then second in command of a kingdom the next. That's a good promotion.

Genesis 41:39 reads: "And Pharaoh said unto Joseph, Forasmuch as God hath shewed thee all this, there is none so discreet and wise as thou art."

Pharaoh learned of Joseph's abilities and talents. The people of Philadelphia heard of James Forten. Both men did good in their lives.

Are you doing good in your life?

October 10

On this day in history in 1973, Spiro Agnew resigned as vice-president of the United States. He became the first vice-president to resign the same day as he entered a plea of no contest to a charge of tax-evasion. Charges of political corruption against him were dropped, but he was also given a fine of $10,000 and three years of probation. A lawyer, he was then disbarred in Maryland. Under the procedures of the 25th Amendment to the Constitution, Gerald R. Ford was then appointed vice-president, and then less than a year later became the 38th president when President Richard Nixon resigned. Ford served as president without being elected by the people or the Electoral College.

The passage of 1 Samuel 13:13 reads: "And Samuel said to Saul, Thou hast done foolishly: thou hast not kept the commandments of the Lord thy God, which he commanded thee, for now would the Lord have established thy kingdom upon Israel forever."

Saul did not follow the Lord. He was evil and went against God's will. His punishment was that his kingdom would be taken from him and his family and he would no longer be King of Israel.

Doing what is wrong in God's sight is a bad thing. You can lose your own personal kingdom for that.

Are you following God? Or is your kingdom going to fail?

October 11

On this day in history in 1984, Kathryn Dwyer. Sullivan became the first female to walk in space from aboard the space shuttle *Challenger*, a walk not to be confused with Michael Jackson's moonwalk.

Onboard the *Challenger,* Sullivan was a NASA mission specialist. Her spacewalk was to work on and in the payload bay. Her workspace was traveling at 17,000 miles an hour about 140 miles above the earth. The Earth Radiation Budget Satellite that she co-invented was also onboard. She and her teammate David Leestma did a trial fluid transfer, a key function in refueling satellites. After her NASA days were behind her, Sullivan took a series of job in the education field.

Acts 1:11 reads: "Which, also said, ye men of Galilee, why stand ye gazing up into heaven? This same Jesus, which is taken up from you into heaven, shall so come in like manner as ye have seen him go into heaven."

This verse tells us that Jesus will one day return to earth to gather his people, to leave through the skies as he did. Then we will be flying in space.

Are you ready for Jesus to come again? Do you trust in God as your savior?

October 12

On this day in history in 1492, Christopher Columbus discovered a new world during an expedition funded by King Ferdinand and Queen Isabella of Spain. Columbus was looking for a route to Asia for spices and gold since the overland route to Asia were closed by the Ottoman Empire. The European world was running low on spices that came from the Middle East and Asia. After exploring the island of Hispaniola, Columbus set up a colony, and then left in March of 1493 for Spain carrying spices, gold, and even Indians. Columbus was the first European to explore the Americas since the Vikings had been here in the 10th century.

Acts 3:6 reads: "Then Peter said, Silver and Gold have I none; but such as I have, give I thee: In the name of Jesus Christ of Nazareth rise up and walk."

Christopher Columbus was looking for worldly treasures, but what about the real treasures of life? In this verse the crippled man was looking for worldly treasures, but what he got was a good faith healing. He had to do something about this treasure, so he leapt up and began walking. He probably shouted and jumped, too, as he cried for joy and sang the praises of the Lord.

Have you had a healing in your life? Are you looking for earthly treasures or heavenly treasures? The choice is yours.

October 13

On this day in history in 1775, the Continental Congress authorized the first American naval force. The first U.S. Navy formally organized on December 22, 1775, with Esek Hopkins appointed by George Washington its first commander-in-chief. Hopkins was to look at the possibility of attacking British ships in the Chesapeake Bay. Instead, Hopkins, with his eight Navy ships, headed to the Bahamas. He raided the port at Nassau, preying on merchant ships and several British warships. For this, Hopkins was relieved of his command upon returning home. After the war was over, the Navy was disbanded. Later, the U.S. Navy as we know it today was created as the Department of the Navy in April of 1798.

When the Children of Israel disobeyed God, it would not go unpunished. Deuteronomy 29:68 reads: "And the Lord shall bring thee into Egypt again with ships, by the way whereof I spake unto thee, Thou shalt see it no more again: and there ye shall be sold unto your enemies for bondmen and bondwomen, and no man shall buy you."

If the children continued to disobey God, then they would be captured and sold into slavery and bondage and scattered around the world.

Are you being scattered today?

October 14

On this day in history in 1962, the Cuban missile crisis began and the United States and Soviet Union were one step closer to nuclear war. America's U-2 spy planes had proof that medium range Russian missiles were now in Cuba and capable of carrying nuclear warheads. All of this was happening only 90 miles from the United States.

After the failed Bay of Pigs invasion, the U.S. and Russia were in more conflict than anyone wanted. Americans wanted the Russians out of Cuba, but the Soviet statesman Nikita Khrushchev wanted a strong stand to raise his popularity at home.

A fearful boy of 14 in South Georgia kept listening for news of war but it thankfully never came. That boy was me, in case you were wondering.

Matthew 24:6 reads: "And ye shall hear of wars and rumors of wars: see that ye be not troubled; for all things must come to pass, but the end is not yet."

We hear of wars and rumors of wars around the world all the time. In 1962, that was especially common, in that Cuba is so close to the United States.

Are you ready for these wars to hit home? How will they affect you? How will they affect your loved ones?

October 15

On this day in history in 1951, the television show "I Love Lucy" began broadcasting. It lasted until 1957. Since this day it premiered, it has been on television on every day through syndication and will probably continue to do so for years to come. The show is a clean comedy that faces everyday situations. The characters in the show are Lucy and her husband Ricky and their best friends, Ethel and Fred. I personally wish that more television shows were as clean and funny as "I Love Lucy."

Proverbs 15:13 reads: "A merry heart maketh a cheerful countenance: but by sorrow of the heart the spirit is broken."

King Solomon, thought to be the wisest man in the world, is telling us to be happy and that happiness makes a good countenance. By contrast, he tells us that by sorrow of the heart, the spirit is broken.

We can make up our minds to be joyful or sorrowful. By living a joyful or happy life, we lift up others also. When we are sorrowful in heart, others around us are also. We are to smile and be happy. If nothing else, it will make people wonder what you are up to.

"I Love Lucy" has an uplifting and happy aura about it. As many times that you see the show, still you'll always smile at Lucy's antics.

Are you lifting up someone? Why not start?

October 16

On this day in history in 1997, Charles M. Shultz, creator of the comic strip "Peanuts," and his wife, Jeannie, gave $1 million toward the D-Day Memorial in Bedford, Virginia. The memorial serves as a tribute to all Allied forces who took part in France on D-Day of June 6, 1944.

The memorial was inspired by the 34 National Guard soldiers who took part in the D-Day invasion, with 19 of them being killed. It also inspired the movie "The Bedford Boys" about the same men. When the memorial was dedicated on June 6, 2001, some 15,000 people in attendance, President George W. Bush was among them. Memorials do not come cheap, especially one that is built on 50 acres of land. But then again, freedom is not cheap either.

Acts 22:28 reads: "And the chief captain answered with a great sum obtained I this freedom. And Paul said, But I was free born."

The Apostle Paul was a Roman citizen. His father was Roman, but his mother was a Jew. So, then, Paul was a Roman citizen and a Jewish citizen. The captain of the guard had to purchase his freedom. I don't know the situation of his birth or nationality, but his freedom had to be purchased. We would say he was a naturalized citizen. One thing that he did realize was that freedom is not free. Someone paid the price.

Salvation in Jesus Christ is not free either. Jesus paid that price for us, and all we have to do is accept it. What better memorial could we leave our loved ones than faith in Christ? What will your memorial look like?

October 17

On this day in history in 1916, the *USS Arizona* was commissioned. During World War I, it served as a training ship and of special note escorted the ship carrying President Woodrow Wilson to the Paris Peace Conference. A quarter of a century later, the *Arizona* was docked at Pearl Harbor in Hawaii on December 7, 1941, when Japan attacked the United States on its home soil. The ship took just nine minutes to sink after being hit.

In 1962, the *USS Arizona* Memorial was dedicated. The flag that flies above it was attached to the original flagpole of the *Arizona*. More than a thousand men are entombed in the wreckage, their remains never recovered.

Exodus 14:26 reads: "And the Lord said unto Moses, Stretch, out thine had over the sea, that the waters may come again upon the Egyptians, upon their chariots, and upon their horsemen."

The sailors who are entombed in the *Arizona* were not the first people in history to be caught up in a lot of water. The Children of Israel had just crossed the Red Sea on dry land with Egyptian army right on their heels. When Moses stretched forth his hand, the waters fell on the Egyptians, and when it was over, not the first Egyptian survivor was to be found.

The sailors aboard the *Arizona* at least had a memorial placed upon their watery grave while the Egyptians did not.

Where is your memorial in your life?

October 18

On this day in history in 1997, the U.S. Service Women's Memorial was dedicated. It is at the ceremonial entrance of Arlington National Cemetery and the only major memorial dedicated to the history of the women who wear the uniform of the U.S. military. Each individual story is checked for accuracy and tells of women such as the first surgeon, a Medal of Honor recipient, the first director of the Women's Auxiliary Army Corps (WAAC) and Women's Army Corps (WAC), and the first woman to lead U.S. troops in combat. The memorial also promotes goodwill and encourages all females serving in the military.

Judges 5:24 reads: "Blessed above women shall Jael the wife of Heber the Kenite be, blessed shall she be above women in the tent."

Jael was a woman who was not a part of the military, but she did great work to help her country and the military. She smote Sisera, the leader of King Jabin's Canaanite army, by driving a tent peg into his temple with a mallet. She should have been a carpenter. In doing this, she helped win the battle. The verse here proclaims her to be blessed above all women, and that same should be said of the women of the U.S. Service Women's Memorial. They should be blessed above others.

Women have in the past have done great work for the men of war. Are you a good servant in your life?

October 19

On this day in history in 1781, British General Lord Charles Cornwallis surrendered and effectively brought the American War for Independence to a close. Cornwallis had successfully beat the Patriots in New Jersey and then in South Carolina. He then moved to North Carolina but was not as successful there. From there he marched on to Virginia toward a coastal town to give his army a needed rest while he went to Yorktown.

General George Washington ordered Frenchman Marquis de Lafayette and his army of five thousand to pin Cornwallis in at Yorktown. Washington and a French army under Count de Rochambeau attacked Cornwallis from the North. With the help of the French Navy, before the end of September, Yorktown was completely surrounded. When the British surrendered, its band played, "The World Turned Upside Down." Peace negotiations began in 1782 and the Treaty of Paris was signed in 1783, a move that made the United States of America a free nation.

Matthew 19:26 reads: "But Jesus beheld them, and said unto them, With men this is impossible; but with God all things are possible."

America with no trained Army had just defeated the most powerful nation in the world, a feat most people and even the leaders of the time thought impossible. And yet hope reigned eternal.

With faith in God and His grace, American prevailed. When Congress of the news of Cornwallis' surrender, they proceeded to a nearby church to give thanks to God.

Has God worked the impossible in your life? When was the last time you said thank-you to Him?

October 20

On this day in history in 1903, the United States purchased the French territory known as Louisiana. The Louisiana Purchase was a great investment, as it doubled the size of the U.S. at a cost of only three cents per acre. Congress quickly approved the action, and divided the purchase into 15 states. Thomas Jefferson was president at the time, and many believe that the Louisiana Purchase was the best course of action he took during his presidency. France had a large war debt and was afraid that the United States or the British would invade the territory and take it anyway.

2 Samuel 24:25 reads: "And David built there an alter unto the Lord, and offered burnt-offerings and peace-offerings. So the Lord was intreated for the land, and the plague was stayed from Israel."

Here King David of Israel bought the land to build an altar to the Lord. David had sinned against God, and this was his choice of punishment. David, as king, could take the land from Araunah if he wanted it; in fact, David told Araunah that he would not offer anything to the Lord that did not cost him anything.

Are we like that? Does what we give God cost us? What is the price of your sacrifice?

October 21

On this day in history in 1879, Thomas Edison invented the lightbulb, so now we're no longer in the dark. The lightbulb was probably the most important invention of Edison's. Some of his others include the phonograph, batteries, an improved telephone, and a motion picture machine. While he created more than a thousand inventions, he also failed more than a thousand times. When asked about his failures, Edison stated, "These are not failures. I know that it is a thousand things that did not work, but we are closer to finding the things that do work."

Edison is also credited with the expression, "Genius is one percent inspiration and 99 percent perspiration."

Edison was educated at home, and his thirst for knowledge always kept him in trouble. He was the first person to set up an experimental laboratory. When it was destroyed in a fire, he built a larger one. He certainly was one to follow his dreams, even if they sometimes ended in failure. But through it all, he was one to never give up hope.

The passage of 1 Kings 9:4-5 reads: "And if thou wilt walk before me, as David thy father walked, in integrity of heart, and in uprightness, to do according to all that I have commanded thee, and wilt keep my statues and my judgments. 5Then I will establish the throne of thy kingdom upon Israel forever, as I promised to David thy father, saying, There shall not fail thee a man upon the throne of Israel."

Verse 4 tells of what must be done for God to bless King Solomon and Israel. God tells Solomon in Verse 5 that a son of David will always be on the throne of Israel.

God does not fail, but do we keep going in spite of our failures? Is it just another thing that doesn't work? When we follow God, our failures will be made bearable.

October 22

On this day in history in 1957, American forces in Vietnam suffered its first casualties of the war when 13 people were injured when terrorists attacked the Military Assistance Advisory Group and U.S. Information Service installations in Saigon. American forces had been in Vietnam since 1951, and by the end of 1957 many terrorist attacks were recorded. Some 75 local officials were assassinated or kidnapped in the last quarter alone.

Judges 16:3 reads: "And Samson lay until midnight, and arose at midnight, and took the doors of the gate of the city, and the two posts, and went away with them bar and all, and put them upon his shoulders, and carried them up to the top of the hill."

Samson was a terrorist in a way. He went to the top of the hill with the attitude of "See me now? What are you going to do?" That would be like up picking up a house door, frame and all, and leaving with it. Samson even showed more terrorism when he defied Delilah and the men who tried to capture him.

Do you know a terrorist? Why not be one? Follow God and resist Satan.

October 23

On this day in history in 1777, the British fleet suffered a defeat at Fort Mifflin, Pennsylvania. The British Royal Navy was trying to open supply lines on the Delaware River when six of its ships were severely damaged from cannon fire from Fort Mifflin. The *HMS Augusta* and the 20-gun sloop *HMS Merlin* were hit by direct fire before running aground and being destroyed.

Even after this fighting, the Americans still had to defend the fort until November, at which time it was abandoned. General Charles Cornwallis took over the fort, where he spent a safe and warm winter. The Patriots, on the other hand, had to spend the winter in a town called Valley Forge, Pennsylvania, with General George Washington. One thing that Washington and his men did not take for granted was that God's providence was upon them.

Philippians 4:19 reads: "But my God shall supply all your needs according to his riches in glory by Christ Jesus."

The Continental Army lost many men at Valley Forge. But while conditions were indeed terrible at best, God still met their needs. They were able to rest, re-train, and re-group, for in the spring would come renewed fighting and trials.

Are you trusting God to supply your needs?

October 24

On this day in history in 1921, in the French town of Colons-sur-Marne, the first body of an unknown soldier was selected for entombment in Arlington National Cemetery. The Army Graves Registration Service had four bodies of unknowns moved to Colons-sur-Marne for the selection. Each of the four men was from a great battlefield. Identification of the bodies was completely unknown.

At 10 o'clock the next morning the American flag-draped caskets holding the remains were lined side by side for display. Sargent Edward Younger was given the honor of making the selection. With a spray of white roses, Younger walked around the caskets three times, then laid the roses on the third casket from the left. He faced the body, came to attention and saluted. Once the selection was made, the casket was brought back to the U.S. and placed in Arlington National Cemetery at the Tomb of the Unknown Soldier.

Galatians 1:22 reads: "And was unknown by face unto the churches of Judea which were in Christ."

Paul, the Apostle of Christ, wrote that people did not know his face. They had heard of him, but had never seen him before.

We have heard of the unknown soldier, but we don't know him. Paul preached the gospel, and the soldier served his country.

What are you doing for Christ? What are you doing for your country?

October 25

On this day in history in 1944, during the battle of Leyte Gulf, the Japanese utilized kamikaze pilots for the first time. This divebombing suicide force was intended to turn the tide of the war in Japan's favor. The first attack was against escort carriers and when they were hit, they sank within minutes.

More than five thousand Japanese pilots were killed by this action, while the United States and British ship losses were at 34. Even at the cost of three thousand lives, the U.S. still controlled the seas and captured the Philippines, Iwo Jima and Okinawa.

Samson was the thirteenth judge of Israel. He had several run-ins with the Philistines and was the victor in all of them except one. He met Delilah and she finally tricked the truth out of him. He was captured and blinded by the Philistines and then put into prison. In prison, he asked God for strength to fight the Philistines.

Judges 16:28 reads: "And Samson called unto the Lord, and said, O Lord God remember me, I pray thee, and strengthen me, I pray thee, only this once, O God, that I may be at once avenged of the Philistines for my two eyes."

After asking God to help him to get revenge on the Philistines for the loss of his eyesight, Samson then became a terrorist. After asking a servant to place his hands on the pillars of the temple, he pulled them in so that the temple crumpled upon itself, killing not only himself but also the Philistines. History tells us this was a successful attack on his enemies.

How do you attack your enemies today? Do you ask God for strength?

October 26

On this day in history in 1942, the last remaining U.S. carrier that was manufactured before the entry of the U.S. in World War II was sunk by the Japanese. The *USS Hornet* was attacked by Japanese airplanes in the Battle of Santa Cruz. This was part of the Battle for Guadalcanal to prevent the Japanese from capturing another island in the chain known as the Solomon Islands. As with the Battle of the Coral Sea, this battle was fought in the air. After two Japanese bombers were hit, they divebombed into the *Hornet*, causing great damage. While American casualties were heavy, the Japanese forces lost 25 of the 27 bombers that attacked the *Hornet*. The Japanese were unable to resupply their troops at Guadalcanal, signaling the beginning of the end for Japan and yet another victory for the Allies.

The spies for the Children of Israel had just returned from the land of the Amorites. The results were split with two for ten against invading the land, and that made God angry. After being told of God's anger, some of the men said okay, that they would go anyway. But Moses stepped in and told them no, that God was not with them.

Deuteronomy 1:42 reads: "And the Lord said unto me, Say unto them, go not up, neither fight; for I am not among you; lest ye be smitten before your enemies."

The Japanese could not reinforce their men, and they also needed supplies, food, clothing, ammunition, and replacement fighters. The Children of Israel had all these, and the only supply they needed was God. The Japanese ran out of supplies, while the Children of Israel ran out on God.

Where are you getting your supplies? If you need more of them, just ask God.

October 27

On this date in history in 1787, the first of a series of newspaper articles was published called the Federalist Papers; eventually they would number 85. Alexander Hamilton, James Madison, and John Jay were the authors. In the first of the Federalist Papers, Hamilton told the readers that for the first time in history a nation's people were given the choice of what kind of government they would have by choosing it themselves. That system is still in place today.

Joshua 24:15 reads: "And if it seem evil unto you to serve the Lord, choose you this day whom ye will serve, whether the Gods which your fathers served that were on the other side of the flood, or the gods of the Amorites, in whose land you dwell, but as for me and my house, we will serve the Lord."

What choices will you make today, tomorrow, or next week? You must make choices every day.

October 28

On this day in history in 1949, Eugenia Moore Anderson was appointed by President Harry S. Truman as ambassador to Denmark, the first woman to ever become an ambassador. She held the post until mid-1953.

Anderson was born Eugenia Moore. She attended Stephens College in Missouri, Simpson College in Iowa, and Carleton College in Minnesota but didn't earn a degree from any of them. After working in state politics and helping Truman get elected as president, she was appointed to the post of ambassador.

Judge 4:4 reads: "And Deborah, a prophetess, the wife of Lapidoth, judged Israel at the time."

Israel was being ruled over by judges who were to keep its people on the straight and narrow path of following God. Deborah was one of those judges, and her position was one of great importance and authority.

Anderson had an important position in Denmark as a representative with much authority.

Both Deborah and Anderson were leaders in a man's world, and both worked out just fine.

Who are you representing today? Do you represent God?

October 29

On this day in history in 1944, the Japanese-American soldiers reached their finest hour in the Vosges Mountains in France. The Germans had 221 men surrounded on a ridgetop with no medical supplies or ammunition. They had gone for three days without food. News sources even referred to them as the Lost Battalion. But then the 100th Battalion of the 442 Regimental Combat team arrived and two days of fighting followed. The Lost Battalion had been found and rescued. The 100/442 was awarded 9,486 Purple Hearts and 21 Medals of Honor.

One member of the 100/442 was Daniel K. Inouye of Hawaii. Inouye was elected to Congress in 1958, and in January of 1959 when new congressmen and women took their oaths of office and were told to raise their right hands. In Hawaii, a hush fell over the crowd, as Inouye could not do this. He had lost his right arm while in the 100/442 while fighting in France. He was one of those 21 Medal of Honor recipients. Inouye would later be elected as senator from Hawaii.

The passage of 1 Samuel 29:4 reads: "And the princes of the Philistines were wroth with him and the princes of the Philistines said unto him, Make this fellow return that he may go again to his place which thou hast appointed him, and let him not go down with us to battle, lest in the battle he be an adversary to us: for wherewith should he reconcile himself unto his master? Should it not be with the heads of these men?"

The 100/442 fought in France as they were not trusted in the Pacific. Similarly, David could not go into battle because he was not trusted. Both units were good at fighting.

The slogan of our local veterans association, of which I am a member, is this: All gave some. Some gave all. That is also the name of a song.

Inouye served his country well, and he gave some while some of his fellow soldiers gave all with their lives.

What are you giving for your country? What are you giving God?

October 30

On this day in history in 1735, John Adams was born. He later became the second president of the United States. At the age of thirty, Adams wrote his dissertation on canon and feudal law, stating, "Liberty cannot be preserved without a general knowledge among the people who have a right, from the frame of their nature to knowledge."

The passage of 2 Timothy 2:15 reads: "Study to shew thyself approved unto God, a workman that needeth not to be ashamed, rightly dividing the word of truth."

John Adams was a very educated man and sought to help his fellow man. He was always in a search for knowledge, but more importantly he also encouraged others to study. Without knowledge and education, we cannot have liberty.

The Apostle Paul felt much the same way. Paul was an educated man and always striving to learn more. Several times in Scripture we find Paul searching out other leaders to learn from them. He also encouraged others, especially a young Timothy who became his protégé. Paul wanted everyone to be able to divide the truth of God's word.

Studying and education go hand in hand and are very important in our lives.

What are you studying? Does it promote liberty or the Word of God? Are you sharing that knowledge to help others?

October 31

On this day in history in 1941, work was completed on Mount Rushmore, a 60-foot tall monolith in the Black Hills of South Dakota that includes the carved faces of four of our presidents. These looming statues serve as a reminder of just how great our presidents and statesmen were and are. Mount Rushmore includes the faces of George Washington, Thomas Jefferson, Theodore Roosevelt and Abraham Lincoln.

The prophet Jeremiah of Israel loved and had compassion for his people and was always telling them to turn from their wicked ways. He was emotional about his people, often crying for their souls, and became known as the Weeping Prophet. Even if he did not approve of the way his people acted, he still had to prophesy against them.

Lamentations 3:22-23 reads: "It is of the Lord's mercies that we are not consumed, because his compassions fail not. They are new every morning; great is thy faithfulness."

Mount Rushmore would not have been built if not for the faithfulness of the workers. We must be faithful in all the things we do.

What are you doing to show your faithfulness? Have you told anyone about Christ this week? God has been faithful to us.

November 1

On this day in history in 1950, President Harry S. Truman survived an assassination attempt by Griselio Torresola and Oscar Collazo. The president was living in Blair House at the time because the White House was being renovated. Truman heard the gunshots downstairs, but the police and the Secret Service were quick to respond. Torresola was killed and Collazo was captured. Truman kept his other appointments that day saying, "A president has to expect these things." Collazo was tried and given the death penalty, but Truman commuted his sentence, leaving him with life in prison.

The passage of 1 Samuel 20:42 reads: "And Jonathan said to David, Go, in peace, forasmuch as we have sworn both of us in the name of the Lord, saying, The Lord is between me and thee, and between my seed and thy seed forever. And he arose and departed: and Jonathan went into the city."

President Truman saved the life of a man who wanted to kill him. Jonathan saved the life of a friend, and he and David were friends until the day Jonathan died. David even took care of Jonathan's son. That is true friendship.

Are you a friend to someone today? If not, why not begin right now.? It may save someone's life.

November 2

On this day in history in 1948, President Harry Truman, a Democrat, defeated New York Governor Thomas Dewey, a Republican, to win reelection. Everyone thought that Dewey would win.

Three weeks before the election, Truman left by train on an ambitious 30,000-mile whistle-stop tour of America. When election night came, Truman went to sleep as usual. Everyone was assured that he had lost. At midnight Truman awoke and turned on his radio. The news was unchanged, so Truman then went back to sleep. At 4 o'clock in the morning, he was again awakened by an aide who told him that he was two million votes ahead. He had won the election against the odds. In fact, the impulsively written headline in the morning's *Chicago Tribune* read: "Dewey Defeats Truman." Talk about fake news.

The passage of 1 Samuel 31:4 reads: "Then said Saul unto his armourbearer, Draw thy sword, and thrust me through therewith; lest these uncircumcised come and thrust me through and abuse me. But his armourbearer would not, for he was sore afraid. Therefore, Saul took a sword and fell upon it."

King Saul and his armourbearer were dead. An Amalekite was nearby, and he went to tell David the news. The Amalekite told David that Saul had asked him to kill him. David then asked the Amalekite if he were scared to kill God's anointed. Realizing that the man was giving fake news, David had him killed.

Are you helping to spread fake news? Are you stretching the truth?

November 3

On this day in history in 1964, residents of Washington D.C., voted in a presidential election for the first time. The passage of the 23rd amendment to the U.S. Constitution, which gave those residents the right to vote passed in 1960 and was ratified in 1961.

Previously the U.S. capitals had been Philadelphia, New York City, and now Washington D.C. In 1790, Congress passed a law allowing George Washington to select a place to serve as the capital. It was first called Federal City, but the name was later changed by Congress to honor Washington.

In 1801 voting rights for Washington D.C. were eliminated and not restored fully until 1963. Washington D.C. gets three electoral college votes, the same number for Wyoming, the state with the smallest population. Efforts to make Washington D.C. a state have failed.

The citizens of Washington D.C. are like the children of the tribe of Levi. The Levites had no land for a possession, only a priesthood for their inherence.

Joshua 18:7 reads: "But the Levites have no part among you; for the priesthood of the Lord is their inherence: and Gad and Ruben, and the half tribe of Manasseh, have received their inheritance beyond Jordan on the East, which Moses the servant of the Lord gave them."

The twelve tribes of the Children of Israel were given land. The Levites were given possessions in their land and tithes to supply their needs. They were what we would call in today's language as preachers. Every tribe needed leaders or preachers.

Are you supporting your spiritual leaders? It is what God commanded.

November 4

On this day in history in 1991, five former U.S. presidents gathered together for the opening ceremony of the Ronald Reagan Presidential Library. Joining Reagan were George H.W. Bush, Jimmy Carter, Gerald R. Ford, and Richard M. Nixon. Until then, five former presidents had never been together before, as that many had never been alive at the same time.

The Ronald Reagan Presidential Library is in Simi Valley, California, and holds letters, papers, artifacts, news reports, photos, and so much more to commemorate the life and history of our 40th president.

Joshua 10:3-4 reads: "Wherefore Adoni-zedek king of Jerusalem sent unto Hoham king of Hebron, and unto Piram king of Jarmuth, and unto Japhia, king of Lachish, and unto Debir, king of Eglon, saying, Come, up unto me and help me, that we may smite Gibeon; for it hath made peace with Joshua and with the Children of Israel."

These five kings wanted to start a war with Gibeon because of a treaty they had with Joshua. They wanted to capture first Gibeon and then Israel. All the power of five kings in one place and all for no good reason. At least the five former presidents didn't have war on their minds. Joshua and his army went to Gibeon's aid, as they had a peace treaty with them. In the end, Israel won the war, and Gibeon and Israel could live in peace.

Do you study war? Do you live in peace with your fellow man?

November 5

On this day in history in 2009, Nidal Malik Hasan killed 13 people and wounded 30 at Fort Hood, Texas. The shooting rampage was the worst mass murder at a U.S. military installation. Hasan, a major in the Army, is a psychiatrist. He is also of the Muslin faith. Armed with a semi-automatic pistol, Hasan started shooting and shouting, "Allah Akbar," which is Arabic for "God is Great."

The shooting took place in a processing center for soldiers about to deploy to Iraq and Afghanistan. Hasan was wounded by police and arrested, but he ended up paralyzed from the waist down from a bullet wound.

Hasan was tried in a military court and served as his own attorney. In court, Hasan admitted that he was the shooter. He called no witnesses, offered little evidence and had no closing arguments. He was sentenced to death after being found guilty of 45 counts of murder and attempted murder. As of 2019, he is still imprisoned.

The passage of 2 Timothy 4:10 reads: "For Demas hath forsaken me, having loved this present world, and is departed unto Thessalonica; Crescens to Galatia, Titus to Dalmatia."

The Apostle Paul was at the end of his life. He had just given his last sermon in which he said that he had fought a good fight. But then he then gives another warning, telling of his former helper, Demas.

Demas and Hasan have both forsaken themselves and others. Demas, for his religion and salvation, and Hasan, for his country and any respect that he had. Both will be outcasts forever.

All men will stand before God. How will you receive your judgment? What will you say?

November 6

On this day in history in 1977, the Toccoa Falls Dam in Georgia gave way and killed 39 people. The day before, on November 5, just hours before the dam broke, it had been inspected by a volunteer fireman. When the dam broke, water thundered down the hill at 120 miles an hour so there was no time to evacuate.

First Lady Rosalynn Carter visited the college after the tragedy to offer her support, later reporting, "I was enveloped by hope and courage and love."

The dam had been constructed in 1887 as an earthen dam and created a 55-acre lake. In 1911, R.A. Forrest established the Christian and Missionary Alliance College beside Toccoa Creek just below the dam. Toccoa means "beautiful" in the Cherokee language.

After Jesus was crucified and later arose, it was a hard time for His disciples, especially for Peter. Before Christ's death, Peter had denied Jesus three times when Jesus needed him most. Peter lost his leader and teacher and felt alone in spite of being forgiven by Jesus. To where would that loneliness lead? When the Day of Pentecost came, Peter, the one probably most affected by Jesus' death, preached a sermon.

Acts 2:14 reads: "But Peter, standing up with the eleven, lifted up his voice, and said unto them, ye men of Judea, and all ye that dwell at Jerusalem, be this known unto you, and harken unto my words."

Peter went on to preach a message of love and repentance. His life had been renewed in strength and power, and he went from denying Jesus to becoming his best evangelist.

Rosalynn Carter said the same thing but in different words. The citizens of Toccoa Falls had lost lives, homes, futures, and friends yet they looked to Christ and His reward in their lives.

A time like this brings hope and joy to your future. Are you living a joyful life?

November 7

Sometimes in history in the first eight days of November, a national election is held on every year that is divisible by four. That day is determined by the fact that national elections are held the Tuesday next after the first Monday in the month, or the first Tuesday after November 1. Zachary Taylor was the first president elected using this system.

November was selected so the people involved in agriculture could vote because by then most farming was over for the year. And Tuesday was selected because some people had to travel overnight away from their homes to vote. Another reason was because November 1 is All Saints Day, and Congress did not want the day to vote to fall on a religious holiday.

The passage of 1 Samuel 8:22 reads "And the Lord said to Samuel, Harken unto their voice, and make them a King. And Samuel said unto the men of Israel, go ye every man unto his city."

Israel had become tired of Judges ruling over them and demanded that Samuel appoint a king. But Samuel warned them about having a king and tried talking with them to no avail. The Children of Israel wanted a king and kept insisting for one. Samuel then went to the Lord to see if He could change their minds. God told Samuel to give them a king so that one day they would learn their lesson. Samuel then went about selecting a king.

The Children of Israel had no say in whom would be their king. At least we in America have a say in who our president is. There are good, valid reasons for our democratic system of voting. We can participate and make a choice.

Is God directing our choice?

November 8

On this day in history in 1892, Grover Cleveland defeated incumbent Benjamin Harrison in the election for president of the United States. Cleveland was the only person to serve as president for two non-consecutive terms. Harrison defeated Cleveland four years earlier, At that point, Cleveland had already served one term. Then Cleveland won again.

While the Constitution does not allow anyone to serve more than two terms, those terms do not have to be consecutive. Since I was not alive in 1892, I have to question this odd occurrence: Why would anyone vote for Harrison over Cleveland, and then four years later vote for Cleveland over Harrison?

Matthew 9:17 reads: "Neither do men put new wine into old bottles: else the bottle will break, and the wine runneth out, and the bottle perish: but they put new wine into new bottles and both are preserved."

When you put new wine into old bottles, the bottle is destroyed because the expansion of the wine causes the jug to burst. Putting new wine into new bottles will not destroy the bottle. Similarly, you cannot put old things into a new body. Once Christ has cleansed and forgiven you of your sins, you are a new person. Putting old stuff into your body just makes you unfit again.

Are you trusting God to keep you from the old things in life?

November 9

On this day in history in 1967, Captain Lance P. Sijan was shot down while over North Vietnam. He suffered a skull fracture, a mangled right hand, and a fractured left leg. Despite Sijan's injuries, he evaded capture for six weeks. When he was found by North Vietnam soldiers, he became a prisoner for several days. As his strength returned, he tried to escape but was recaptured. He was sent to Hỏa Lò Prison, the notorious prison American soldiers called the Hanoi Hilton, where he contracted pneumonia and died. On March 4, 1976, President Gerald Ford presented the Medal of Honor to Sijan's father at a ceremony at the White House.

Mark 5:15 reads: "And so Pilate, willing to content the people, released Barabbas unto them, and delivered Jesus, when he had scourged him, to be crucified."

Jesus was a just man but He was also a prisoner and a person about whom many untruths had been told. Barabbas was a crook, pure and simple. Why would anyone want Barabbas walking around and Jesus being a prisoner? Jesus was going to be put to death.

Pilate was afraid for his job. He did not want any trouble with anyone else yet refused to do what was right. Sometimes going along with the crowd will take pressure off yourself but the end result will be very different. If Pilate had taken the high road and done what was right, we may feel more honored about him today.

Are you doing what is right? How much pressure are you bowing to?

November 10

On this day in history of every year, the United States Marine Corps celebrates its birthday. The Marines seem almost like a bunch of children playing and singing, "Happy Birthday to me!" Marines also go around slapping each other on the back and saying, "Happy Birthday!"

Don't get me wrong, I love Marines. The veterans association of which I am a member has been led thus far by two Marines as president and vice-president. Bless their hearts. I always tell them that their birthday was the day before Veterans Day to help them remember.

Has anyone ever heard of a Marine Corps birthday sale? Marines are very polite people and are always thanking the Navy for the ride. Even when two Marines meet, they say to one another, Semper Fi, which is Latin for "always faithful." That part is true. We cavalry men just always know that it is truly Semper Fidelis. I could go on but a Marine friend of mine just said that his pants were not glued to the seat of his chair.

Happy Birthday, Marines. We hope that you have many more. Always remember the old saying: There is the right way, the wrong way, and the Marines way.

Ephesians 4:16 reads: "From whom the whole body fitly joined together and compacted by that which every joint supplieth, according to the effectual working in the measure of every part, maketh increase of the body unto the edifying of itself in love."

Our military is made up of five branches of service, and each one has special duties and assignments. We often pick on each other. After all, not everyone can be a cavalry man. But when times get rough, we all depend on one another and then join together for the common good.

In our Christian lives, are we working together for the common good? Let us work together and lift up one another.

November 11

On this day in history in 1918, the World War I—the Great War—finally ended. The Germans were exhausted, and there was turmoil on their home front, plus the surrender of their allies had left them little else to do.

In early November German Chancellor Prince Max Von Badem sent representatives to Compiegne, France, to negotiate the agreement to end the war. While it was signed at 5:10 in the morning, the official surrender would take effect at 11 o'clock in the morning of the 11th day of the 11th month of the year. It became known as the first Armistice Day, but in 1954 Congress would change the name to Veterans Day to honor all veterans from all wars.

The words, "Hello, veteran," have a nice ring to them even if you stayed stateside during your entire tour. It really has a good ring to it if you were stationed overseas or in a war zone. Being away from our loved ones is not what we wanted, but it had to be done and we veterans we did it well. Because of our veterans, we can say that we are truly in the land of the free.

The passage of 2 Samuel 23:16 reads: "And the three mighty men broke through the host of the Philistines, and drew water out of the well of Bethlehem, that was by the gate, and took it to David: nevertheless, he would not drink thereof, but poured it out unto the Lord."

These three mighty men did what David wanted them to do, and David, being overwhelmed by their deeds, would not drink of the water. Instead he offered it as a sacrifice and an offering unto the Lord in honor of his men.

What an act of a good deed that was done by David. He sacrificed of himself for the pleasure of a drink of water so that others could be blessed of the Lord.

Do we honor others who sacrifice for us? Thank you, veterans, for your service. May your lives be a blessing to others.

November 12

On this day in history in 1954, Ellis lsland in New York was closed after processing more than 1,2 million immigrants since it opened in L892. An estimated 40 percent of all Americans can trace their heritage to Ellis lsland. ln the first year that Ellis lsland opened, then President

Benjamin Harrison designated it as the nation's first immigration center. Before then immigration was left up to the individual states.

Egypt also had an immigration center. Joseph was in Egypt when the famine started. The children of lsrael and all of Joseph's descendants came into Egypt. His family numbered 66 plus himself, his wife and two sons for a total of 70. We get these numbers from Genesis 46 26-27.

Pharaoh said yes to their immigration into Egypt, and for the next 400 years the children of lsrael lived and prospered in Egypt, going from a favored people to slavery. When God wanted them released from bondage, the population of the children of lsrael greatly increased.

Genesis !2:37, reads "And the children of lsrael journeyed from Rameses to Succoth, about six hundred thousand on foot that were men, beside children."

Some Bible experts say that the number of the children of lsrael leaving Egypt was between 1-1/2to 21-/2 million. The passage in Genesis tells us that 600,000 of them were men but does not take into account old and young women, old men and children. Where did your descendants come from? Are they leaving a mark on history? What about us and our descendants? Are we making a mark for our Christian life?

November 13

On this day in history in 1982, the Vietnam Veterans Memorial was dedicated in Washington D.C. The memorial is a simple black granite wall inscribed with the names of 57,939 Americans who died in the conflict. The names are arranged in order of death and not rank or alphabet as are most memorials.

Maya Lin, a daughter of Chinese immigrants, was the winner of a nationwide contest to design the memorial now known more commonly as The Wall. Public opinion was against the design at first, as the memorial has no statues or stirring words inscribed on it. But a shift in public opinion began when veterans started visiting the wall and finding names of their loved ones, friends, and heroes. Visitors leave items at the site, things like pictures, dog tags, flowers, and other personal items. The wall has helped to draw Americans together to heal the wounds and emotions of the Vietnam conflict.

Matthew 21:12-13 reads: "And Jesus went into the temple of God, and cast out all them that sold and brought in the temple, and overthrew the tables of the money changers and the seats of them that sold doves. And he said unto them, It is written, My house shall be called the house of prayer: but ye have made it a den of thieves."

The temple to which Jesus is referring is in Jerusalem. It was built in 20 B.C. and then destroyed in 90 A.D. Its western wall is about all that remains of it today. The cracks in the ancient wall serve the same as the names on the wall in Washington, D.C. The western wall is a place for remembrance, healing, and forgiveness.

Have you asked God to forgive you?

November 14

On this day in history in 1910, Eugene Ely became the first pilot to take off from a ship, the *USS Birmingham*, which was anchored off the coast of Hampton Roads, Virginia. In January of 1911, Ely flew from San Bruno, California, and landed on a ship, the *USS Pennsylvania* that was anchored in San Francisco Bay. It was the first landing on a ship and proved that it could be done. It put Ely in the record books once again.

On October 11, 1911, while at an exhibition in Macon, Georgia, the plane Ely was piloting went into a nosedive. He couldn't pull up the plane and it crashed. While Ely had ejected from the plane, his neck was broken in the fall. He died minutes later. Congress posthumously awarded Ely the Distinguished Flying Cross in 1933.

The passage of 2 Samuel 23:8 reads: "These be the names of the mighty men whom David had: The Tachmonite, that set in the seat, chief among the captains; the same was Adino, the Eznite he lifted up his spear against eight hundred, whom he slew at one time."

Adino was perhaps the greatest, bravest, and most honorable of King David's mighty men. He went up against eight hundred enemies of the king at one time. Certainly, he had no ship on which to land a plane, but that didn't diminish his accomplishments at all. Ely was brave in one way, while Adino was brave in another.

Are we being brave in telling others about Jesus? Why not start?

November 15

On this day in history in 1777, the Articles of
Confederation were adopted, but it wasn't until March 1, 1781,
that Maryland became the last state to vote to approve the
agreement.

When the debates first began on the Articles of
Confederation, the legislature was cautious about infringing on
states' rights. Congress couldn't levy taxes but could regulate an
army and declare war and peace. But in a few short years, the
government and its Articles of Confederation were overthrown by
peaceful means. The American people were about to choose what
type of government they wanted, and in 1787 a legal body met in
seclusion to create a new government. On March 4,1789, the
modern United States were established when the Constitution
replaced the Articles of Confederation.

Genesis 26:5 reads: "Because that Abraham obeyed my
voice, and kept my charge, my commandments, my statues, and
my laws."

America is ruled by a set of laws, so accordingly we don't
have a king to whom to bow down. These laws protect us from
others and from society.

God also gave Abraham a set of laws that essentially said,
"If you will, I will," with an emphasis on "if." The three branches
of our government make, interpret and enforce our laws. God
enforces His own laws with either blessings or curses.

Do we keep our laws? More importantly, do we keep God's
law?

November 16

On this day in history in 1952, in the comic strip Peanuts, the character of Lucy held a football for Charlie Brown. As Charlie Brown approached to kick the football, Lucy jerked it up. Charlie Brown missed it and landed on the ground. Lucy was always the great deceiver, and in all those years since, Charlie Brown never does get to kick the football.

The late Charles Schulz, the creator of Peanuts, did a great job with the comic strip. It was popular and is still a favorite among newspaper readers everywhere. Real life is woven into the stories. For example, Charlie Brown and his gang often played football. Lucy wants to do and thinks she can do anything the boys can, including holding the football.

Genesis 27:36 reads: "And he said, is not he rightly named Jacob? For he hath supplanted me these two times: he took away my birthright; and behold, now he hath taken away my blessing. And he said, Hast thou not reserved a blessing for me?"

Jacob was the deceiver, and he had help from his mother, Rebecca. She did neither Jacob nor Esau, her sons, any good. Jacob had to leave his mother behind and learn a few things on his own. He eventually met a man who was a better deceiver than he was when he went to see his Uncle Laban. Then through trickery, he met and married Leah, and then later married for love with Rachel. Just as Charlie Brown was being tricked by Lucy, Jacob was tricked by Laban.

Are you being a trickster? Is God happy with you? Ask Him to lead you.

November 17

On this day in history in 1990, a mass grave was found near the River Kwai Bridge in Thailand. While the numbers of how many are actually buried there, they are believed to be prisoners of war (POW) from World War II. The railroad and bridge were built by Japan by POW and slave labor beginning in 1942 as a supply route for the planned invasion of India. But it stopped in Burma (now Myanmar). Kanchanaburi War Cemetery in Thailand holds more than seven thousand graves of POW. Allied forces bombed the bridge in 1944, and now parts of the bridge are in a war museum in Kanchanaburi. Today the railroad and parts of the bridge are tourist attractions.

2 Kings 13:21 reads: "And it came to pass, as they were burying a man, that, behold they spied a band of men; and they cast the man into the sepulcher of Elisha: and when the man was let down, and touched the bones of Elisha, he revived and stood up on his feet."

This was not a mass grave and Elisha did not want it to become one. When another man's body was put inside of Elisha's grave and touched his bones, the "dead" man stood up, clearly not dead at all. I would have left in a hurry. But Elisha just wanted to rest in peace, and no one knows where his grave is today.

This story proves two things. The first is that you can throw your loved one in a grave and he might come back to life; or two, you can cover up the grave and let the dead be dead.

Mass graves are a fact of life, especially in war zones, and no one likes to hear of them. But it's even worse to have dead bodies lying around.

Ask God to give peace to those families of those who are in mass graves. May they never be another.

November 18

On this day in history in 1928, the animated movie "Steamboat Willie" debuted and was the first movie that had sound that starred Mickey Mouse. Disney, who produced it, was facing bankruptcy a year earlier in 1927 when "The Jazz Singer" was released with sound and dialogue. Disney then decided to stake everything on Mickey Mouse as a mouse that spoke. The gambit paid off. Since then, generations have been entertained by Disney cartoons. By then, it seems Walt Disney had it made and had only to give names to his animal characters of dogs, cats, mice, ducks and so forth.

But Adam had a much more difficult job.

Genesis 2:19-20 reads: "And out of the ground the Lord God formed every beast of the field, and every fowl of the air; and brought them unto Adam to see what he would call them: and whatsoever Adam called every living creature, that was the name thereof. [20] And Adam gave names to all cattle and to the fowl of the air and to every beast of the field; but for Adam there was not found an help meet for him."

Adam had to name all the animals, even the gnats. Too bad he didn't just swat them. It is not known if he gave them scientific or common names. Either way he had a big job to do.

Has God given you a job to do? Are you doing it?

November 19

On this day in history in 1863, President Abraham Lincoln delivered the Gettysburg Address only four months after the Battle of Gettysburg. The speech lasted only two minutes but went down in history as one of the greatest ever delivered.

(Attention all longwinded pastors: two minutes, still quoted, and still effective.)

Lincoln was in Gettysburg to dedicate a national cemetery for those killed in battle, and today it's known as the Gettysburg National Cemetery and its graves are of soldiers from every war and conflict since the cemetery was dedicated in 1863.

The passage of 2 Chronicles 6:12-13, reads: "And he stood before the alter of the Lord in the presents of all the congregation of Israel, and spread forth his hands: [13]For Solomon had made a brazen scaffold, of five cubits long, and five cubits broad, and three cubits high and had set it in the mist of the court: and upon it he stood, and kneeled down upon his knees before all the congregation of Israel and spread forth his hands toward heaven."

When Solomon was king of Israel, he dedicated the temple where he preached with a short sermon and then a prayer that lasted longer than Lincoln's speech. He asked God to bless Israel, to protect them from their enemies, and to guide him in his leadership.

What do we ask of God? Do we praise Him before we ask for blessings?

November 20

On this day in history in 1789, New Jersey became the first state to ratify the Bill of Rights and took the first steps in approving the Constitution. These were reforms brought about by the Declaration of Independence.

Critics of the Constitution were afraid that it would set up a form of government that was heavy on federal control and low on states' rights. These same critics wanted a Bill of Rights that could not be infringed upon before they ratified the Constitution. Congress kept its promise—yes, really—and wrote the Bill of Rights to amend the Constitution. It was first ratified by thirteen states and then amended as necessary even until today.

Jeremiah 36:28 reads: "Take thee again another roll, and write in it all the former words that were in the first roll which Jehoiakim the king of Judah hath burned."

Jeremiah had written God's laws for King Jehoiakim. When the king read the law, he burned a few pages at a time. The Lord then told Jeremiah to write the law again and add some to it. The last part tells of Israel being taken captive by Babylon. King Jehoiakim nor his successor followed these laws.

When you fail to follow God's laws, bad things could happen to you. Are you going to be led away into captivity?

November 21

On this day in history in 1922, Rebecca Ann Latimer Felton was appointed to a seat as one of the two U.S. senators from Georgia. The seat was vacant because of the death of Senator Thomas Watson. Felton was the first woman to serve in the U.S. Senate and also the oldest freshman senator at 87 years, 9 months, and 22 days old. Reports of Felton's length of service varies. Some claim she served only one day, while others state its length from October 3, 1922, until November 22, 1922.

When Felton was appointed on October 3, 1922, the Senate was in recess, so the appointment was largely ceremonial. Walter F. George won the special election to fill the seat but refused to take office until after the Senate came back in session and first swore in Felton. He then took office the next day. Even until now, Felton is the only woman to serve as a senator from Georgia. She died in Atlanta in 1930.

Genesis 17:17 reads: "Then Abraham fell upon his face and laughed, and said in his heart, Shall a child be born to him that is a hundred years old? And shall Sarah, that is ninety years old bear?"

Felton was well advanced in age, as was Sarah. The chances of Felton ever being a senator were from very rare to it ain't gonna happen. But Sarah, the wife of Abraham, outdid Felton, as she was with child at the age of 90. God kept his promise to Abraham that his descendants would be as numerous as the sands of the sea. Everyone laughed, even Abraham, but they would all be proved wrong when Sarah gave birth to a son and named him Isaac.

This lesson gives us reason to be faithful in our decisions. Are you faithful to God's word?

November 22

On this day in history in 1963, every American of any cognitive age knows where he was when he heard the news that President John F. Kennedy had been assassinated. Kennedy and his wife, Jackie, and Texas Governor John Connally and his wife, Nellie, were in a Lincoln convertible in Dallas when Kennedy was killed. A few hours later, Vice-President Lyndon B. Johnson was sworn in as the nation's 36th president.

Lee Harvey Oswald was Kennedy's alleged assassin. Two days after the president died, Oswald was shot and killed by Jack Ruby as he was being transferred to another jail. Ruby was tried and sentenced to death, but the Texas Court of Appeals reversed the decision. While he waited for a new trial, Ruby died from lung cancer.

Mark 15:43 reads: "Joseph of Arimathea, an honorable counselor, which also waited for the kingdom of God, came and went in boldly unto Pilate and craved the body of Jesus."

How would you react if your leader were killed? Reactions always vary from person to person. When Jesus was crucified, Joseph of Arimathea became a bold follower of Christ. The Apostle Peter stood from afar, wishing he could do something. The women set about washing and preparing Jesus' body for burial. Some disciples went into hiding while others left town. Judas Iscariot, who had betrayed Jesus, an act that led to Christ's death, had already hanged himself.

How you act will determine your outcome in life. Jesus allowed us to be forgiven and start anew. Will you start again? Will you accept His salvation?

November 23

On this day in history in 1749, Edward Rutledge in born in Charleston, South Carolina. He was to become the youngest person to sign the Declaration of Independence, but he would also come to be known as the Reluctant Patriot. Rutledge urged caution and slowness in declaring independence from England.

Edward Rutledge and his brother, John, had both studied in England and both were lawyers. Neither wanted to sever ties with Great Britain. Edward Rutledge signed the Declaration of Independence in an effort to create unity. He later served as the 39th governor of South Carolina.

The passage of 2 Kings 22:1-2 reads: "Josiah was eight years old when he began to reign, and he reigned thirty and one years in Jerusalem. And his mothers, name was Jedidiah, the daughter of Adaiah of Boscath. And he did that which was right in the sight of the Lord and walked in all the ways of David his father, and turned not aside to the right hand or to the left."

Josiah was another young ruler like Edward Rutledge. They both had a great responsibility to their countries, and both put away the mentality of "what I want," for the good of their countries.

Being young is no crime nor sin. How you treat your youth may be a crime or sin. When Josiah was repairing the temple, he found God's laws. The workmen brought them to the king, who proclaimed that they be read in the temple for the people to hear.

Do you read God's laws? What are they telling you? Should you repent?

November 24

On this day in history in 1944, U.S. B-29 Superfortress bombers, 111 of them, raided Tokyo. This was the first time the Japanese homeland had been bombed in World War II since Captain's Jimmy Doolittle's raid in 1942.

Two weeks before the Tokyo raid, the U.S. had dropped tons of bombs on Iwo Jima in order to keep their planes on the ground and not mount a counterattack. Next was Tokyo and the Nakajima aircraft engine works, led by General Emmett "Rosie" O'Donnell. The use of radar was useless because of cloud cover, so only 50 bombs hit the target with the loss of only one aircraft. Clouds can be a good or bad thing. For the bad, the U.S. didn't hit its target. For the good, the Japanese couldn't hit our planes.

Exodus 13:21 reads: "And the Lord went before them by day in a pillar of a cloud, to lead them the way; and by night in a pillar of fire to give them light; to go by day and night."

The cloud by day was not just for shade. God was leading them to freedom. The fire by night was for them to see and for a place for God to watch over them while they were on their way. Pharaoh couldn't see through the cloud and he was also afraid of the fire. The Children of Israel were safe from the Egyptians and also knew that their God was watching over them.

As we go through this adventure called life, is God protecting you?

November 25

On this day in history in 1783, British soldiers withdrew from New York City. It had been three months after the treaty had been signed that ended the War of Independence. General George Washington entered the city amidst cheers from happy New Yorkers.

New York was declared the capital of the new United States of America, but in 1790 Philadelphia became the second capital under the Constitution. The New York Loyalists were evacuated to other countries, primarily Canada. The move shifted the balance of power from French to the British. Cheers went up in New York City for General Washington and his men and were well deserved.

The passage of 1 Samuel 21:11 reads: "And the servant of Achish said unto him, Is not this David the King of the land? Did they not sing one to another of him in dances, saying, Saul hath slain his thousands, and David his ten thousand?"

Sometimes others were jealous like King Saul, who was angry and rejected by his people. The cheers for David were well deserved, just as they were for Washington and his men. Both men had the leadership ability to serve their countries.

Do we love our leaders? Do we pray for our leaders today?

November 26

On this day in history in 1941, President Franklin D. Roosevelt signed a bill establishing the fourth Thursday in November as Thanksgiving Day. Celebrating Thanksgiving goes back to the days of Plymouth and Massachusetts Bay Colonies. Most days of Thanksgiving were held on weekdays and included feasts and topical sermons.

Thanksgiving has been significant on many dates. In 1621, Plymouth Governor William Bradford invited local Indians to join them. President George Washington was the first president to proclaim a day of Thanksgiving. In 1863, President Abraham Lincoln and Confederate President Jefferson Davis both proclaimed days of Thanksgiving. In 1941, celebrating Thanksgiving on the fourth Thursday in November became official and has occurred on that day ever since.

Psalms 92:1 reads: "It is a good thing to give thanks unto the Lord, and to sing praises unto thy name, O most high."

Ever since and even before the foundations of our nation were solidified, our leaders have given us many reasons to give thanks. Now that the foundation of this nation has been more firmly established, we still proclaim to give thanks to God for His blessings. We, as a nation, have even set aside a special day to give thanks.

We should give thanks every day, as each of us surely has something for which to give thanks. I have had cancer two times, but I don't hear you telling me that I shouldn't be thankful. For me, every day is Thanksgiving. Think about this country. It is not perfect, but I don't know where a better one is. Give thanks for our country. Give thanks for our salvation.

November 27

On this day in history in 1911, Elizabeth Jaffray, a White House housekeeper, wrote in her diary about a conversation between President William Howard Taft and his wife, Nellie. The subject of Taft's presidential waistline was being discussed along with the fact that it was ever expanding. The White House Historical Association also reported that Jaffray, in her book entitled "Secrets of the White House," tells even of what Taft, who weighed up to 332 pounds, had for breakfast: two oranges, a 12-ounce beefsteak, several pieces of toast with butter, and a vast quantity of coffee with cream and sugar. When Jaffray and Nellie Taft commented on his eating habits, the president responded, "Things are in a sad state of affairs when a man can't even call his gizzard his own."

Taft served a full term as president. When he lost his reelection bid, the new president, Warren Harding, appointed him to Supreme Court in 1921. Taft was the first and only person to serve as president and a Supreme Court justice. He served until a month before his death from cardiovascular disease.

Exodus 18:17 reads: "And Moses' father-in-law said unto him, the thing that thou doest is not good."

Moses' father-in-law spoke to him from the perspective of an older and wiser man, and the younger Moses was smart enough to listen. Now Moses got only the most important problems.

Taft was in charge of leading his people. He did a good job of it in spite of his need to eat. But he wouldn't listen to his wife and housekeeper about his weight, although at times he didn't feel well.

Do we pray for our leaders, even the ones who eat a large breakfast?

November 28

On this day in history in 1925, the Grand Ole Opry began broadcasting live from Nashville, Tennessee. It is still a live program that never missed a broadcast since its beginnings. The Opry is a mix of several kinds of music but mostly country and gospel. It was patterned after the National Barn Dance from Chicago, a program that had started only a year earlier. Both shows jumpstarted the careers of many musicians and singers. The Opry helped make country music an enduring part of American culture.

Psalms 9: 11 reads: "Sing Praises to the Lord, which dwelleth in Zion: declare among the people his doing."

King David was a singer and songwriter, penning songs that are still used today. He wrote the songs of Zion and plenty of them. When David did wrong, he turned to God and repented with truthfulness and then turned away from that sin.

Are you a psalmist? Are you a sinner? Have you turned away from your sin? Have you used a passage from Psalms to confess and praise God for forgiving your sin?

November 29

On this day in history in 1997, the legendary coach Eddie Robinson coached his last football game. He had been coaching at Grambling State University in Louisiana for 55 years. His career record was 408 wins, 165 losses, and 15 tie games. He is the second winningest coach in college football after John Gagliardi of St. Johns University in Minnesota. Robinson sent 220 players to the National Football League and four to the Pro Football Hall of Fame in Canton, Ohio. Robinson molded every man he coached. Once he sent his entire team to help his star running back pick cotton so he would be through with that chore before a championship game. Grambling won that game.

Proverbs 22:6 reads: "Train up a child in the way he should go: and when he is old, he will not depart from it."

I believe that Robinson lived by this verse. He wouldn't have been such a success without it. Being a coach is more than teaching a sport like football, basketball, baseball or soccer. You must train people, because training lasts a lifetime.

In my younger years, I coached Little league Baseball for ages 7-12. I was not very good at it but at least I loved it. Ten years after I quit coaching, one of my former players who now stands at six feet, three inches and weighs in at 220 pounds, came up to me, lifted me off the ground, and then asked, "Hey, Coach. Do you remember me?"

I was thrilled, but I did have a problem. How do you remember a 12-year-old child ten years later?

How are you raising your children? Are you teaching them by your words? What about your actions?

November 30

On this day in history in 1804, Samuel Chase, an associate justice on the U.S. Supreme Court, was impeached. Chase, one of the signers of the Declaration of Independence as a representative of Maryland, was charged with letting his partisan leanings affect his court decisions. He was acquitted by the Senate and remained in office.

I could really get started on this one. Why would you go through the trouble and time and effort to impeach anyone and then not remove him from office? That tells me that you really don't care.

Imagine if a sheriff sworn to enforce the law is convicted of a malicious murder. What if he were then found guilty, but his punishment was nothing except to be free to go back to work? He could murder again, but his constituents would think that he would only be freed once again.

Daniel 5:27 reads: "TEKEL; thou art weighed in the balances and art found wanting."

Belshazzar was a Babylonian king. Babylon had captured Jerusalem and had taken all its gold and silver cups from the temple. Belshazzar had a party and used those same cups that had been dedicated to the Lord.

Then came forth fingers from a man's hand and wrote on the wall. That will sure end a party. Belshazzar looked for someone to interrupt the writing, so he called Daniel. His interpretation is Verse 27. That very night Belshazzar was slain and Darius the Median took the kingdom.

Are you misusing what God has given you?

December 1

On this day in history in 1779, George Washington and his army settled in Morristown, New Jersey, for the winter that turned out to be the worst of the 1700s. The economy was at rock bottom. With no money to pay the soldiers or to feed them, many deserted. Life was bleak for the citizens as well. British and Indians raided villages so the British were no better off. Washington's army even had to requisition supplies from farmers, but it wasn't long before they quit farming because of the money crisis. The British were in the same fix. Back in London, the populace no longer wanted to pay for the war to save the Colonies, and a war of attrition was fast approaching.

The passage of 1 Kings 17:12 reads: "And she said, As the Lord thy God liveth, I have not a cake, but a handful of meal in a barrel, and a little oil in a cruise: and behold, I am gathering two sticks, that I may go in and dress it for me and my son, that we may eat it and die."

Hard times and famines happen all the time. The Lord sent Elijah, to a city where God had commanded a woman to sustain him, but she had only enough for her and her son for one last meal. Afterward, there would be nothing left for her to eat. Elijah asked for water and a morsel of bread. The look on the woman's face must have been one of "Are you kidding me?" At least she was honest. But Elijah assured her that she would be okay, and she acted on faith. She gave a stranger what little she had left at the risk of the life of her own child.

Is your faith that strong? On whom do you depend, God or yourself?

December 2

On this day in history in 1982, retired dentist Barney Clark became the first person to have a permanent artificial heart. He lived 112 days after the transplant. The operation was the first of its kind and took place at the University of Utah. Perhaps the worst thing Clark had to deal with was the media circus with reporters scrambling for his story. Those 112 days were a record at that time. Another gentleman from Indiana named Bill Schroeder lived 620 days with the same type of artificial heart.

Luke 7:12 reads: "Now when he became nigh to the gate of the city, behold there was a dead man carried out, the only son of his mother, and she was a widow: and much people of the city was with her."

This so far is nothing unusual and happens every day, but this time it would be different. Luke tells us that he had compassion for the widow so he touched the casket and told the man to arise. Imagine the miracle when the young man's heart started beating again. While the woman gave glory to God, I'm sure I would have left the area as quickly as I could.

Has Jesus touched your heart? Will you allow Him to heal you?

December 3

On this day in history in 1805, Captain William Clark of the trailblazing duo of Lewis and Clark wrote, "I wrote my name and the day of the month and year on a large pine." After nearly 19 months and traveling eight thousand miles, Meriwether Lewis and William Clark finally reached the Pacific Ocean in their efforts to cross the West.

President Thomas Jefferson had sent Lewis and Clark to see what was in the unexplored land west of the Louisiana Purchase. Did the United States get its money's worth from the expedition? Before they reached the Pacific, they crossed raging rivers, the snow-capped and looming mountains of the Rockies, and dangerous terrain. They saw just about every animal that was in the West and sent some back to Jefferson. The pair made maps of the routes they traveled. They met with Indians, and at times nearly starved or froze to death on those vast, open lands. Yes. We seem to have our money's worth in the beauty that we now call the West.

Genesis 13:10 reads: "And Lot lifted up his eyes, and beheld all the plains of Jordan, that it was well watered every, where, before the Lord destroyed Sodom and Gomorrah, even as the garden of the Lord, like the land of Egypt, as thou comest unto Zoar."

Abraham and Lot had so many animals that the land would not sustain them, so Abraham, in order to stop a fight, let Lot choose the land he wanted. Lot chose the best land that faced Sodom and Gomorrah. Abraham took the rest and built an altar upon it in the plains of Mamre. He prospered because he worshipped God. Lot was in Sodom the night before it was destroyed. Did he get his money's worth?

Do you get your money's worth? Trust God and He will bless you.

December 4

On this day in history in 1780, the Quaker cannon was used near Camden, South Carolina. Patriots under the command of Colonel William Washington cornered in a house and barn some Loyalist forces led by Colonel Rowland Rugeley. Washington, lacking sufficient artillery, ordered his cavalry to surround the house and barn to prevent escape. His men then cut down a pine tree and made it look like a cannon and faced it toward the house and barn. When told to surrender, Rugeley saw the "cannon" and surrendered without a shot being fired.

The passage of 1 Samuel 14:10 reads: "But if they saw thus, come up unto us; then we will go up: for the Lord hath delivered them into our hand: and this shall be a sign unto you."

Jonathan, being an ambitious young man, slipped off from his father. He and his armorbearer went on an adventure and hoped to capture some Philistines. They walked straight into the camp of the enemy. Twenty Philistines were all killed, and then they began beating up on each other. Fear will make you do strange things. The Philistines were defeated that day, with little effort from the Children of Israel.

Are you facing an overwhelming force? Do you follow God's instructions in your life? God can and will make strange things happen when you call upon Him.

December 5

On this day in history in 1964, Captain Roger Donlon is awarded the Medal of Honor by President Lyndon B. Johnson. Donlon and his Special Forces team were at a mountain outpost named Nam Dong in Vietnam when they were attacked on June 6, 1964. Donlon was wounded in the stomach, but then stuffed it with a handkerchief to stop the bleeding and kept fighting. Even though he was wounded three more times, he continued fighting with mortars and hand-grenades and refused medical treatment. When the battle was over, Donlon allowed himself to be evacuated to a hospital in Saigon. When he was presented the Medal of Honor, his team was there with him. He told Johnson that the medal belonged to them, too.

Psalms 23:4 reads: "Yea, though I walk through the valley of the shadow of death, I will fear no evil; for thou art with me; thy rod and thy staff they comfort me."

We are all familiar with this verse. I have prayed it many times in my life, both at home and when I was stationed in Vietnam. Walking through the valley of the shadow of death is a terrifying experience, but knowing God is with you makes it a lot easier. For Donlon and his men, they came home was a rewarding experience.

Is God with you in your trip through a valley? Are you facing a fear today? God will comfort you.

December 6

On this day in history in 1941, President Franklin D. Roosevelt sent Emperor Hirohito of Japan a message. Based on reports that the Japanese fleet was headed to Thailand, Roosevelt wrote, "For the sake of humanity, to prevent further death and destruction in the world."

This was a request for Hirohito, but little did we know that the Japanese fleet was making a U-turn in the Pacific and headed to Pearl Harbor. A Royal Australia Air Force pilot spotted the Japanese fleet and sent the message before he was shot down. The British had received a coded message about "raffles" and for its fleet to be on alert. I don't know about "raffles," but I do know that the Japanese were about to "ruffle" some feathers and change the world.

The passage of 2 Chronicles 32:11 reads: "Doth not Hezekiah persuade you to give over yourself to die by famine and by thirst, saying, the Lord our God shall deliver us out of the hand of the king of Assyria."

Sennacherib, the king of Assyria, was set on capturing the land of Judah. His show of force didn't work, and now he was using words to make them afraid. Roosevelt had asked the Japanese to not go to war for the sake of humanity. Neither Japanese nor Judah listened to the warning. Judea had God to protect them while Japan had America to defeat them.

Of course, I believe that God was with America. The Japanese ruffled feathers when they attacked Pearl Harbor, but at least they were warned, as was Sennacherib when he faced Judea. When Sennacherib went home and to his place of worship, he was murdered by his own sons.

Are you treating God's, people, right?

December 7

On this day in history in 1941, Japan attacked the United States of America at Pearl Harbor in Hawaii, with President Franklin D. Roosevelt calling it "a day that shall live in infamy." The U.S. knew the attack was coming, as we had received a coded message, but we didn't know when it would happen.

Until then, the U.S. had also placed high economic sanctions on Japan, which were to be removed when certain conditions were met. First, the Japanese had to withdraw from China. Second, Japan had to withdraw from Indo-China. Third, Japan had to renounce its alliance with Germany and Italy.

The attack on Pearl Harbor was planned and led by Japanese Admiral Yamamato. Approximately 360 Japanese warplanes were launched from six aircraft carriers, then came another 200 aircraft to bomb the U.S. ships anchored in the harbor.

Eighteen U.S. ships were sunk or badly damaged, with180 planes destroyed on the ground and another 150 damaged. At the end of the day, only 43 U.S. planes were operational. American casualties were 2,400, with another 1,000 wounded. More than a thousand men were killed on the *USS Arizona* alone, their remains forever entombed in the wreckage of the ship.

Deuteronomy 3:11 reads: "For only Oz, king of Bashan remained of the remnant of giants; behold his bedstead was a bedstead of iron, is it not in Rabbath of the children of Ammon? Nine cubits was the length thereof, and four cubits the breath of it after the cubic of a man."

King Oz was a giant who often intimidated the Children of Israel because of his size. In World War II, Japan thought they were giants, too, and could intimidate America and the rest of the free world. But it was proved they could not. King Oz was destroyed by Israel, while Japan was destroyed by America and her allies.

Are you facing a giant? Put your faith in God. The giant may not be as big as you thought, for I know that the giant you are facing is not as big as my God.

December 8

On this day in history in 1941, Congresswoman Jeanette Rankin of Montana cast the only vote against the United States entering World War II. Rankin, a dedicated Pacifist, was the first woman elected to Congress. She also voted against going to war when it was declared for World War I.

Following that, Rankin was defeated for re-election. Her opponent said that she had no stomach for war. She had won re-election just two years earlier, right in time to cast another no vote to go to war. I'm not sure which language Rankin wanted to speak, German or Japanese. One of the nicer names that she was called was "Japanette Rankin."

Luke 6:29 reads: "And unto him that smiteth thee on the one cheek, offer also the other; and him that taketh away thy cloak, forbid not to take thy coat also."

Rankin lived this verse. She voted for Germany in World War I and World War II. The Germans slapped her twice, much to the displeasure of the men who were fighting the war.

Have you turned the other cheek? God will help you turn the other cheek and forgive others.

December 9

On this day in history in 1917, Turkish troops moved out of the Holy City of Jerusalem. The keys to the city were offered to the British Army under the command of General Edmund Allenby. Allenby waited two days to enter the Holy City after being instructed how to not offend its inhabitants. He entered on foot as compared to Kaiser Wilhelm's entrance on horseback. No flags of the Allies were flown over the city, but Muslin troops were dispatched to guard the Dome of the Rock, a religious landmark. The proclamation declaring martial law was read in English, French, Arabic, Hebrew, Russian, and Greek. Church bells in London and Rome rang out, celebrating the arrival of the British.

Israel ultimately gained its independence in 1948 when England granted its freedom. The United Nations further declared that Israel was a free and independent state that same year.

The passage of 2 Kings 24:13 reads: "And he carried out thence all the treasures of the house of the Lord, and the treasures of the king's house and cut in pieces all the vessels of Gold which Solomon King of Israel had made in the temple of the Lord, as the Lord had said."

In the year 600 B.C., another army came to Jerusalem led by Nebuchadnezzar, the king of Babylon. (Because of my typing ability and the length of Nebuchadnezzar's name, I'll refer to him as Neb, in keeping with my Southern heritage.)

Neb invaded Jerusalem, as he has no respect for any of the people living there. He moved the best and brightest young men to Babylon, but those left in the city were made slaves and servants. He destroyed the Jewish temple and stole all of its gold and silver cups. Anyone who had a talent or a good job or trade was sent to Babylon. Neb showed no respect for the Holy City, but the British did.

Do you have respect for God's house? Do you have respect for God's children?

December 10

On this day in history in 1967, the Georgia-born Otis Redding died in an airplane crash. He had written "Sitting on the Dock of the Bay," and was almost finished with it but had to leave to catch the plane. The part of the song that now has whistling in it had not yet been written. After Redding's death, the song, with the whistling, was an instant number one hit.

Redding mostly sang blues and was just getting started in pop music when he died. His song "Sitting on the Dock of the Bay" was popular in Vietnam because most of us in the military who went there had departed from the "'Frisco Bay," what Redding called San Francisco Bay. As Redding had done, I left my home in Georgia, but I was headed for the snowcapped mountains of Seattle, Washington. Somehow that doesn't have the same ring as "'Frisco Bay" in Redding's song.

Matthew 6:34 reads: "Take therefore no thought for the morrow: for the morrow shall take thought for the things of itself. Sufficient unto the day is the evil thereof."

Redding's song was almost written and recorded and then he had had to leave before it was finished. That gives us something to think about. Tomorrow is not promised. For him, the song was not finished, and there was no tomorrow.

Do you worry about tomorrow? Why should you when you have enough problems for today? If tomorrow is as bad as yesterday then your problems will be multiplied. Trust God for tomorrow, and give Him today.

December 11

On this day in history in 1872, William Fredrick Cody made his first stage appearance in "Scouts of the Prairie" as Buffalo Bill Cody. Born in 1846, Cody held a variety of jobs. He was a messenger and later claimed to work for the short-lived Pony Express, served in a variety of irregular militia groups supporting the North, was in a cavalry regiment in 1864-65, worked as a scout for the U.S. Army in the American-Indian Wars, and earned a living as a guide for the wealthy who wanted to enjoy the wild west. He was serving as a guide when he met Ned Buntline, who had written popular dime novels. Buntline made copies of the novels, and often they were produced as stage plays. He talked Cody into starring in a play in Chicago. Cody never looked back after he began working as an entertainer. He started the "Buffalo Bill Wild West Show," which was still going strong when he died in 1917.

The passage of 2 Samuel 23:9 reads: "And after him was Eleazar the son of Dodo the Ahohite, one of the three mighty men with David, When, he defied the Philistines that were there gathered together to battle, and the men of Israel were gone away."

Eleazar was one of the mighty men who went to Bethlehem to get water for David. As a warrior, Eleazar had many jobs, much like Cody did. He wasn't an actor but an elite soldier who fought in many battles, some of them covertly. He just didn't meet a writer of dime novels as Cody did.

Would you rate as a mighty man of your church? Why not start?

December 12

On this day in history in 2000, the Supreme Court of the United States ruled that the Florida Supreme Court ruling of the recount of presidential votes was unconstitutional in the race between presidential candidates Al Gore and George W. Bush. Gore conceded the election the next day, and Bush became the nation's 43rd president. The electoral vote was close, with Florida as the fighting ground. If Gore had won the electoral vote for Tennessee, his home state, he would have been president instead of Bush.

The passage of 1 Samuel 16:11 reads: "And Samuel said unto Jesse, Are here all thy Children? And he said, There, remaineth yet the youngest, and behold, he keepeth the sheep. And Samuel said unto Jesse, Send and fetch him: for we will not sit down until he comes hither."

The Lord told Samuel to go to Bethlehem to the house of Jesse for the next king. Jesse sent his oldest seven sons before Samuel, but Samuel didn't pick any of them. Then Jesse sent for David, and he was selected.

This happened the same way in the presidential election. All the candidates were put before us, and then we chose the final two. Then we chose Al Gore by the popular vote, but the electoral votes are what counts. George Bush won by four votes of the Electoral College. It is my belief that Bush was God's choice also.

Do we seek God's choice in our lives? What about your political life? Are you selecting a chance to be a child of the king?

December 13

On this day in history in 1636, the Massachusetts Bay Colony organized into three regiments, then scattered militia companies for villages around Boston.

Today's National Guard, Army National Guard and Air National Guard are made up of 450,000 men and women from all walks of life and from every state and the District of Columbia. Each guard member takes the same oath as the regular service men and women. The National Guard and Army National Guard are a part of the U.S. Army, while the Air National Guard is part of the U.S. Air Force. In peacetime, the guard is commanded by the state's governor. In wartime, the guard can be called up to active duty. The guardsmen's motto is "Always ready. Always there."

The passage of 2 Timothy 4:2 reads: "Preach the word; be instant in season, out of season; reprove, rebuke, exhort, with all longsuffering and doctrine."

This could be the start of the National Guard for Massachusetts. The National Guard is ready for service at any time, just as a Christian should be. The Apostle Paul tells his young friend, Timothy, to always be ready.

This verse applies to us, too. Are we ready to proclaim Jesus and His saving grace? How would you react if you were asked to speak on one hour's notice? We all need to heed the motto of the guard: Always ready. Always there.

Can you say that?

December 14

On this day in history in 1799, George Washington, our first president, died at the age of 67. He had been a lieutenant colonel in the Virginia Militia and fought in the Ohio River Valley against the French. When the American Revolution erupted in 1775, he became the commander-in-chief of the newly established Continental Army. Washington's army was called ragtag by the British. I wonder what they called them when General Charles Cornwallis, commander of the British, surrendered at Yorktown.

In 1789, Washington was elected as our nation's first president and served two terms before refusing to run for a third. Two years after his presidency ended, he died at his home in Mount Vernon in the Virginia countryside south of what is now Washington, D.C. His friend Harry Lee gave the eulogy, saying of him, "First in war, first in peace, and first in the hearts of his countrymen."

The passage of 1 Kings 12:16 reads: "So when all Israel saw that the king hearkened not unto them, the people answered the king saying, What portion have we in David? Neither have we inheritance in the son of Jesse: to your tents, O Israel: now see to thine own house, David. So Israel departed unto their tents."

Here is the beginning of the division of the Children of Israel into two nations, Judea and Israel. This division came after the death of Solomon, and the Jewish nation destroyed itself. At least when George Washington left office, our young nation did not separate, nor did it happen after his death.

Are you helping to keep our nation together? Are you working to keep God's nation united?

December 15

On this day in history in 1939, the movie "Gone with the Wind," patterned after Margaret Mitchell's bestselling book of the same name, made its first showing at the Loew's Grand Theater in Atlanta. Produced by David O Selznick and staring Vivian Leigh as Scarlet O'Hara and Clark Gable as Rhett Butler, the four-hour long movie covered the War Between the States from start to finish.

The beloved movie shows the hopes and dreams of young men and women in this thing called war. Most of the movie was about the upper crust society of the South. And in an historic move, in 1940 Hattie McDaniel won an Academy Award for Best Supporting Actress for her role of Mammy in the movie and became the first-ever African-American to win an Oscar.

Genesis 12:5 reads: "And Abram took Sarai his wife, and Lot his brother's son, and all their substance that they had gathered, and the souls that they had gotten in Haran; and they went forth to go into the land of Canaan; and into the land of Canaan they came."

Abraham followed God to the point of being called a friend of God. Sarai went forth with her husband, and their lives were brought together in full color. When Sarai gave birth to Isaac, she then became the mother of the Hebrew Nation. As she taught Isaac, she was teaching the nation of Israel. Her role in life became bigger and bigger.

There were no movies in the time of Abraham and Sarah. No doubt if there were, then Sarai would have won all the supporting roles.

Are you a supporter of God? Do you support Him? Does He have a leading role in your life?

December 16

On this day in history in 1773, the Boston Tea Party took place. Everyone loves a party unless they want tea to go with it. The Colonists had dressed as Mohawk Indians, boarded three English ships loaded with tea, and then dumped 342 chests of it into Boston Harbor. Not only was there a high tax on tea, but also you could buy it only from the East India Company.

You are not going to make me like something that I don't like. Forcing me to use one store over another is going to be hard. That is the gist of what happened here.

Samuel Adams led the tea party. The British then closed Boston Harbor, established military rule, made British officials immune to prosecution of crimes, and then required the Colonists to house British soldiers and officers—and all of this without tea that the British enjoy so well.

Matthew 2:16 reads: "Then Herod, when he saw that he was mocked of the wise men, was exceeding wroth, and sent forth, and slew all the children that were in Bethlehem, and in all the coast thereof, from two years old and younger, according to the time which he had diligently enquired of the wise men."

What does this have to do with the Boston Tea Party? Consider this: Britain used only one tea company, and higher taxes made the price climb. Not having tea was the next option. At least the Loyalists had no tea either.

The children who were killed by Herod were a captive people. To Herod, they meant nothing. Getting rid of a king meant everything.

Both of these examples went against the people, both were uncalled for, and both hurt the economy of their countries.

What are you doing to help people? Have you told them about Christ?

CARROLL WALKER

December 17

On this day in history in 1903, it took 12 seconds, 120 feet, and one flimsy aircraft to introduce the world to flight. In Kitty Hawk, North Carolina, Wilbur and Orville Wright became the first people in the world to fly with their contraption. The Wright brothers made and repaired bicycles in Dayton, Ohio, but their first love was flying, first with gliders, then unmanned flights, and finally that famous manned flight.

Kitty Hawk was chosen by the brothers because of its steady wind currents. On one of their gliders they put an old fan blade on a wooden box and an old washtub to make a wind tunnel. Then they mounted a gasoline engine to a plane, and finally on that cold December morning Orville Wright climbed into plane, moved a lever, and the plane took off. The age of flight had begun.

The passage of 1 Thessalonians 4:16 reads: "For the Lord himself shall descend from heaven with a shout, with the voice of the Archangel, and with the trump of God: and the dead in Christ shall rise first."

This verse alludes to Christ's return to earth. When Jesus leaves Heaven and comes back to earth, the Archangel will shout, the trumpet will blow and then we will be gone. The dead in Christ will be first, followed by the folks who are alive and believe in Christ. We will not even need an air traffic controller. Imagine that. There will be no need for a fan, a washtub, an engine, or wooden box. Just us and God and we're off to our new home.

Are you ready to fly?

December 18

During World War II, the U.S. military was segregated. Blacks were taught and trained in separate units from whites. Blacks were not allowed to become fighter pilots, but pressure from black leaders and Congress led the Army Air Corps to open a base in Tuskegee, Alabama, with its main purpose to train blacks as pilots, navigators, bombardiers, mechanics and other occupations having to do with aircraft.

In 1943, the Army Air Corps sent 450 Tuskegee pilots to North Africa and Europe to fly escort for long range bombers. The Tuskegee Airmen painted the tail sections of their planes red. They then became known as Red Tails or the Red Tail Angels. Pilots of bombers soon asked for Red Tails to escort them. The Tuskegee Airmen proved they could fly with the best and helped open the door to desegregation of the military.

Acts 10:28 reads: "And he said unto them, ye know how that it is an unlawful thing for a man that is a Jew to keep company, or come unto one of another nation; but God hath shewed me that I should not call any man common or unclean."

Peter started out this verse very rudely, saying that it was unlawful for Jews to "keep company" with other nations, but that God showed him differently. Cornelius needed some direction, so he sent for Peter, who came knowing that the man was from Caesarea. Peter's actions proved him a better man.

The Tuskegee Airmen were different at first just because they were black. They were taught the tools of their trade and did them very well. There was nothing common about these men.

How do you treat others? Do you love your fellow man?

December 19

On this day in history in 1776, Thomas Paine published a pamphlet called *American Crisis*. General George Washington was at MacConkey Ferry on the Delaware River camping for the winter. His men were again starving and moral was low. Washington was losing men every day due to desertion. He had lost several battles and things were not getting any better with time.

Along comes Thomas Paine, who had already written another pamphlet named *Common Sense*. Paine's *American Crisis* would again stir up Washington's men, just as *Common Sense* had. After *American Crisis* was read to the Army, the men crossed the Delaware and defeated the Hessian Army, many of them hung over from drinking heavily on Christmas night. Then on January 2, 1777, the army defeated British General Charles Cornwallis at the Battle of Princeton. If you need encouragement, you should read Thomas Paine's work. He sure does know how to stir a nation.

Deuteronomy 6:6-7 reads: "And these words, which I commanded thee this day, shall be in thine heart: and thou shalt teach them diligently to thy children, and shall talk to them when thou sitteth in thou house, and when thou walkest in the way, and when thou liest down, and when thou riseth up."

Moses talked about knowing God's laws and even told us how we should react in teaching our families. These instructions have not changed over time. Talk to your children about God. You are to teach your children every single day and have time with God and your family.

Do you live God's laws? That's more important than teaching. Do you follow God's law? What will your children say about you?

December 20

On this day in history in 1989, U.S. Army Captain Linda Bray became the first female officer to lead troops into combat. During the invasion of Panama, Bray commanded a military police company of thirty men and women. She was also assigned to capture a kennel holding guard dogs. When the Panamanian Defense Force started firing and defending their position from a command post a half-mile away, Bray issued orders to return fire. Using a ditch as cover, she left her command post and joined her troops. When threatened by artillery fire, the Panamanians escaped into the woods. The kennel had rifles, ammunition, maps, and other valuable information inside of it. For her efforts, Bray was awarded the Army Commendation Medal for Valor and the Combat Infantryman Badge.

The passage of 2 Kings 22:14 reads: "So Hilkiah the priest, and Ahilam, and Achbor, and Shapan, and Asahiak went unto Huldah the prophetess, the wife of Shallum the son of Tikvah, the son of Harhas, keeper of the wardrobe; (now she dwelt in Jerusalem in the college) and they communed with her."

The young King Josiah ordered the temple cleaned and repaired. It was during this time that the Book of the Law was found by Hilkiah, who read it to King Josiah. King Josiah then asked the priest what it meant and to find its purpose. Huldah was a prophetess in Israel. She told the priest the book's meaning and explained what God was going to do to Israel, but because the king had repented, the punishment would be less severe. The book was then read to the people.

From leading troops in combat to rocking the cradle at home, women have had a major role in helping others. Do we lift them up in prayer?

December 21

On this day in history in 1945, General George S. Patton, often called "Old Blood and Guts," died in a car accident. Patton was commander of the Third U.S. Army. By the time of his death, World War II was over and mop-up operations were underway.

Patton graduated from West Point in 1909. He represented the U.S. in fencing in the 1912 Olympics but did not place. In World War I he was a tank commander. His most famous military action came at the Battle of the Bulge when he moved his Third Army to relieve the Americans there and for reinforcement. That battle was the last offensive of the war from the Germans.

Patton was a tough character. He was also mean but his troops respected him and they fought hard under him.

First Kings 16:30-31 reads: "And Ahab the son of Omri did evil in the sight of the Lord above all that were before him. And it came to pass, as if it had been a light thing for him to walk in the sins of Jeroboam the son of Nebat, that he took to wife Jezebel the daughter of Ethbaal king of the Zidonians, and went and served Baal, and worshipped him."

Ahab was the worst king Israel ever had, and his bad character was preceded by that of his wife, Jezebel. Elijah met Ahab and discussed the drought and famine and even accepted the challenge from the prophets of Baal. Here came Jezebel, and Elijah left town fast. Until the death of Ahab and Jezebel, Elijah stayed on the run. He may have been the first to say, "Hell hath no fury like a woman scorned."

We all know evil people. Let us pray for them.

December 22

On this day in history in 1864, General William T. Sherman gave President Abraham Lincoln a gift for Christmas, and that gift was the city of Savannah. Sherman had captured Savannah, where he ended his infamous March to the Sea through Georgia. He had destroyed almost everything in his path from Atlanta as he moved into Savannah.

In Sherman's telegraph to Lincoln, he wrote: "I beg to present you, as a Christmas gift, the city of Savannah, with 150 heavy guns and plenty of ammunition and also, about 25,000 bales of cotton."

Savannah was the last major Confederate seaport left unscathed. After the first of January, Sherman then turned north from Savannah to meet his compatriot General Union Ulysses S. Grant and attack Confederate General Robert E. Lee from the rear.

Luke1:31 reads: "And behold, thou shalt conceive in thy womb, and bring forth a son, and shall call his name Jesus."

The time for the long-awaited Messiah had come. God sent His angel Gabriel to take a message to earth to a young virgin named Mary. She could be found in Galilee in the town of Nazareth. Gabriel told her that she was blessed of God and would have His son. She was to name him Jesus.

Mary was confused. She had never even known the physical love of a man, but Gabriel soothed her by saying, "Don't worry. The Holy Ghost will come upon you and your child will be God's son."

Imagine getting a message like that.

When Lincoln's telegraph message arrived from General Sherman, he was probably glad, but think of how much gladder Mary was when she received her message from Gabriel.

Are you open to hear God's message for you?

December 23

On this day in history in 1823, the poem "The Night Before Christmas" was first published. There is some confusion as to whom the poem rightfully belongs or by whom it was written. Most historians believe the poet to be Clement C. Moore, but some now think that Henry Livingston wrote it. It doesn't matter to me who wrote it. I enjoyed it as a child and later I enjoyed reading it to my sons. After all the hustle and bustle of Christmas, it's a nice story to read to children on a cold winter's night.

Luke 2:4-5 reads: "And Joseph also went up out of Galilee, out of the city of Nazareth, into Judea, unto the city of David, which is called Bethlehem; (because he was of the house and lineage of David) to be taxed with Mary his espoused Wife, being great with child."

Yes. I know that this is not the night before Christmas. Joseph and Mary had to travel for some time to get to Bethlehem. Think of a vacation you took with your loved ones. Did you make that trip in one day? Joseph and Mary were much like us and probably made plans for their lives as a couple. But despite the difficult journey, it was a good trip. As Mary's time to give birth approached, she probably became more anxious but Joseph was with her and offered comfort.

Now that the long journey was about to end, they could find no room at an inn and were offered a manger. Joseph probably thought that his world was turning upside down.

Has your life been turned upside down? Jesus, once a child in a manger, can help straighten it out.

December 24

On this day in history in 1968, the crew of Apollo 8 broadcast a Christmas message from outer space. America was in troubling times with the unpopular Vietnam War raging on, segregation issues taking front and center, and the assassinations of Robert Kennedy and Dr. Martin Luther King Jr. causing great fallout in America.

It was Christmas Eve and Apollo 8 was orbiting the moon with astronauts Frank Borman, Jim Lovell and Bill Andes at the helm. Andes was the first to speak in the broadcast, quoting Scripture from Genesis1:1-10. The other astronauts also took turns reading Scripture, with Bowman ending the broadcast by wishing everyone a merry Christmas and blessings from God.

Luke 2:13-14 reads: "And suddenly there was with the Angels a multitude of the heavenly host praising God and, saying, Glory to God in the highest and on earth peace and good will toward men."

This passage is part of the Christmas story, and the world-changing events at the manger were just getting started while surrounded by peace on earth.

Every year in Vietnam, a truce was called for Christmas. Sometimes that truce was broken, but in 1968 it was not—or at least that's what the news reported. One of the more wonderful songs of Christmas is "Silent Night," and on that Christmas Eve night I went to chapel. As we were singing "Silent Night" by candlelight, things became not so silent and not so holy as rockets and mortars began falling all around. The chapel seemed to be the target, and shrapnel fragments hit the church but there was little damage and no death or injuries. Ever since that night, I cannot sit in a church and sing "Silent Night" by candlelight.

Please pray for our servicemen and women around the world this Christmas.

December 25

On this day in history every year, we celebrate Christmas. Merry Christmas, everyone!

Christmas is a day set aside to worship the Baby Jesus, who was born in a manger in Bethlehem. He grew up to be called Jesus of Nazareth and died on the cross for our sins.

Why December 25th was chosen as the date for Christmas, I don't know, but it probably has to with the winter solstice and the coming new year.

There are many stories I could tell about this date in history. It's when General George Washington crossed the Delaware River. And it's known for Bing Crosby singing "White Christmas." It's also about Elisha Hunt Rhodes, a soldier from Rhode Island who kept a diary during the War Between the States and told about spending his four Christmases in the uniform of the Union.

Another story focuses on Christmas in 1914 in France during World War I. In the early morning hours, the Germans laid down their weapons and began to sing. Thinking it was some sort of trap, the Americans were slow to respond. But soon they left their trenches and began socializing with the Germans, playing soccer and exchanging food. At the end of the day, both sides returned to their trenches and the war began anew.

Luke 2:1-20 tells us the true story of Christmas, with Verse 17 reading: "And she brought forth her first born son, and wrapped him in swaddling clothes, and laid him in a manger; because there was no room for them in the inn."

Why not take a few minutes to read this story to your family? It is the true meaning of Christmas and means Christ worship.

December 26

On this day in history in 1944, General George S. Patton employed a strategy to relieve Bastogne, Belgium, during the Battle of the Bulge. The Germans had attacked the American lines through the Ardennes Forest. If the line broke, then the Germans had a way north to be able to expand. The Germans, under a flag of truce, asked the Americans to surrender. But General Anthony C. McAuliffe met the German demand with one type written word: Nuts.

Patton and his Third Army broke through the German lines and started pushing the Germans back across the Rhine River. The Allies were relieved that the line was bent but it was never broken.

Matthew 2:1-2 reads: "And when Jesus was born in Bethlehem of Judea in the days of Herod the King, behold there came wisemen from the east to Jerusalem. Saying, where is he that is born King of the Jews? For we have seen his star in the east and are come to worship him."

The wisemen came to worship the Jesus. When Herod heard about Jesus, he wanted to find this king, not to worship Him, but to destroy Him. After the wisemen left, Joseph, Mary and their baby Jesus fled to Egypt to escape Herod's wrath. But a Hebrew living in Egypt was not an easy thing. That line was bent many times but it was never broken. After Herod's death, Joseph, Mary, and Jesus returned to Nazareth.

Is the line between your life and Jesus bent or broken? Call upon Jesus, and He will reinforce your line.

December 27

On this day in history in 1941, a little town made a big mistake that paid off royally. In the few days after Japan attacked Pearl Harbor, the townspeople of North Platte, Nebraska, heard their own Company D of the Nebraska National Guard was coming through town. They gathered at the train station to greet the men with cookies, candy, and small gifts. When the train stopped and the troops got off, the townspeople realized a big mistake. The soldiers were from Company D of the *Kansas* National Guard, not the *Nebraska* National Guard. Someone in the crowd shouted, "Well, what are we waiting for?" They began to share their gifts with the Kansans.

Beginning on Christmas Day in 1941 until the end of the war, the people of North Platte met every train and gave every soldier gifts, sandwiches, candy or cookies until April 1, 1946. More than six million men came through North Platte during the war.

James 2:15-17 reads: "If a brother or sister be naked, and destitute of daily food. And one of you say unto them, Depart in peace, be ye warmed and filled: notwithstanding ye give them not those things which are needful to the body; what doth it profit. Even so faith if it hath not works indeed, being alone."

The soldiers traveling through North Platte didn't leave hungry. Oh, I'm sure they were not stuffed, but being cared for is very appreciated. The same thing goes for James. If we meet someone without clothes, food or shelter, we are to help them. Our works prove our salvation. An age-old question is explained well in Verse 17. We can all have faith, but if we never put that faith to work, it is worthless or dead.

Is your faith dead today?

December 28

On this day in history in 1941, Rear Admiral Ben Morrell requested authority to create the Navy Seabees. Those chosen for this battalion had to have experience in construction of every kind. Seabees were also trained as infantrymen and worked around the world to help the war effort. In Guam, for example, they built airfields for the B-29 Bomber and enlarged ports to get supplies to land. They also built pontoons for the Allies to use for troop landings and sent demolition units to destroy obstacles set up by the Germans on D-Day. The motto of the Seabees is "We build. We fight."

Exodus 28:3 reads: "And thou shalt speak unto all that are wise hearted, whom I have filled with the spirit of wisdom, that they may make Aaron's garments to consecrate him, that he may minister unto me in the priest's office."

Moses used his people like the Seabees. While the Seabees were trained in a certain trade, Moses selected people with a wise heart and who were filled with wisdom and also trained so that they could make Aaron's garments and other things in the tabernacle.

Are you being trained to serve God?

December 29

On this day in history in 1940, President Franklin D. Roosevelt held one of his renowned fireside chats, speaking to the people about how our American civilization was in danger. World War II had already begun in Europe and things were not looking good. Roosevelt said, "If Great Britain falls, we will be living at the point of a gun."

Roosevelt then stated that we had no choice but to industrialize our nation to help the Allies. He further stated that we must be the great arsenal of democracy.

In the next month the United States started making planes, tanks, guns, and ships. Alistair Cooke, a British journalist, wrote, "The Allies would not have won the war ... without the way the American people with amazing speed created an arsenal no coalition of nations could come close to matching."

The passage of 2 Kings 4:7 reads: "Then she came and told the man of God, and he said, Go, sell the oil, and pay the debt, and live thou and thy children on the rest."

A widow was about to lose her house. She called on a man of God for help and then did what he told her to do. She borrowed vessels for oil and then sold the oil to pay the bills and meet her own needs.

Americans have helped her allies during the war, and the Allies then helped the Americans win the war.

Are you helping someone?

December 30

On this day in history in 1951, the "Roy Rogers Show" made its debut. Most of us of my generation remember watching this show, or at least its reruns on Saturday mornings. The show always opened up the same way with Roy Rogers, known as the King of Cowboys; Trigger, his golden palomino; Bullet, the wonder dog; and Dale Evans, Queen of the West, all interacting with Pat Brady, the comical sidekick of the show. On the show, no one ever was killed but the prisons were filled with the bad guys, who never had a chance against Roy Rogers. That was good television entertainment.

Second Kings 6:17 reads: "And Elisha prayed, and said, Lord, I pray thee, open his eyes, that he may see. And the Lord opened the eyes of the young man; and he saw: and behold the mountains were full of horses and chariots of fire round about Elisha."

Elisha and his servant were well protected from the opposing army as the chariots of the Lord were all around. No one was killed. The enemy was blinded and led to Samaria where the Lord opened their eyes. Elisha told the king to feed them. They then returned to their country, never to go back again.

Roy Rogers put the bad guys in jail or at least stopped them before they became hardened criminals.

How do you treat your enemies? If you love your enemy, it will drive him crazy, and you will also feel better about yourself.

December 31

On this day in history in 1929, in New York City, Guy
Lombardo and the Royal Canadians introduced America to the
custom of playing "Auld Lang Syne" on New Year's Eve.

As this day comes to a close, so does this book. It is my
desire that as you have read it each day, you have learned a little
more about history. And I also hope you have had a laugh or two or
maybe three. Perhaps the Bible verses have touched your heart.

I started the book off on January 1st writing of the need for
salvation from our past sins. Now as I close this book, let us look
ahead to Christ's return.

Revelation 22:20-21 reads: "He which testifieth these
things saith, Surely I come quickly. Amen, even so come Lord
Jesus. The grace of our Lord Jesus Christ be with you all. Amen."

Jesus will again return to this earth to gather His loved ones
home. Will you be ready when He comes? We know not the time,
but we know that He will return. If He comes before you are ready,
then it will be too late.

Please. Accept Jesus Christ as your Savior today.

Bibliography

Internet Sites

Arlington National Cemetery. www.ArlingtonCemetery.mil.

Birthplace of Anesthesia. www.CrawfordLong.org.

Bible Study Tools. www.BibleStudyTools.com

Biography. www.Biography.com.

Bob Hope Foundation. www.BobHopeFoundation.org.

Home of Crazy Horse Memorial: Crazy Horse Memorial. www.CrazyHorseMemorial.org.

International Skydiving Museum and Hall of Fame. www.SkyDivingMuseum.org.

Military and Veterans Benefits, News, Veterans Jobs. www.Military.com.

National Parks Service. www.NPS.gov.

Naval History and Heritage Command. www.History.Navy.mil.

On-This-Day.com – Daily History, Famous Birthdays and Music History. www.On-This-Day.com.

Strategy Page Military News Humor Photos. www.StrategyPage.com.

Vietnam Veterans Memorial, National Park Service. www.NPS.gov/vive/index.htm.

Wikipedia. www.Wikipedia.org.

Women in Military Service for America Memorial. www.WomensMemorial.org.

Books

Bennett, William J. and Cribb, John T. The American Patriot's
     Almanac: Daily Readings on America. Thomas Nelson
     Publishers. 2013.

Lockyer, Herbert. Nelson's Illustrated Bible Dictionary: An
     Authoritative One Volume Reference Work on the Bible.
Thomas
     Nelson Publishers. 1968.

The Scofield Study Bible. King James Version. Oxford University
     Press. 1909, 1917, 1937, 1945, 1996.

Young, Robert. Young's Analytical Concordance to the Bible.
     Eerdman's Publishing Company. 1970. Reprint 1974.

A Patriot's Devotional

CARROLL WALKER

CPSIA information can be obtained
at www.ICGtesting.com
Printed in the USA
BVHW041914130919
558404BV00016B/198/P